ALL
IN

ALL IN

The (Almost) Entirely True Story of
The World Series of Poker

JONATHAN GROTENSTEIN
STORMS REBACK

THOMAS DUNNE BOOKS
ST. MARTIN'S PRESS   NEW YORK

THOMAS DUNNE BOOKS.
An imprint of St. Martin's Press.

www.stmartins.com

Design by Phil Mazzone

Library of Congress Cataloging-in-Publication Data

Grotenstein, Jonathan, 1970–
    All in : the (almost) entirely true story of the World Series of Poker /
Jonathan Grotenstein, Storms Reback.—1st ed.
      p. cm.
    Includes bibliography (page 285).
    Includes index (page 301).
    ISBN 0-312-34835-5
    EAN 978-0-312-34835-9
    1. World Series of Poker—History. I. Reback, Storms. II. Title.

GV1254.G76 2005
795.412—dc22

                                             2005045505

First Edition: October 2005

10 9 8 7 6 5 4 3 2 1

For Kristen and Sara, who know all too well about deadlines and bad beats. The wives of writers have it hard; the wives of poker players have it worse. These poor women have somehow ended up married to men who are both. God help them.

CONTENTS

FOREWORD

This book has been a long time coming, and it is one that has been sorely needed. The authors have spared no expense in delivering to readers the stories of the pioneers of the poker industry from the beginning of the World Series of Poker up to the present.

The World Series, that's where all the notoriety is, and for me it's always been about getting through the first day. That's where you run up against a lot of these strange players. One year I had the best starting hand in Texas hold'em, two aces, against a 7-6. We got all the money in, and he made a flush. Another time I had A-K and he had A-Q, a big underdog to my A-K, but my opponent got a queen on the river.

I'll tell you a little story. In the 2000 World Series, I came in second. That's where I had Chris Ferguson "dead to a 9," that is, only if a 9 came could I lose the hand. In the very next tournament I played I got down to heads-up (one-on-one), and once again I had the man dead to a nine and he caught it. Then, in the Tournament of Champions, I played Brian Saltus heads-up, and I had him dead to a 9 with one card to come. He caught a 9 to make a straight. I lost three no-limit hold'em final events in a row when my opponents heads-up were dead to one card and they all caught it. It was a difference of about $2 million in my pocket, and I didn't say boo. In the next six months I might have listened to two hundred bad beat stories, and all the pots in those stories together didn't add up to $2,000. I always get a kick out of that. It's just the way it goes.

A lot of people don't like how big the tournament has gotten. Before the recent explosion in the size of the fields, you used to be able to say, "Well, I got a hell of a chance of winning it." Now you just hope, hope you get there deep. Me, I don't care about there being so many more players because you still have to play one table at a time. That's all you can do.

I have known or played with almost everyone mentioned in this book, the old-timers who learned to play by "fading the white lines" on the highways between games and rehashing the key hands of each session with their road buddies, and the modern book- and TV-learned players who rely mostly on tutorials. I can attest to their being as unique as individuals as they are gifted as players.

I recommend this book to everyone, as it not only gives an accurate account of the World Series of Poker, but also of the many different people who have been part of its fascinating history.

T. J. Cloutier
Richardson, Texas

NOTE FROM THE AUTHORS

What follows is an entirely true account of the oldest and grandest poker tournament in the world. Almost.

Many years, the tournament has attracted television coverage and great writers to provide blow-by-blow descriptions of the action. Other years have been ignored by nearly everyone but the players themselves. Official records—who won, how they won, how much they won—were not kept until the 1980s.

The authors have done their best to piece together the history of the World Series of Poker from whatever fragments they have been able to unearth. Often they have been forced to rely upon the recollections of the players themselves, men and women who misdirect and mislead one another for a living. Sometimes their memories contradict one another. Several key hands have been lost to obscurity, certain biographical details may be apocryphal or anecdotal.

The authors have in every instance striven for the truth, processing these stories in a way that made the most sense to them as poker players and in a style that appealed to them as writers. If they are guilty, in regards to a hand or two, of using bluff and bluster to capture the spirit of this unique and amazing event, well, that's poker.

ALL IN

INTRODUCTION

Binion's Horseshoe never looked like much from the outside. There were no pirate ship battles or erupting volcanoes to lure you inside the casino. Chances were good that a light bulb on its façade had burned out and had yet to be replaced. Like most of its competitors in downtown Las Vegas, it refused to pander to a highfalutin crowd. At the Horseshoe, what you saw was what you got, and what you got most often was a no-attitude attitude and a very practical outlook: no need to build a roller coaster on the premises when the casino's bread-and-butter clientele—gamblers—had much simpler means of seeking thrills.

Inside it had even less to recommend it. What was left of the threadbare carpets reeked of cigarette smoke and beer. The cocktail waitresses looked like real human beings, in stark contrast to the supernatural beauties employed along the glitzier Las Vegas Strip. The restaurants offered hot dogs and chili and not much else. The lighting remained perpetually dim, not in an elegant or romantic way, but in the seedy kind of way you'd expect from an old-fashioned gambling hall.

The Horseshoe was always a fair reflection of the family that owned it. Its history was their history. Like tumbleweeds, the Binions were uprooted from their native Texas soil and drifted west with the wind, settling in Las Vegas in 1946, just as the city was discovering its vast potential as a gambling destination. As the city grew, so did the family's little casino, attracting a steady stream of customers despite, for many years, only having one real concession to tourism, a large Plexiglas horseshoe stuffed with $1 million in cash. For visitors to Las Vegas, a trip downtown wasn't complete until they'd had their picture taken in front of that famed horseshoe.

Besides the usual casino accoutrements, blackjack tables and roulette wheels, there wasn't much else to look at inside the ramshackle building until the Binions started adorning one of the walls in the back with framed photographs. Every year, another photograph, dating all the way back to 1970. Each picture was essentially the same, a close-up of a man smiling for the camera. Although it looked no more rarified than a series of employee of the month plaques in an ice-cream parlor, poker players regarded this as hallowed ground, for this was the Gallery of Champions, and the men smiling at the camera had all won the world championship of poker.

To be considered a poker player, you must only know how to play the game. To be a professional, you must win at it on a consistent basis. To be a world champion, you must win the main event of the World Series of Poker, held each spring, for the first thirty-four years of its existence, at Binion's Horseshoe.

The World Series, as its name implies, is actually a succession of tournaments that takes the better part of a month to run. In 2005, there will be forty events spread over six weeks. Each tournament tests a player's skill in a particular game, such as seven-card stud, Omaha, and razz, with "buy-ins"—the entry fee—beginning at $1,000.* The winner of each event receives a gold bracelet engraved on the back with the date of his victory, as well as a very large stack of

---

*Throughout the text we will be referring to many different poker tournaments, each of which will be preceded by the amount of the buy-in, e.g., a $5,000 Limit Hold'em event is a limit hold'em tournament with a $5,000 buy-in.

bundled hundred-dollar bills, its size determined by the number of entrants and cost of the buy-in.

While tens of millions of dollars will change hands during these preliminary tournaments, they are all warm-ups for the crown jewel of the World Series of Poker, the $10,000 No-Limit Texas Hold'em event. Not only does it have the biggest buy-in—and hence the biggest prize pool—but it has always determined whose picture will hang in the Gallery of Champions.

Unique as the game of poker itself, the championship, unlike those of similar pastimes that profess to encompass the world, has never discriminated against amateurs. Anybody can enter, provided he is able to muster the $10,000 entry fee. Imagine being able to step on to the first tee at the Augusta National Golf Club to compete for the Masters title with no greater credentials than a love of the sport. Or, after sitting out the entire football season, suiting up for the Super Bowl and throwing the winning touchdown. The vast majority of human beings will never experience either of these thrills. But any "Joe Blow from Idaho" can enter the World Series of Poker and, every once in a while, one of these nobodies actually wins it.

The players come from all corners of the world. What used to be an event dominated by weathered Texans with cold eyes and evocative nicknames is now just as likely to feature daring Norwegians and charismatic Vietnamese, feisty grandmothers and college students too young to know they are supposed to be intimidated.

The root of its universal attraction is obvious—the prize money at the World Series has always dwarfed that of all the other major championships of individual pursuits, such as golf, tennis, and chess, *combined*. The 2004 champion took home $5 million. Then again, it took him a whole week to earn it.

The nature of the contest makes it clear how difficult the work actually is. Each player starts with $10,000 worth of chips, or "checks." Once a player loses all of his checks, he is eliminated from the tournament. One of the boldest plays available to a player is to go "all in," raising with all of the checks he possesses, leaving the critical decision whether to call or to fold up to his opponent. As strong as this move is, it also has a rather unpleasant downside. If your opponent calls your all-in bet and shows a better hand, you're gone. During the course of the World Series, a player will have to make thousands of such crucial decisions. One bad move and, in the memorable words of one champion, "It's all over, baby!"

As the first true poker tournament ever played, the World Series of Poker has rightly been credited with creating the modern poker industry. Before it was devised, poker was a game played in smoky back rooms away from the watchful eyes of the laws. There were no tournaments, at least not as we know them today. Casino poker was a relative novelty. The idea that poker could be enjoyed on television was inconceivable. Being a professional poker player was far from respectable work, while actually calling yourself one was more likely to attract derision than admiration.

That all changed after the World Series was conceived and gradually evolved into the most recognized poker tournament in the world. Casinos that, only a few years ago, replaced their poker rooms with row after row of slot machines are now sprinting to reopen them. Millions aspire to master the game well enough to be considered professionals, and those who achieve this lofty status are looked upon as celebrities. Poker is on television nearly every night of the week, and new tournaments are popping up wherever there is a yearning for hot poker action, which is to say, *everywhere.*

The last several years have seen the genesis of literally hundreds of new poker tournaments, but any professional player will tell you that the World Series remains the most coveted championship. It carries a prestige that transcends the prize money and the baubles, and it is regarded in the same way as Wimbledon is by tennis fans or the Masters by those who love golf. Other poker tournaments may create millionaires, but only the World Series creates legends.

Until the recent explosion in poker's popularity, the World Series was dominated by the professional players. Despite leading lives without schedules or conventional obligations, this fraternity of brave souls has always treated the tournament as the one can't-miss event of the year. For them it is a homecoming of sorts. Many of the players have spent more time with one another than they have with their families, having intersected too many times to count at other tournaments or in high-stakes cash games where thousands, sometimes millions, of dollars are won and lost. Even though there is a highly competitive bent to their work (all of these men and women are ferocious competitors) there is a remarkably communal feeling among them.

Maybe it's the intimate relationship to the vagaries of luck they share, the knowledge that a night of hot cards might be followed by a month of cold ones. Or perhaps it's the awful sinking feeling that strikes all of them equally as soon as they get knocked out of the main event of the World Series, a time widely acknowledged in the professional ranks as being "the worst poker day of the year." For those fortunate enough to win the world championship, it is the crowning achievement of their poker careers. For everyone else, there is pain and suffering, mitigated only slightly by a passing thought: *Wait until next year.*

1

TWO THE HARD WAY

Johnny Moss was not a handsome man. He was almost entirely bald, while failing eyesight towards the end of his life required he wear a preposterously thick pair of glasses. Without them, his face lacked any distinguishing features, unless you count its utter lack of expressiveness. So impassive was Moss, he often fooled others into thinking he had fallen asleep at the table.

If his bland appearance won him no friends, his brusque disposition helped to lose them. In the words of frequent rival Thomas "Amarillo Slim" Preston, Johnny "had the type of personality that was well suited to a poker game but not much else." Fortunately for Moss, after discovering that he not only had the ultimate poker face but also an unparalleled capacity for winning at the game, he rarely had to do much else.

Life hadn't always been so easy. Shortly after Johnny's birth in 1907, his father John Hardie Moss lost his job as sheriff's deputy in a small West Texas town and was forced to take the family on the road in search of work. A burst appendix killed Johnny's mother along the way. John Hardie eventually found a job as a lineman for the telephone company in Dallas, but lost it when a falling pole crushed his right leg, rendering him a cripple. To help put food on the table, Johnny dropped out of elementary school to work full-time selling newspapers for a penny apiece. What free time he had he spent studying the only men who seemed to be prospering in his dirt-poor neighborhood—the back-alley dice shooters, the gamblers who played dominoes at the parlor on Ackard Street, and the poker players at the Otter's Club, a private house of chance—and he eventually mustered the nerve to join their freewheeling fraternity. It quickly became clear that the gambler's lifestyle, marked by long, odd hours and an ever-fluctuating bankroll, was in no way compatible with that of the working stiff, a point that John Hardie made to his son in the form of an ultimatum: quit gambling or quit his job.

"Daddy, if I don't work, how can I get money to gamble?"

"Son, that's what gamblers got to figure out."

In 1923, at the age of sixteen, Johnny found a temporary compromise. The owner of the Otter's Club began paying him three dollars a day to act as a lookout man in the poker room, protecting the players from cheaters. The education he would receive proved far more valuable than the salary.

"The owner of the place was the best draw [poker] man around and the first thing you know, I learnt myself to be a real fine draw player," recalled Johnny. "I hung on there for about three years and then moved on to the Elks Club 'cause there was some shrewd players in there who could learn me hold'em. I lied about my age to get into the place. It was two-dollar-limit hold'em. During the day I made enough money at the domino parlors to support my hold'em lessons at night."

His schooling was briefly disrupted when he caught the eye of Virgie Ann Mouser, the girl who worked behind the counter of the neighborhood drugstore. They were married after a six-month courtship. As wives of gamblers are wont to do, she quickly tired of his late nights and the unpredictability of his financial situation and insisted he find regular work. Hoping to appease her, he took a job driving a truck for the National Biscuit Company during the week, relegating his poker playing to the weekends; but the arrangement only upset her further, as she now saw him even less. It wasn't long before she issued a familiar ultimatum. Choose one: the job or the gambling. After taking a long motorcycle ride to think it over, Johnny gave his notice at the biscuit company. Confident that his skills at the poker table would pay their bills, he took to the road as a professional player.

It was the perfect time and place to do so. Not unlike the gold and silver rushes that sustained the Western cardsharps of the previous century, an oil boom had transformed much of Texas into a gushing well of loose money. Looking to separate these overnight millionaires from their newfound wealth, an entire generation of gamblers "faded the white line," traveling the state highways that connected rough-neck boomtowns, such as Tyler, Longview, Kilgore, Breckenridge, and Graham, in search of action.

The circuit was littered with dangers. Getting busted by the Texas Rangers was the least of a road gambler's fears—cheaters and hijack-ers were commonplace. Moss took to carrying a .38 with the hammer removed, enabling him to pull the pistol out of his pocket that much faster. Occasionally, he even had to use it.

Like the time he noticed a peephole in the ceiling while playing in a poker game in an unfamiliar small town. "So I pull out my gun," Johnny recalled, "and said, 'Now, fellas, do I have to go and shoot a bullet in the ceiling? Or are you going to send your boy down without any harm?' Hell, they thought I was bluffing," he laughed. "Ended up shooting the guy in his ass."

Other incidents were less light-hearted. Asked if he had ever killed a man, Moss flatly replied, "I don't know if he died."

The life of a road gambler came with its highs and lows, and it was often Virgie who took the brunt of such volatility. The pattern was set on their wedding night when Johnny, stuck in a poker game, pulled her engagement ring off her finger and used it as collateral to win a huge pot.

"If'n ah hadn't [allowed him to take the ring]," Virgie later de-clared, "Johnny would've ripped mah whole finguh off."

No occasion was too sacred to prevent him from gambling. The night before she was to deliver their first child he chose to play craps, losing all his ready cash in the process. Unable to pay for the room she had reserved at the local hospital, Virgie was forced to have the baby at home. Then there was the night Johnny won $250,000 in a particularly juicy poker game. Flush with cash, he instructed Virgie to start looking for a new house, but by the time she'd found one to her liking, it was too late. Johnny had already squandered his winnings.

Of his many setbacks the most devastating may have been when, during a single session, he lost $80,000 of *credit,* money he didn't even have. With limited options, he contemplated skipping town to avoid the debt, but could not bring himself to actually do it. Contrary to popular belief, most gamblers of the old school valued honor above all and considered a handshake deal more binding than any written contract. Swallowing his pride, Johnny turned to the one person he knew could help him—his childhood pal Lester Ben "Benny" Binion. Understanding well the life of a road gambler, Benny not only loaned Johnny the $80,000 he needed to pay off his debt, but $20,000 on top of that so he'd have a bankroll big enough to get himself back in the game.

Benny Binion and Johnny Moss first met as paperboys in east Dallas, two street urchins with dreams of better days. While Johnny sought his fortune as a gambler, Benny saw clearly the benefits of the other side of the equation—the house always wins.

Gone were the storied gambling saloons of the Old West, having fallen to the wave of moral reform that swept through the country at the dawn of the twentieth century. But while the reformers may have limited the means, they couldn't quench the desire to gamble.

Benny grew up in Pilot Grove, a small Texas town near the Oklahoma border where gambling was an intricate part of everyday life. "The men of Pilot Grove," writes Dallas historian Jim Gatewood, "gambled with dice, on dominos, cock fights, greyhound races, bare-knuckle fights, card games, foot races, dog fights, elections, the weather, which tree a dove would land in—anything with an unknown element affecting the result."

A fight with a local bully intent on revenge spurred a teenage Benny to leave his hometown, eventually making his way to Dallas. As a tough kid who understood the principles of gambling, Benny soon found himself rubbing elbows with the informal league of gangsters who ran the city's card games and dice parlors.

In his twenties, Benny started a "numbers policy"—an illegal neighborhood lottery—occasionally turning an extra dollar selling bootleg whiskey on the side. He ultimately chose gambling over liquor, driven as much by personal preference as the repeal of Prohibition: "The bootlegging, to me," he'd later recall, "was never no good."

He learned the ins and outs of running a craps game from Warren Diamond, a racketeer who for years operated a no-limit game out of the St. George Hotel, located, ironically, a stone's throw from the Dallas County courthouse. In 1926, the twenty-two-year-old Benny severed relations with his mentor and started his own no-limit craps game in room 226 of the Southland Hotel. When the arrangement attracted too much heat, he turned it into a "floating" game that appeared wherever there was a thirst for action. Using specially designed tables that could be folded quickly into crates that, at least according to the labels on the outside, contained hotel beds, the entire operation could be packed up and moved to a new location with just a half-hour's notice. These mobile casinos were, despite the humble trappings, the only real game in town—the birth of Las Vegas as we know it today was still a decade or two away—and Benny's tables often attracted the likes of H. L. Hunt, Clint Murchison, and Howard Hughes, millionaires who weren't afraid to gamble and, more important, lose vast sums of money. At the height of his success, Benny earned as much as $1 million a year from the operation.

With financial security came the desire to keep it. Like Johnny Moss, Benny occasionally had to resort to violence to protect himself and his assets. His motto was, from a very early age, "Do your enemies before they can do you."

"I ain't never killed a man who didn't deserve it," he often bragged.

In 1931, he shot and killed bootlegger Frank Bolding in a dispute over stolen liquor, but managed to slide by with only a two-year suspended sentence. Five years later, he shot and killed Ben Frieden, a rival numbers operator. This time he avoided imprisonment by pleading self-defense. He did, however, earn a nickname, thanks to his prowess with a gun—the Cowboy.

Aside from the murder raps, Benny successfully evaded conviction on numerous other charges that included bootlegging, theft, and possession of a concealed weapon. "I had a lot of very high, influential friends in Texas," he would later confess. They included Sheriff R. A. "Smoot" Schmid and his deputy Bill Decker. While Smoot was perfecting his jailhouse chili, it was Decker who really ran the show. And if Decker wanted some unsavory character run out of town, he had Benny do it for him. In return Benny was allowed to maintain his gambling operation with minimal interference from the law. Twice a week an officer from the vice squad would visit Benny's game and do a head count on how many customers he had. The next morning Benny was expected to pay the fines: ten dollars a head.

"There actually never was no arrangements made," said Benny, "but they had a real good city administration. So they just come in and raid us, and wouldn't tear up nothin', or do nothin', and we'd pay big fines. And I think we paid somethin' like, oh, six hundred thousand dollars a year for fines, for a few years there. So we helped the city out, just with no arrangement. There wasn't no graft or nothin' to it."

Politics will always be politics, and the 1946 election of a sheriff who couldn't be bought forced Benny to beat a hasty retreat from his home state. He packed his wife Teddy Jane, their five children, and $2 million in cash into his maroon Cadillac and headed for the only city where his vices were virtues—Las Vegas, Nevada.

What he found upon his arrival seemed like a little piece of paradise. "The most *enjoyable* place that you can imagine," he'd later say. "Everybody was friendly, and there wasn't none of this hijackin', there wasn't no stealin'—hell, you couldn't get robbed if you hollered 'Come rob me!'"

He wound up partnering with J. Kell Houssels, a fellow Texan, on a downtown casino called the Las Vegas Club. When Houssels decided to move the operation into a building he owned on the other side of Fremont Street, he sold the space to Benny and a new set of partners, who used it to open a gambling hall called the Westerner.

In Texas, Benny had grown used to running things in a certain way, predicated on the belief that customer service was the best way to keep a high-rolling gambler coming back. On occasion, this involved returning money to players who had lost big in hopes they might remember the gesture and come back and lose again. You can't fleece a sheep once it's been slaughtered. "I'm kinda freewheelin'," Benny explained, "and sorta like the old sayin', of bread cast upon the water come back. . . . There's a lot of people don't understand that."

His new partners were among them. Their relationship quickly soured, the Westerner was shuttered, and in 1951 Benny turned his attention to a failing casino down the street called the El Dorado. Under the eye of his wife Teddy Jane, the decrepit building, renamed the Horseshoe, was given a makeover. Benny spent $18,000 to cover the floor with carpets, the first downtown casino to do so.* He dressed his waitresses as cowgirls and outfitted his bartenders with string ties, creating an atmosphere akin to a slightly seedy cowtown saloon. No matter. The décor was not what attracted its devoted clientele. The sign Benny placed on the outside for all to read—THE WORLD'S HIGHEST LIMITS—was largely responsible for that.

This wasn't some idle boast or fallacious come-on. Not only was the limit at the Horseshoe's craps tables ten times that of any other casino, but an ambitious gambler could wager as much as he dared, as long as he announced his intention before placing his first bet.

NO LIMITS

Benny acquired his willingness to accept any wager, no matter how large, from his old mentor in Dallas, Warren Diamond. Benny loved to tell the story of the time an oilman from Texarkana paid a visit to Diamond's craps game and threw a thick envelope down on the table, announcing his intention to bet it all.

"Diamond," said the oilman, "I'm gonna make you look," referring to what was undoubtedly a large sum of money in the envelope.

Diamond refused to take the bait, barely glancing at the oilman or his envelope as he instructed his stickman to pass the man the dice.

Only after the oilman crapped out in two rolls did Diamond look inside the envelope, casually pocketing the $170,000 it contained.

---

*Aside from improving the joint's aesthetic appeal, the carpeting further reinforced Benny's maxim concerning bread cast on water: the man who installed the carpet turned out to be a gambler as well, and on his first visit to the Horseshoe proceeded to lose exactly $18,000—the very price Benny had paid him.

Benny surrounded himself with a team more sympathetic to his style of management—his family. His two sons, Jack and Lonnie (who everyone knew by his nickname "Ted"), were installed as casino bosses as soon as they turned twenty-one. "They still mind me just like they was six-year-olds," Benny would brag. His wife Teddy Jane knew what she was getting into from the time she started dating him. "If I marry Benny Binion," she said, "I'll spend my life in a room above a two-bit craps game." Sure enough, once all five of their children had grown old enough to leave home, Teddy Jane began working in the casino cage, helping to look after the books.

Binion's Horseshoe remained a true family business well into the next millennium, one of the last Las Vegas casinos to do so. There were financial partners, but they tended to remain behind the scenes. One of them was Nick "the Greek" Dandalos, or as Benny described him, "the strangest character I ever seen."

No one was entirely sure where Dandalos had found his fortune. It was rumored that he had broken every high roller on the East Coast, including gangster Arnold Rothstein, the man who had fixed baseball's World Series in 1919.* Benny's attempts to press him for specifics were met with inscrutability. After the Greek was informed that his sister had died, Benny tried to take advantage of the man's fragile emotional state to solve the mystery, but the Greek wasn't fooled.

"If I outlive you, I'll tell it," he said, wiping away his tears and grinning, "but if I don't outlive you, it won't go any further. I'll *never* tell it."

"He never did tell me," recalled Benny. "And there don't nobody know."

Whatever deep secrets the man chose to keep, on the surface Nick Dandalos appeared to be the consummate gentleman gambler: refined, well educated, blessed with abundant charm.

"He told stories by the hour," recounted the other "Greek," famed oddsmaker Jimmy Snyder. "He recited poetry. . . . He was beautiful

---

*This will be the sole reference to that *other* World Series. Anytime the World Series is mentioned in the text it can safely be assumed that it is the World Series of Poker that is being discussed.

with women. He made Omar Sharif look like a truck driver. . . . He had a deft touch with a phrase and said things like, 'I would rather fall from a mountaintop than die of boredom on the plain.' It was remarkable, really, to watch him in action. He attracted people like fish to a flashpan, people who begged him to play with their money. It was the legend and the charm and, no doubt, the idea of sharing winnings with Nick the Greek."

Shortly after the Horseshoe opened, Dandalos expressed his desire to play a poker game for the highest stakes in history, and asked Benny if he'd host it. It was an easy decision for Binion—regardless of the outcome, the publicity alone would make it worthwhile. Finding a worthy opponent for the Greek was even easier. All he had to do was get on the phone to his childhood friend in Texas, who had since earned a reputation for being one of the finest poker players in the state.

"Johnny," Benny said, "they got a fellow out here calls himself Nick the Greek. Thinks he can play stud poker. Johnny, I think you should come out here and have some fun."

Johnny Moss had never been to Las Vegas before. He was also bone-tired from having played poker for four consecutive days. Neither aspect of his condition was enough to give him even a moment's pause.

"No point in putting it off when there's money to be made," declared Moss, who made a beeline straight for Binion's Horseshoe and, upon his arrival, immediately sat down to play.

The legendary duel between Johnny Moss and Nick Dandalos began on a Sunday night in January of 1951 and would not end until the calendar reached May. A change of dealers every twenty minutes or so kept the game moving at an efficient pace; the players did their part by rarely straying from the table, often playing for days on end without taking a break. During the infrequent pauses in the action, Johnny tended to sleep more than the Greek, who spent much of his time away from the poker table playing craps. Fifteen years older than the forty-four-year-old Moss, the Greek jumped at every opportunity to needle the younger man.

"What are you going to do?" he once greeted Johnny upon his return to the table. "Sleep your life away?"

As the battle raged on, Benny took full advantage of the Greek's larger-than-life personality and Johnny's ample poker skills, placing their table in a prominent position at the very front of his casino. Spectators flocked to the rails, standing five and six deep most of the day. A few of the wealthier and more brazen were allowed to "change in" to the game for the agreed-upon minimum of $10,000. None lasted more than a day or two.

When the players tired of one game, they simply switched to another. Finally, after five months of battle, the cagy Texan managed to break his charming foe. As dashing in defeat as in victory, the Greek rose from his chair and said famously:

"Mr. Moss, I have to let you go."

"That Greek was a real gentleman," Johnny later recalled. "He never said nothing else. He just got up, and he smiled, and he set off to bed."

Moss was rumored to have beaten Dandalos to the tune of two or three million dollars, while Benny Binion likely reaped an equally gaudy sum from all the walk-in traffic the drama attracted. The two former street urchins, neither of whom had advanced past the second grade, had done the unthinkable, hosting—and winning—the biggest game in Las Vegas history.

Eighteen years later, in 1969, Benny Binion accepted an invitation from another transplanted native of the Lone Star State, Tom Moore, to attend something called the Texas Gamblers Reunion. The brainchild of casino insider Vic Vickrey, the get-together was a marketing ploy to attract high rollers to Moore's new Holiday Hotel in Reno, Nevada during a slow time of year. The country's best card players, as well as some Las Vegas casino bosses and professional bookmakers, gathered at the hotel for a series of high-stakes poker games.

In the time that had passed since the Moss–Dandalos affair, Benny had enjoyed steady success, marred only by a brief prison sentence. Convicted on charges of tax evasion by the authorities in Texas in 1953, he had his chauffeur, the wonderfully named Gold Dollar, drive him from Las Vegas to Dallas where he surrendered to his old friend Bill Decker. He spent the next three years in the federal penitentiary at Leavenworth. Upon his parole he returned to Las Vegas, but as an ex-felon he was no longer allowed to maintain a gaming license.

Although Benny had no official title, everyone knew who was calling the shots from behind the scenes. Just as they had throughout his absence, his two sons Jack and Ted remained responsible for the day-to-day operation of the Horseshoe. While the more reserved Jack was officially named casino president in 1964, many who knew the Binions believed that Ted—the one who most resembled Benny—would one day assume control. Ted liked to dress like a cowboy and often carried a pistol. But he also liked to take drugs, a severe handicap when it came to running a multimillion-dollar business.

The trip to Reno gave Benny the chance to reunite with many of the most feared poker sharps from his home state, men like Moss, Amarillo Slim, Doyle Brunson, Jack "Treetop" Straus, Brian "Sailor" Roberts, even the notorious Charles Harrelson, a convicted contract killer who also happens to be the father of actor Woody Harrelson. There were plenty of notable non-Texans there as well, including Tennessee's Walter Clyde "Puggy" Pearson, New Yorker Jimmy Casella, Ohio's own Jimmy "the Greek" Snyder, and Rudolph Wanderone, better known as "Minnesota Fats."

Doing what they liked to do best, these men played poker for an entire week straight. To diminish the edge maintained by any specialists, they frequently alternated games, switching between five-card stud and draw, seven-card stud, seven-card hi-lo split, and lowball, both ace-to-five and deuce-to-seven, but the most popular proved to be a variation of seven-card stud called Texas hold'em.

"THE GAME IS TEXAS HOLD'EM"

While the numerous tournaments that make up the World Series of Poker cover a wide range of games, the $10,000 buy-in Championship Event tests a player's skill in the contest often referred to as "the Cadillac of poker"—no-limit Texas hold'em.

Each player receives two "hole" cards facedown, which he uses in combination with the five "community" cards placed faceup on the table to make the best five-card hand.

Although the house generally supplies the actual dealer, the dealer's position—the most advantageous seat at the table, as this player gets to act last during each round of betting—is represented by a plastic "button."

In addition to any antes, two players have to post bets before the cards are even dealt. The player sitting to the left of the button, the "small blind," has to pay a portion, usually half, of the opening bet, while the player to his left, the "big blind," has to risk the full opening bet. These positions are relative, changing after each hand as the button moves clockwise around the table. In tournament poker, the blinds and antes are increased in regular intervals, forcing players to risk larger and larger portions of their checks.

The rest of the players can "limp in," simply matching the opening bet; raise the pot, forcing everyone else to match or increase their bet; or fold. The next round of betting comes after the "flop," the first three community cards placed simultaneously on the board. There is another round of betting after the next card—called "fourth street" or "the turn"—is delivered, then a final round of betting follows, once the last card—"fifth street" or "the river"—is laid on the table.

Despite its apparent simplicity, hold'em is a surprisingly difficult game to master. "As opposed to other forms of poker," Doyle Brunson once wrote, "you can represent a lot of different hands in hold'em. You can also put your opponent on any one of several hands.* You're forced to do a lot of guessing. So is your opponent."

One of the more credible stories surrounding the origin of this variation of poker credits a bunkhouse full of ranch hands. With only one deck of cards available to them, they devised a game in which as many as twenty-three players could participate at the same time. As its name would suggest, Texas was undoubtedly the land of its birth, but the game quickly moved into neighboring Louisiana and Oklahoma.

The game would remain a mystery to most of the rest of the world until Felton "Corky" McCorquodale, a native of Forth Worth, Texas, introduced it to Las Vegas's California Club in 1963. It spread like wildfire to the other popular poker rooms of the day: the Golden Nugget, the Stardust, and the Dunes.

Most chose to play "limit" hold'em, a game where the amount a player was able to bet or raise at any point in the hand was restricted to a specific amount. The Texas road gamblers, however, saw limit poker as a repetitive exercise that could only be stomached by accountant types and "leather asses," players who carved out a meager existence waiting for a great hand to play. A *true* gambler preferred "no-limit" hold'em, where a player could risk his entire stack of chips at any time by declaring himself to be "all in." While limit poker tends to be a very mathematical game whose correct play is usually dictated

---

*In poker's distinctive vernacular, to "put on" means to make an educated guess as to the strength of an opponent's hand.

(continued)

by odds, no-limit incorporates a larger palette of skills, including controlled aggression, a deep understanding of human psychology, and a certain elevated class of courage that players refer to simply as "heart." Perhaps Crandell Addington, an accomplished no-limit player from San Antonio, Texas, put it best when he said,

"Limit poker is a science, but no-limit is an art. In limit you're shooting at a target. In no-limit the target comes alive and shoots back at you."

At the end of the Texas Gamblers Reunion in Reno, the poker players who had gathered there named Johnny Moss the best overall player. He was awarded a silver cup proclaiming him to be the "King of Cards." Benny Binion also left the reunion with something: inspiration fueled by what he had seen. Forever seeking new ways to promote his casino and remembering how successful the Moss–Dandalos affair had been in achieving that objective, he conferred with his son Jack about the possibility of hosting a similar gathering.

"That was a good thing up there in Reno a few months ago. It sure brought in a lot of people, and I'm certain there will be even more next year. The more I think about it, that might be a good thing to have here at the Horseshoe."

From a conversation with Vic Vickrey the following spring, Jack gleaned that there were no plans to host another reunion at the Holiday Hotel. The Binions were further encouraged when Jimmy Snyder volunteered to promote such an event at the Horseshoe for free. Benny had a great deal of confidence in the man's abilities. A bookmaker who had earned a national reputation, thanks to a series of articles in *Sports Illustrated*, Jimmy "the Greek" had gone legit in the early 1960s, amidst repeated attempts by Attorney General Bobby Kennedy to link him to the Mafia. He began writing a column on sports wagering for the *Las Vegas Sun* that was eventually syndicated to newspapers around the country. Having awakened to the power of the press, Snyder opened a public relations business, and in early 1970 included the reclusive Howard Hughes among his clients.

Benny's trust in Snyder proved well founded. Thanks to Snyder, the inaugural tournament received mention in thousands of newspapers across the nation. All Benny had to do in return was comp the expenses of any reporters who bothered to show up. The only obstacle that remained was, in the grand scheme of things, a relatively minor detail: the Horseshoe didn't have a poker room. Casino floor space was far too precious to waste on a game in which players vied for each other's money, leaving the house only a small percentage of each pot. After converting his casino's baccarat alcove into a temporary card room, Benny sent out invitations to the top poker players in the country, requesting them to meet at the Horseshoe in May 1970 for what he called in his usual grandiose style the "World Series of Poker."

For Johnny Moss, word of Benny's gathering couldn't have arrived at a better time. His life had been growing progressively duller since his card-playing marathon with Nick the Greek.

He reportedly won $10 million playing poker in Las Vegas during the 1950s, only to lose it—and then some—playing craps. By the end of the decade, having gone a half-million dollars into debt to various casinos, he was forced to leave the city. "I told them I'd pay them back in five years," said Moss, who returned to the circuit in and around Texas. "I did it in a year and a half."

Moss continued to improve his already formidable skills. "I learned all the poker games, because that's what a professional gambler has to do." During one stretch he flew to Gardena, California every day to get "lessons" on how to play ace-to-five lowball, using his newfound skills to destroy the game in Vegas every night.* He went on a tear, once winning $848,000 in a single session, so many racks of $100 chips he had to stack them on the floor around his chair.

Virgie Moss, having little desire to return to their early days of financial insecurity, took over as his money manager. "I give my wife a

---

*Thanks to a series of landmark court decisions, "draw" poker became legal in Gardena in the late 1930s. Both the city and the game enjoyed a heyday until the 1980s, when another series of legal decisions legalized all forms of poker—including Texas hold'em—throughout California, opening the floodgates for state's currently thriving cardroom scene.

big percentage of every win," Johnny once said. "Getting any of it
back from her is like trying to get gold from Fort Knox." She wisely
sunk a good portion of his winnings into real estate, mostly apartment buildings in Texas. "Now I may be broke or as near to broke as
can be, but Virgie—well, Virgie's a millionaire."

Thanks to Virgie's prudence, sixty-three-year-old Johnny was enjoying a comfortable retirement in Odessa. Sort of. The boredom was
nearly killing him. He could only find small games on the weekends
and was forbidden from hosting bigger ones at home.

"I won't let Johnny play poker in the house," said Virgie. "They
just get so nasty when they're playin', droppin' cigarette butts on the
rugs and ever'thing."

With Johnny growing increasingly irritable, Virgie actually offered to pay him a thousand dollars a week to sit at home and drink
whiskey.

"What good is money if you can't gamble with it?" he grumbled.

When Benny's invitation reached Odessa, Virgie practically
pushed her grumpy husband out the door.

Moss was joined by a who's who of the poker world: Doyle Brunson,
Puggy Pearson, Jack Straus, Jimmy Casella, Sailor Roberts, Amarillo
Slim, Bill Boyd, Crandell Addington, Curtis "Iron Man" Skinner, Titanic Thompson, and twenty-six other highly skilled players. For three
straight days they tested each other's prowess in a variety of games.

"It was open to everybody," recalled Doyle Brunson, "and we
played for ten days or so. . . . Many times a game would go on for
two, three days straight."

"You just kept playing until you got too tired to play any more,"
said Amarillo Slim. "And if you were hungry, you ate at the table. I sat
there with a big ol' jar of pure honey. People thought I was able to play
for days without eating, but I just kept fortifying myself with honey."

There was no formal schedule of events. "If seven seven-card stud
players arrived at the Horseshoe at the same time, they'd play the
seven-stud contest—provided one of them wasn't asleep," said Eric
Drache, who would later run the World Series for the Binions
through most of its first two decades.

The hospitality the players received from the Horseshoe proved an unexpected pleasure for these men who were used to playing in shady backrooms in the dicey parts of town. Even the usual security issues could be set aside, as Doyle Brunson discovered when he noticed a group of potential hijackers eyeing one of the games. He passed the word to Benny, who immediately told the outsiders to stand back, that they were making the players nervous. When they refused, Benny approached the one who appeared to be in charge.

"I know you're a young man who thinks he's tough. I'm an old man and I know I'm tough. If you want to see who's tougher, let's go to the garage and figure it out."

"Right about then," recalled Doyle, "those guys left."

As organized as the event was, compared to the backroom games these players had been weaned on, this World Series still seemed more like a fraternity meeting than a competitive sport. Over a steak dinner in the Horseshoe's restaurant, the Sombrero Room, nearly everyone got an award. Jack Straus was named "Most Congenial Participant." Curtis "Iron Man" Skinner and "Doc" Green—the only two amateurs who had dared to join the mix—earned honors as "Nonprofessional Champions."

Jack Binion then asked the participants to vote for the best all-around player.

"I couldn't understand why the fuck anybody would vote," scoffed Slim. "We played for a lot of money and that was the vote."

Everyone else voted for themselves.

So Jack refined his approach. "I asked them to vote for whom they thought was second best."

They elected Johnny Moss, who had already been named "Best All-Around Hold'em Player" and "Deuce-to-Steven Lowball Champion." He could now add the title "World Champion Poker Player" to his list of accomplishments.

"Moss was the best I had ever played with," said Doyle. "He was the Grand Old Man of Poker and he deserved it."

"It was pretty nice," said Johnny, "because there were a lot of good players in town," he said. "But most good players are only good at one game, and I was good at them all."

Not everyone, however, had as good a time as the gamblers. Ted Thackrey, a feature writer covering the event for the *Los Angeles Times*, observed that this "World Series" was hardly as grand as its name suggested. Watching emotionless people pass chips back and forth for days at a stretch was, in a word, boring. The election of a gruff, uncharismatic champion by popular vote didn't help.

"You've got to find some way to make it a contest," advised Thackrey. "If you want to get the press involved and turn the World Series into a real sporting event, you need to give it some structure, create some drama, and make it a real tournament."

By his own account, it was Amarillo Slim who hit upon the idea of making it a "freezeout." The players would begin with a fixed quantity of chips that could not be replenished. Once a player had lost them all, he was out of the tournament. The last remaining player would be crowned champion.

Thackrey liked the idea. That winter, Jimmy the Greek—who had been fired by Howard Hughes in a massive purge as mysterious as the man himself—redoubled his efforts to promote the tournament. In 1971, they were going to be hosting a true poker championship, the first of its kind.

The idea that they were making history, however, couldn't have been farther from the minds of the seven men—Johnny Moss, Jack Straus, Puggy Pearson, Jimmy Casella, Sailor Roberts, Doyle Brunson, and Amarillo Slim—who sat down to play. What could be more unremarkable than a poker game among these all-too-familiar faces? The stakes were high but hardly extravagant. Johnny Moss's coronation as "world champion" the previous year hadn't changed his life a lick. And the new winner-take-all format, while good for drama, actually represented more of a risk for the participants, as all but one would be leaving the table empty-handed.

No one bothered to take notes or keep records. The details of what happened over the next two days have for the most part been lost to history. What is remembered is that the cards fell in a way that only reinforced what everyone already suspected.

"[Johnny] Moss won that event," Doyle later recalled of the 1971 championship, "so it does show that we voted [in 1970] for the right guy."

The new format worked. Now all that was left to do was convince the rest of the world to start paying attention.

2

FADING THE WHITE LINE

It was hardly surprising that the first world champion of poker hailed from the Lone Star State. The backroom games that flourished in Texas throughout the 1950s and 1960s created expert poker players the way the University of Miami produces NFL prospects.

These "outside" or "road" gamblers made their living driving from town to town across the state in search of action in much the same way that today's professional poker players follow the tournament trail. Rarely making much money off each other, the road gamblers instead relied on "producers," suckers with a lot more money than skill.

An ambitious player could find a high stakes poker game nearly every night of the week, assuming he was familiar with the area's "boss gambler." Some of these bosses used fraternal organizations, such as the Elks Lodge or Redman's Club, to hide their illegal operations from the authorities. Others ran games right out of their houses. Every Tuesday and Friday night Hugh Briscoe hosted the biggest game in Denton. On Wednesday and Thursday nights Martin Cramer's house in Brenham was the place to play. It was at one of

Cramer's games in 1957 that three players—Amarillo Slim, Sailor Roberts, and Doyle Brunson—decided to pool their resources and form a team. Traveling together and playing off the same bankroll, they shared both the wins and the losses. It proved a historic partnership.

"I doubt if there will ever be three poker partners with the kind of talent we had," brags Slim. "Any one of us could pinch-hit for the other when he was tired or just not feelin' right. Doyle, Sailor, and I dedicated ourselves to becoming the best three poker players in the world.

"After a long session, none of us could hardly sleep from being so wound up, and we would just stay awake for hours talking about the hands we played that night, the players in the game, and all different sorts of strategies. Imagine what it would have been like if Paul "Bear" Bryant, Vince Lombardi, and George "Papa Bear" Halas traveled together for ten years and did nothing but talk football. Or if Warren Buffet, Peter Lynch, and George Soros went around the world picking stocks together and exchanging investment ideas. Let's just say there was a lot of knowledge changing hands."

The team lasted seven years, until a disastrous trip to Las Vegas—more specifically, the no-limit Kansas City lowball game at the Dunes—nearly wiped out their entire bankroll, some $100,000. They went their separate ways after that, but the three would butt heads at the poker table many times in the future, most notably at the World Series of Poker, where, thanks to all the knowledge they had amassed together, each would claim his rightful share of personal success.

For much of its early history there were always two events at the World Series of Poker—the tournament itself and the "side games" that regularly sprung up around it. Side games, as the name suggests, are informal cash games played off to the side of a poker tournament. Whereas the tournament players were playing with chips that had no value outside of the tournament, those playing in the side games were playing with actual cash. The bigger cash games offered players the chance to earn, with a single pot, what the World Series champion made for a full day of work.

So it should have come as no surprise that, although twelve players signed up for the 1972 championship, only eight of them actually made it to the table. The others were presumably lost to the lucrative action on the fringes. In what should have come as even less of a surprise, six of the eight players were Texans.

While it was announced that the entry fee had been raised to $10,000, twice what it had been the year before, the entrants themselves still only had to pony up $5,000—Benny Binion quietly subsidized the rest, believing that a bigger buy-in would make for bigger headlines. Relentless in his efforts to promote the Horseshoe, he spent much of the tournament regaling Ted Thackrey and the rest of the newsmen seated in a special section close to the action, while Jimmy the Greek, with microphone in hand, narrated the play, and Benny's son Jack ran the show. A poker player himself, Jack enjoyed a special camaraderie with most of the players, often starting the games himself and remaining forever willing to hear suggestions as to how the tournament could be improved.

Six hours into the 1972 championship, Johnny Moss sat on more chips than any of his opponents. He appeared to be on his way to another title when he called a small opening raise from Doyle Brunson, who held pocket aces. While two aces in the hole represent the most powerful starting hand in hold'em, it's a hand which often delivers as much heartache as joy. Poker players quickly learn that aces are good for winning little pots—or losing big ones. In making a small raise, Doyle was hoping to lure one of his opponents into raising him, building a large pot that he would be heavily favored to win, but neither Johnny nor Jack "Treetop" Straus fell for the trap. Both merely called, hoping to improve their modest hands, and both did. The 9-7-2 flop made top pair for Straus, who had J-9, and he called when Doyle made yet another small bet. Johnny held an even bigger hand, as his pocket deuces had connected with the board to make a "set"—three of a kind—and he fired a huge raise back at Doyle, one large enough to force Doyle to risk the last of his chips. With his tournament life on the line, Doyle took his time before he finally called.

"Well, if this hand's not any good," he said with resignation. "I'm ready to go home."

After Straus folded, Johnny showed Doyle his three deuces. Only an ace would save Doyle, a long shot as there were only two remaining in the deck. As Doyle rose from the table, preparing to leave, Moss peeked at the "muck"—the messy pile of discarded cards—and discovered that one of those two aces had already been thrown away. Doyle had his jacket on by the time a 10 fell on the turn and was all but out the door when the dealer turned over the river card—the last ace in the deck!

Doyle's reaction was about the same as it would have been if he had been eliminated on the hand, which is to say, steady as she goes. If they are to maintain their sanity, professional poker players learn not to get too emotionally invested in individual hands, and the unflappable Doyle is about as professional as they come.

Johnny had a few chips left, but they wouldn't last long. As luck would have it, he moved all in before the flop with a pair of 9s on the very hand that "Jolly" Roger Van Ausdall, a farm equipment salesman from Missouri, moved in with the other two 9s. Unfortunately for both, Puggy Pearson had a pair of kings and was only too happy to call. The duplicate pairs of 9s made it all but impossible for either to draw out a winner, Puggy's kings held up, and it was assured that for the first time in the short history of the tournament somebody other than Johnny Moss would be crowned champion.

With only four players remaining, Puggy seemed firmly in control of the action with nearly half the chips on the table. At the back of the pack limped Amarillo Slim, who was down to his last $1,775 after losing a big hand to Jack Straus. An entrepreneurial spectator who had been taking odds on the players throughout the tournament loudly declared Slim to be a 25–1 underdog.

Where others saw futility, Slim saw opportunity.

"Well," he responded with his usual enthusiastic confidence, "I'm taking a hundred dollars of that."

The fact that Amarillo Slim was born in Johnson, Arkansas has never stopped him from claiming to be a Texan. Thomas Austin Preston, Jr., was just a baby when his parents "saw the error of their ways" and moved to the town that would engender his famous nickname. He would spend the rest of his life trying to atone for the sin of having been born elsewhere, in the process becoming more Texan than most of the natives.

He certainly dresses the part. He habitually adorns his toothpick-thin frame—Slim was once described as "the advance man for a famine"—with all sorts of stylish Western wear. He has a special fondness for boldly colored suits and custom boots stitched from the skins of exotic animals: alligators, ostriches, kangaroos, even ant-eaters. The blandest shirts in his wardrobe sport emerald buttons, the louder ones dollar gold pieces. Wound around the brim of his favorite Stetson is a stuffed rattlesnake, the same creature that made the fatal error, once upon a time, of biting him on the hand.

To write off his fashion choices as reflective of a questionable aesthetic sensibility is to overlook the calculating mind of one of the greatest "proposition" gamblers who ever lived. "It never hurts," says Slim, "for potential opponents to think you're more than a little stupid, and can hardly count all the money in your hip pocket, much less hold on to it. People everywhere assume that anyone from Texas in a ten-gallon hat is not only a billionaire, but an easy mark. That's just fine with me, because that's the impression I'm trying to give. This approach puts those dudes in the category of guessers, and guessers are losers. That's my meat, to make the other guy guess."

Never one for the grind of a regular job, Slim decided at an early age to follow in the tradition of the legendary "Titanic" Thompson, the most famous proposition gambler of his day. "I like to bet on anything—as long as the odds are in my favor," wrote Slim in his memoirs, *Amarillo Slim in a World Full of Fat People*. "I've bet big money that I could pick any thirty people at random and two of them would have the same birthday, that a stray cat could carry an empty Coke bottle across the room, and that I could hold on to a horse's tail for a quarter of a mile. I even wagered $37,500 that a fly would land on a particular sugar cube. At the fanciest casino in Marrakech, Morocco, I bet that I could ride a camel right through the middle of it." He won every one of those bets, having figured out, well in advance of the actual event, some angle that would ensure his victory.

Sitting at the 1972 championship table with less than $2,000 left of the $10,000 he had started the tournament with, Slim knew his only angle was to find a situation that would allow him to grab as many chips as he could. It didn't take long to find it. After Doyle Brunson opened with a $700 bet that was called by both Puggy and Treetop, Slim glanced at his top hole card—a king—and decided it was time to make his move, pushing all in. If everyone folded, he would more than double his stack of chips; and if someone called, that was fine too, as he was getting a huge "overlay" on his money, risking just $1,775 to win more than $5,000.

"Well, there ain't no need of me looking at that other card," he told his opponents as he pushed all of his chips into the middle. "I can get action for my money *now*. It makes no difference what that other card is."

"Amarillo Slim's moving in," announced Jimmy the Greek.

"It feels better in!" yelled Slim, much to the crowd's delight.

His bluster failed to frighten any of his opponents. They all called his bet. The flop delivered two 5s and a 3, all of different suits. Confident that his pocket 10s were the best hand, Doyle bet $4,000, forcing Straus and Puggy to fold.

Slim flipped over his second hole card with a flourish and discovered, to the delight of nearly everyone other than Doyle, the 5 of hearts. Slim's trip 5s held up, and he was right back in the thick of the action.

Play adjourned at three in the morning, recommencing at two the following afternoon. When Jack Straus was eliminated four hours later, the three remaining players—Doyle, Puggy, and Slim—asked for a timeout and reconvened in the Sombrero Room, which during tournament time became the de facto players' lounge.

As close as they were to the ultimate prize, the surviving aspirants maintained a few reservations about winning it. These were men accustomed to living lives of quiet anonymity. Aside from the cash—a relatively average day at the office for a high-stakes road gambler—it wasn't at all clear that being labeled the "world's greatest poker player" carried any tangible benefit. A higher profile might make it more difficult to find willing opponents, or even worse, place a target on a suddenly visible bankroll.

"People were concerned about the IRS and the tax law," recalls Eric Drache. "They might have thought that a win at the Series would mean an instant audit."

Saying he had an upset stomach, Doyle asked his opponents if they'd allow him to cash out his remaining chips and go home. With no rule, as there is today, prohibiting such a move, Puggy and Slim readily gave their consent, happy to see the departure of such a formidable player.

Of the two men left, Puggy arguably possessed the better poker skills. He also had nearly twice as many chips as his opponent, but Slim's long history as a hustler had made him a master of these sorts of confrontations.

"Amarillo Slim Preston is a fine player, although I don't consider him among the cream of the crop," once observed veteran rounder "Oklahoma" Johnny Hale. "His best skill is that he's a good psychologist. He can 'interview' his opponents with such a degree of skill and read their verbal responses better than anybody I've ever seen. Slim will talk about anything in the world to get the other man to respond so that he can hear his voice. And if he can hear him, he can read him. He can read his intonations along with his body language. When he's head-up in a hand or in a big game and he's putting down that line of bullsquat, it isn't bullsquat. He's getting information and putting it in his computer bank and coming up with answers."

Or, as Slim describes his fondness for riling his opponents in order to get them to reveal their strength: "Some of these guys play the games real uptight, but I like to put a rattlesnake in their pocket and ask 'em for a match."

When Slim sat down to play heads-up for the championship, he wasted no time trying to get under Puggy's skin, jawing at him incessantly. Not one to back down, Puggy threw Slim's words right back in his face.

"You better play 'em tight, you skinny son of a bitch," Puggy said, "because I'm gonna break you before the night's over."

"Take your best shot, partner," responded Slim. "I've been broke in bigger towns than Vegas, and lost to better men than you."

Despite Puggy's bravado, something in his demeanor suggested to Slim that he was going to start out playing conservatively. One of poker's most widely held maxims suggests that if you can put your opponent on an easily definable style, your best bet, so to speak, is to do exactly the opposite. Slim began "coming over the top" of Puggy, aggressively raising and reraising him, often without bothering to look at his hole cards. The strategy worked, as Slim took down pot after pot, and within an hour the chip count was even.

Dismissing the impartiality he was supposed to be maintaining as the tournament's emcee, Jimmy the Greek whispered to Puggy that he needed to stop Slim from stealing all the pots. Overhearing the remark, Slim knew it was time to change gears. He made a mental note, telling himself the next time he made a powerful hand to "sell it to him real high," playing it exactly like all the bluffs he had been throwing Puggy's way.

The opportunity came just a few hands later when Slim, with a K♥J♣, called Puggy's $700 raise before the flop. The flop brought two 8s and a king, and Slim was confident that his pair of kings was better than whatever Puggy had. Under different conditions, Slim might have made a reasonable bet in an attempt to elicit a call from his opponent. Instead, he pushed all in, knowing full well Puggy would suspect him of trying to steal another pot with a big bluff.

Sure enough, Puggy called with his remaining chips, holding nothing more than a pair of 6s in the hole. He would need another to win the hand, but the turn was a deuce, the river a third 8, and with his full house, 8s over kings, Amarillo Slim Preston became the 1972 world champion. He handled the victory with his usual flair, only this time with the volume turned up even louder.

"I'm looking for a game, any game at all, as long as it's for real money," he shouted. "Seems like a fella should be able to get a game in a town like this. But I swear I can't find a thing to occupy my time!"

While his credentials as the world's best poker player were debatable, there was little doubt that Amarillo Slim was the greatest ambassador the game had ever known. His easygoing charm and natural gift for gab catapulted him into the national spotlight. He wrote a bestselling book, *Play Poker to Win,* and his exploits inspired Kenny Rogers to write a chart-busting song *The Gambler.* Robert Altman cast him in his movie *California Split,* ironically, as an easy mark. But no medium served the garrulous and charismatic Slim better than television. He would make eleven appearances on the *Tonight Show* and three on *60 Minutes.* After accidentally neglecting to mention the Binions on one of the *Tonight Show* spots, Slim made amends to Benny by inviting him to join him on the *Tomorrow Show.* In Slim's words, he and Benny "put on an hour's commercial for the Horseshoe."

"Benny," asked host Tom Snyder, "why is it that those places out there on the Strip in Vegas have a $500 limit and you've got no limit?"

"Well, they got great big hotels and little biddy bankrolls," Benny replied. "I got a little biddy hotel and a great big bankroll."

"But Mr. Binion, aren't you afraid that somebody will break the bank?"

"Well, not really. I've got a derned good head start on 'em."

Binion's Horseshoe—and with it, the World Series of Poker—was finally on the map.

The press flocked to the 1973 World Series, beginning what would become for many of them an annual pilgrimage. Two books—Jon Bradshaw's *Fast Company* and David Spanier's *Total Poker*—devoted entire chapters to detailed account of the event, as did seven thousand newspaper and magazine articles. Television cameras also appeared for the first time as a crew from CBS News filmed a documentary narrated by Jimmy the Greek.

The tournament itself had been expanded to five events, including seven-card stud, razz, and deuce-to-seven lowball, but the featured event remained the $10,000 No-Limit Hold'em tournament, as it decided the world champion. This time around, all thirteen players who signed up actually played, and each of them produced the full $10,000 entry fee without any assistance from Benny Binion. He could not have been more pleased, both by the turnout and the tournament's future prospects.

"We had seven players last year, and this year we had thirteen. I look to have better than twenty next year. It's even liable to get up to be fifty, might get up to be more than that. . . . It will eventually."

As the scope of the tournament grew, so did the need for more efficient mangement. The World Series, despite its increasing stature, still unfolded like a casual game among old friends. Just ask Eric Drache (pronounced "Drake"), a New Jersey native who had dropped out of Rutgers University in 1970 to try and make a living as a professional poker player. During his first four months in Las Vegas, he built the $600 he had arrived with into a $70,000 bankroll, large enough, he decided, to take a stab at the 1972 $5,000 Seven-Card Stud event. When he went to sign up, however, he couldn't get any sense of how many others were entered or how big the prize pool was going to be. As it turned out, it didn't matter—the tournament was cancelled shortly before it was set to begin, as Johnny Moss, having played poker all through the previous day and night, was too tired to participate.

"I was really surprised by what looked like a lack of organization," recalls Drache, who politely said as much to Jack Binion. "He told me if I thought I could do a better job, then why don't I do it?" In 1973, Drache was named the World Series's first tournament director, a post he would retain until 1989.

While he may not have been aware of it at the time, Drache was trailblazing a brand-new occupation—today, nearly every poker room has a tournament director, many of whom learned the trade under his tutelage. He created official schedules that were mailed to players in advance, and set clearly defined blinds and limits for each of the games. He also worked hand in hand with Benny and Jack to ensure the World Series's consistent expansion.

"We made a decision that we were going to show some growth rate in the final event every year, regardless of how we had to do it," says Drache. "I always felt if it's not going up, it's going down—in the eyes of the players, anyway." Sometimes this meant staking a player or two at the last minute. Mostly, however, Drache's persuasive personality was enough.

"There is no one who understands tournament poker the way Eric Drache does," claims Henri Bollinger, who served as the World Series's official publicist for over a decade. "He understands what a serious poker player is all about. He knows, when they talk about integrity, what they mean by that. He knows also that even the most 'honest' of poker players has a bit of the larcenist in him, that poker players do whatever needs to be done to win, and to do it in a way that appears to be honorable is a trick. He's able to deal with people who other people could never deal with because of that. It's a rare talent—people who will trust absolutely no one else trust Eric."

During Drache's sixteen years as director, the number of entrants in the championship event grew more than tenfold. And never once did it decline.

· · ·

In addition to his duties as tournament emcee, Jimmy the Greek was the 1973 Championship Event's unofficial bookmaker. He made Johnny Moss, Jack Straus, and Puggy Pearson the cofavorites at five-to-one odds, which didn't sit well with any of the players.

"Hey, Greek," said Puggy, "with three of us as equal favorites, it sounds to me like you couldn't make up your mind."

Amarillo Slim was even more riled up, having failed to crack the trio of favorites. "Lookee here. I'm the world champion at this here game. The world *champeen*. How come you're only making me eight-to-one? Ain't you read my book? It says right there on the cover in plain English—Amarillo Slim, the world *champeen* of poker shows you how he beats 'em all. Can't you read, Greek? Hell, I'd get better odds in a spelling bee."

"That Slim," responded Johnny Moss with his typical grouchiness. "He always had a lot of country con. . . . That book of his is a joke. He may have won last year, but he was lucky. He's good, but he ain't great. He ain't gonna last out this tournament."

While Jack Binion and Jimmy the Greek hustled to set up the tables and lay out the chips just prior to the four o'clock start, Puggy and Slim were quick to resume the row they had started the previous year.

"Slim, let me tell you something. I'm playing this game a lot better than I did last year. And let me tell you something else—there wouldn't be no Texas if there wasn't a Tennessee. You're lucky to be here in the first place."

"If there wasn't no Tennessee, there wouldn't be no Texas, huh?" Slim fired back. "Well, if you folks in Tennessee could suck as well as you blow, we wouldn't need to be shipping no oil there."

The players cut cards for position and took their respective seats, which, for the first time, were divided among two tables. "They ought to figure up a way to seed 'em like in tennis or something," grumbled Jack "Treetop" Straus. "That table o' mine's about twice as tough as that other one."

Slim played to the crowd, at one point pretending to toss a handful of $100 black chips into their midst while substituting them for dollar chips at the very last second. He was the chip leader at the first break, but, as Johnny predicted, there would be no repeat performance. Minutes before midnight, Treetop caught a heart on the river to complete an unlikely flush, knocking Slim out of the tournament.

"Oh, them cold, cold hearts," he warbled before waving his hat to the crowd and exiting the room, looking somewhat miserable.

"Better stop the world *champeen* before he jumps off the roof," Doyle said to Treetop.

"Let him jump. He's got too much hot air in him to do him any harm."

Benny Binion attempted to placate Slim, pointing out how incredibly lucky Straus had been to outdraw him.

"Well, it's not too unusual," said Slim glumly. "Occasionally the lamb slaughters the butcher. That's just part of it. If you're going to play that hand, you're gonna play any hand. Anyhow, only women and children give up, and I'm neither of those. I'll be back."

Benny laughed. "I know you will. Tomorrow, in fact."

The familiar grin returned to Slim's face as he spied an empty seat in one of the side games. "Tonight, in fact."

In 2002, Bill Miller, a highly successful fund manager for Legg Mason Capital Management, addressed a classroom full of eager students at Columbia Business School, telling them that all of the skills necessary to become a brilliant investor could be summed up in a single quote. Expecting some nugget of erudition from Peter Drucker or Warren Buffett, the students were hardly prepared for what emerged from Miller's mouth:

"Ain't only three things to gambling: knowing the 60-40 end of the proposition, money management, and knowing yourself. Even a donkey knows that."

The author of the quote obviously wasn't some highly educated financier—in fact, he had been lucky to see the eighth grade. Nor was he an investor, at least not in the traditional sense of the word.

Walter Clyde Pearson was born in southern Kentucky, the son of a sharecropper who supplemented his income selling bootleg whiskey until a competitor removed his pinky with a shotgun blast. When Walter was five, his father moved him, his eight siblings, and their mother south to Jackson County, Tennessee, where it was rumored a nine-fingered farmer might find steady work. Such false reports led the itinerant family on a trail that seemed to have no end—before Walter was ten he had lived in nineteen different places and still had yet to see his first loaf of bread. The family settled into a familiar if uncomfortable pattern of sneaking away in the middle of the night before the rent came due in the morning.

When he was twelve, Walter took a hard fall while horsing around at a construction site and landed hard on his nose. The resulting disfigurement provided him with the nickname that would stick with him the rest of his life: "Puggy."

"Puggy's looks fool you," Jimmy the Greek once noted. "That pug nose and round face, that unbrilliant look of any sort. You just cannot conceive that a man like that is smart at anything. And he *isn't* smart at anything. Except one thing, and that's cards."

Puggy discovered his talent at an early age. Just thirteen years old, he hitchhiked all the way to Tampa with three dollars in his pocket, and in just two weeks he turned it into a thousand. He performed the same sort of magic in the navy, emerging at the end of his tour with $20,000, the bankroll that sustained him along a circuit similar to the one followed by the Texas road gamblers—Salina to Hopkinsville, Bowling Green to Louisville, Atlanta to Chicago. From 1951 to 1957 he played nearly every night of the week. He harbored the usual concerns—cheaters and hijackers—but otherwise considered his to be an idyllic life.

"Why hell, there ain't a breeze in the sky floats freer than I do," he once boasted.

Puggy's freedom was based largely on the fact that he wasn't a "donkey," although his defeat at the hands of Amarillo Slim the year before had left him feeling like one. While he was an expert at stud poker, he was relatively new to Texas hold'em and its many subtle nuances. Puggy spent the following year analyzing every aspect of the game.

"I couldn't play this game a lick last year," he said. "But I'm a sponge. I learn."

All the hard work was starting to pay off—he had already won two of the smaller events leading up to the championship. And while Jimmy the Geek might denigrate his play as the performance of some kind of idiot savant, the truth was that Puggy had hit upon a few of poker's deepest and most powerful truths. This was never more evident than it was in a hand against Crandell Addington, a dapper millionaire from San Antonio who was admired as much for his dress as his skill at cards—"Dandy Crandell" was known to change his cream-colored silk suits, mink jackets, and impeccably knotted ties up to three times in a single day.

With ten players left, Addington had the misfortune of getting dealt a pair of 9s when Puggy had a pair of queens. The flop came with three "undercards" to Puggy's queens, 10-8-6. A year earlier, he might have pushed all his chips into the pot at this point in the hand, but this was a different Puggy Pearson, more analytical and less rash. Wary of the possibility that his opponent might have flopped a straight, Puggy made a small "feeler" bet. Addington gave away little information about the strength of his hand when he merely called. The turn brought a queen, which while improving Puggy's hand—he now had three of a kind—did little to allay his fear of a straight.

"Do you know how big my two queens were at the start?" Puggy said afterwards, spreading his hands wide as if describing the length of a prize-winning bass. "They were that big! And when that third queen fell, do you know how big they were then?" He brought his finger and thumb close together. "That small! The queen is a perfect card for a straight."

When Puggy timidly checked the turn, Addington pushed all of his chips into the middle. While he suspected Addington had him beat, Puggy had to entertain the idea that his opponent was on a draw or bluffing. Adding that possibility to the chance of improving his own hand—he could pair the board on the river for a full house, or even spike, that is, to catch unexpectedly, the fourth queen—and comparing the combined odds to the amount of money he stood to win, Puggy determined that, regardless of the outcome, the correct play was to call. The man who hadn't made it past the eighth grade was using what economists with graduate degrees and six-figure salaries call "game theory."

"Everything is pricewise and percentagewise, understand?" is the way Puggy explained it.

As it turned out, Addington was "semibluffing" with his pocket 9s. He hoped to take the pot with his intimidating bet, but also knew he had "outs," cards remaining in the deck that would improve his hand, should Puggy call—a jack or a 7 would complete his straight. The river produced neither, bringing Addington's run to an abrupt end. However, the day wasn't a total loss for him. Before the start of the tournament he had bet $50 to Jimmy the Greek's $1 that his tie would remain tightly knotted throughout the event. He pocketed the Greek's dollar and, like a Chicago Cubs fan, immediately started thinking about next year.

There are as many different ways to win a poker tournament as there are types of poker players. The very cautious simply concentrate on surviving and hope everyone else knocks themselves out. Bobby Brazil, a swarthy twenty-five-year-old from Lake Tahoe, was just such a player. Befitting the huge diamond he wore on his pinky, Brazil played like a "rock," poker jargon for a tight player who refuses to give any action unless he's quite certain he holds the best hand. While rocks are usually able to bleed a small profit from a cash game, their style of play often fails miserably in tournaments, where ever increasing blinds and antes will quickly erode a stack of chips left unplayed. When he finally made his move it was with a less-than-desirable hand, and he was eliminated by Puggy's three jacks. Brazil's was the fifth scalp Puggy had claimed.

In fact, it seemed as if Puggy were on a mission to eliminate all of the other players himself. By nine-thirty of the second day he had knocked out three more players. Yet he was far from celebrating, as he still had to deal with the most aggressive player at that or any other table, Jack Straus, as well as the Grand Old Man of Poker himself, Johnny Moss.

For all his laurels, Moss felt like he was being picked on, as his younger opponents kept pecking away at his stack of chips with timely raises. He needed to take a stand, and, dealt a pair of aces, he had a hand that would allow him to do so. Opting to play them in an eerily similar fashion to the way Doyle had the previous year, he opened with a raise that wasn't big enough to scare anyone; he wanted callers, and he got them. Treetop Straus called with 10-9, Puggy with Q-J.

When the flop delivered both a queen and a jack, no one was more excited than Puggy. He checked, hoping Johnny would bet for him, and Johnny didn't disappoint, shoving nearly $12,500, the last of his chips, into the pot.

Treetop leaned back in his chair and frowned. A man who was

usually the life of the party, he had turned uncharacteristically testy that evening, perhaps because the loss of his glasses the day before had cost him some company.

"Got propositioned from the rail last night and couldn't even read the damn note," he grumbled.

Johnny's large bet did nothing to lift his spirits. Treetop stared at the pot and considered the odds of drawing to his open-ended straight. With less than $20,000, he decided it wasn't worth it and mucked his hand with a scowl.

It was now up to Puggy. If Johnny had made a hand that could beat two pair, Pearson thought he would have tried to "slowplay," checking or making a smaller bet in the hopes of attracting a call. Johnny's big bet seemed to indicate that he wanted Puggy out of the pot *right now*.

"Well, Johnny," Puggy said, "what do you got? I think you got two kings or two aces in the hole. You ain't got nothing else, you know. At least, I hope you ain't got three queens or three jacks."

Puggy called, and with no more betting possible, they turned up their hands. Moss seemed unfazed to see Puggy's two pair. He pulled out a handkerchief and began wiping his glasses. He needed help—a third ace, or for one of the two other cards on the board to pair—and the turn didn't bring it. Moss was now down to his last card, but the way Puggy reacted you would have thought he was the one desperately needing to catch a card.

"Get on with it, dealer," he said anxiously. "Deal."

The dealer did and delivered one of the eight cards Johnny needed to stay alive, another ace. The crowd burst into an excited cheer. Moss's long-suffering wife Virgie jumped out of the gallery and kissed him on the cheek. Johnny just shook his head and wiped his glasses again, as amazed by his good fortune as anyone. For a player who relied as much as he could on skill, getting saved by luck was a strange experience for him.

"I ain't drawed out on nobody in a long time. . . . My wife always says, 'Why don't you outdraw anybody?' Because I start with the best hand, that's the reason. I usually got the best hand when I get my money in there. And I can't help it if they outdraw it."

·   ·   ·

Soon after Johnny Moss knocked Jack Straus out of the tournament in third place, Benny Binion strolled into the room to watch the heads-up match between Johnny and Puggy.

"Sure, I want Johnny to win," he said around the toothpick in his mouth. "Ain't no two ways about it. We Texans, we stick together. Only fair, boy. In Texas, justice means 'just us.'"

Switching to a more aggressive style of play, Puggy wrested the lead from Johnny and nearly took him out after flopping two pair, but the resilient Moss managed to make a bigger two pair on the river, again earning the enthusiasm of the crowd and another kiss on the cheek from Virgie. Puggy appeared shaken and accepted the advice of Jimmy the Greek, who suggested he take a break. Puggy went for a short walk down the street, trying to collect himself.

"I thought I was goin' to bust him right there," he said ruefully. "That was a real brutal draw. He runs lucky, that ole boy, but when he's goin' for cards he's paid for 'em, so he has a right to get 'em I guess. But it don't matter none. It'll just take longer now, and time is on my side. I'll grind him for two, three thousand a pop. I'll get him in the end. That's one *tired* man you see in there."

Johnny was indeed tired. He hadn't slept very well the night before, and now here it was almost one o'clock in the morning. At sixty-seven years old, he was feeling every bit his age. He would have been wise to request a break until later in the morning, an appeal that surely would have been granted, but he prided himself on being able to play through exhaustion, and with a healthy three-to-one chip lead over his opponent, had to think that Puggy couldn't survive much longer.

In that regard Moss severely underestimated his opponent. Each time Johnny made a large raise, Puggy simply threw his hand away, content to lose a small pot and wait for a spot where he might win a big one from his increasingly impatient opponent.

One such occasion arose at two in the morning, and Puggy was quick to capitalize on it. With only a lowly 9♦3♦, Johnny tried to bluff Puggy three times, betting heavily on the flop, turn, and river into a king-high board with three spades. The last bet was enough to put Puggy all in.

Puggy had a strong hand—he made two pair on the river—but was wary of the possible flush. However, reviewing the hand in his head, he thought that Moss would have played any hand that could have beaten him with less aggression in the hopes of trapping him. Having played with Moss countless times before, he knew the man's habits like a farmer knows his animals.

"You know how cows always take the same path to the watering hole, one behind the other?" Puggy later ruminated. "Well, we're the same way. Poker players are just the same."

He believed that Johnny's huge bet on the river meant he *didn't* have a hand.

"Well," he said, calling with the last of his chips. "I don't think you got spades, Johnny. You might have kings and treys or queens and treys, even three treys, but I don't think so." He shook his head. "No, I don't think so, Johnny."

The crowd edged forward, hoping for the kill, but all Johnny could do was throw his hand in the muck. The $84,000 pot belonged to Puggy. It was a devastating blow to Johnny's chip stack as well as his psyche, and Puggy was quick to take advantage. By four o'clock in the morning he found himself with better than a three-to-one chip lead over the thoroughly exhausted Moss.

On the final hand Puggy bet all of his chips into a Q♠10♠3♣ flop and Johnny called. Remarkably, both men had risked everything "on the come": Johnny's K♣J♠ gave him an open-ended straight draw; Puggy's A♠7♠ offered four of the five spades needed for the "nut," or, best possible, flush. The last two cards failed to help either man, and Puggy's lone ace was good enough to knock out Johnny Moss and make him the new world champion.

"My gawd," he said upon realizing what he'd accomplished. "I've done it."

Johnny stood up and shook Puggy's hand. "If it had to be anybody other than me," he said, "I'm glad it was you, Pug."

"Thank you, Johnny, thank you," said Puggy. "I just want to tell you, that was the best game I can remember, and I'd have said so even if I lost. That's one they won't forget for a while."

With no prizes awarded for any place but first, Puggy received the entire $130,000 in the form of one thousand three hundred hundred-dollar bills stuffed inside a large silver cup. Jimmy the Greek informed the crowd that it was the richest poker payout of all time.

Despite the hour, some of the less fortunate players started a game of stud within minutes of the tournament's end.

"Hey, Puggy," one of them shouted. "Bring some of that cash over here and sit down."

"I'm going home, boys," he responded. "I'm all wore out."

Puggy would dip into his winnings to buy the "Rovin' Gambler," a multi-colored, thirty-eight-foot-long, diesel-powered mobile home he still uses to travel the country. Painted across the outside is a poker hand showing a royal flush, a pool cue, and the following quote:

I'LL PLAY ANY MAN FROM ANY LAND ANY GAME THAT HE CAN NAME FOR ANY AMOUNT THAT HE CAN COUNT.

Then, in much smaller letters, PROVIDED I LIKE IT.

As if his devastating defeat at the hands of Puggy Pearson weren't enough, Johnny Moss had to endure an earful from his wife.

"I think you simply gave it to him, Johnny," Virgie said.

"He did outdraw me in some good pots, Mama."

"Why don't you outdraw some of them once in a while then?"

"If I had to outdraw them, you wouldn't be rich."

Johnny promptly announced his retirement. "I'm not going to play in tournaments no more. *Never.* I'm too old."

This turned out to be the latest in a lifetime of bluffs, as Johnny was among the sixteen players who entered the 1974 World Series. The sixty-eight-year-old endured two long days of play, culminating in a grueling heads-up finale against Crandell Addington that took four hours to decide. And when all was said and done, the Grand Old Man of Poker had won his third title in the five-year history of the event.

Moss received $160,000, a silver cup, and, for the first time, a gold bracelet with the date engraved on the back. Given to the tournament's winner every year since, the gold bracelet remains poker's most coveted prize, equivalent in prestige to the green jacket presented to the winner of golf's Masters Tournament.

In hopes of earning a gold bracelet of their own, twenty-one players entered the 1975 tournament, a field large enough to necessitate the use of three tables for the first time in the event's history. None of the three former champions would survive the first day. Jesse Alto, a car dealer from Houston, jumped into a seemingly commanding lead on the second day, but was eliminated in sixth place shortly after the dinner break. After Aubrey Day of Tuscaloosa, Alabama, got knocked out in fourth place, a triumvirate of Texans prepared to fight it out for the championship: Brian "Sailor" Roberts of San Angelo, Bob Hooks of Edgewood, and Crandell Addington of San Antonio.

Had it been a fashion show instead of a poker tournament, "Dandy Crandell" would have won in a landslide. He was looking as dapper as ever, his current costume always a bit more splendid than the last. Early in the tournament he wore an all-gray outfit that matched the color of the $500 chips; later he switched to a beige silk necktie that had been custom-made to match his beige silk suit with blue stitching.

Sailor's fashion sense must have made an interesting contrast to Crandell's haute couture. His uniform of choice was a tailored short-sleeved jumpsuit made out of rough fabric that gave him the look of an auto mechanic, minus only the grease.

"They're comfortable to move around in, that's all," he said when quizzed about his wardrobe. "I have dozens of 'em in dozens of different colors."

Roberts had earned his nickname during a four-year hitch in the United States Navy. History will discover the navy to be not merely a branch of the armed services, but a breeding ground for some of the finest poker players in the world. Both Amarillo Slim and Puggy Pearson claim to have improved their games during their time at sea, and a shrewd young lieutenant commander named Richard Nixon reportedly won so much during his tour of duty he was able, upon his return to civilian life, to finance a run for Congress.

Sailor would not use the poker winnings he amassed while serving during the Korean War for any political gain but as a bankroll to fund his play on the Southern circuit. After his famous partnership with Amarillo Slim and Doyle Brunson dissolved, the freewheeling Sailor moved to Las Vegas in the 1960s in search of bigger scores, not just at the poker table.

"Boy, did Sailor love the girls and the parties," reminisces legendary pro T. J. Cloutier. "I remember one time when he was older and drove to San Angelo, Texas, to play poker. Over about a three-month period of time, Sailor beat the game out of $85,000 . . . but by the time he left town he had less money than he had brought to town with him—that's how much he liked to party with the girls. I mean, he was a party animal. He loved three things: playing golf, playing poker, and going out with the girls. And I'm here to tell you that the good times took him for every dime he had. And Sailor knew it, but he didn't care—he just wanted to live life to the fullest."

Sadly, living his life to the fullest is what would end Sailor's life prematurely. For years he battled a serious drug addiction, and he took to running with a bad crowd. "The dirtier, rowdier, lousier a son of a bitch was," says Amarillo Slim, "the better Sailor liked them." Remarkably, his lifestyle never seemed to affect his play. In his prime he was one of the best hold'em players in the world, and he proved it at the 1975 World Series of Poker.

Despite winning the biggest pot of the tournament—$60,000—and pummeling his opponents in the fashion wars, Crandell would be the next to go, paving the way for a heads-up battle between two Texans of a less refined nature. Bob Hooks had spent about as much time on the road as Sailor had; Sailor's advantage was that much of his time had been spent with two masters of the game, Slim and Doyle.

On the final hand, when the flop came 7♥6♣2♣, Hooks shoved the rest of the $59,500 he had started the hand with into the center of the table. With $150,500 in chips and pocket jacks in the hole, Sailor could lose the hand and still win the championship. Believing Hooks wouldn't have pushed so hard with any hand that could actually beat him, he decided to call.

Sure enough, Hooks only had two "overcards"—cards higher than the highest card on the board—and a flush draw with his J♣9♣. The 9♠ on the turn gave him a few more outs—besides any club, the two remaining 9s in the deck would win the hand for him. But it wasn't to be. The dealer turned over the 10♥ on the river.

Earning $210,000 and the now traditional gold bracelet, Sailor became the second member of the famed triumvirate of Texas road gamblers to win the championship. Only Doyle Brunson had yet to win a world title.

3

TEXAS DOLLY

Beyond hosting the premier poker tournament in the world, what set the Horseshoe apart from all the other casinos in Las Vegas was the Binions's insistence upon enforcing the law themselves. While Jack was busy looking after his fellow poker players and tending to the World Series, his brother Ted was playing the role of sheriff inside the casino, doing surveillance and settling disputes in any way he saw fit. It was the Binions' way, or what Benny called the Golden Rule: he who has the gold makes the rules.

This isn't to say that they had a poor relationship with the police. In fact, by some accounts, they enjoyed an excellent one. During the 1970s, whenever detectives in the narcotics division of the Las Vegas police department needed to get their hands on a large amount of cash on very short notice—to use in a sting operation, for example—they always knew they could borrow it directly from the cage at the Horseshoe.

When the Binions caught cheaters and pickpockets on their premises, however, they preferred to handle the situation with their own personal touch. Large security guards armed with baseball bats seemed to send a more emphatic message than mere jail time. There were rarely repeat offenders.

Not every crook got roughed up. When special circumstances required it, exceptions were made. One Saturday night Benny was informed by his chief of security that the Classon brothers, two of the most notorious casino cheats in Las Vegas history, had been apprehended inside the casino. Benny made straight for the back room in which they were being held, but instead of threatening them as every other casino boss had done, he apologized to them for any rough handling they might have experienced. Genuinely admiring the skill they exhibited at their trade, he treated them to a nice meal in his restaurant, during which he offered them a deal.

"Anytime you guys get broke," he said, "you present yourselves at the casino cage. You ask to see the boss working whatever shift it is, and you tell him your problem. He will give you a thousand bucks each. In return, I just ask you to leave my casino alone."

The Classons agreed and avoided the Horseshoe yet they continued to work downtown. The other casinos stepped up their efforts to stop them through more traditional means, leading Henry Classon to respond to what he saw as personal harassment by squeezing glue into as many of their slot machines as he could. Every casino on Fremont Street was hit except one—Binion's Horseshoe.

The next day Henry visited the Horseshoe and asked for the cage manager. Recognizing him, the manager placed two packets of $1,000 on the counter for Henry to take, but Henry wasn't interested in the money. He wanted to talk to Benny.

"What can I do for you?" Benny asked after shaking Henry's hand.

"Nothing," said Henry. "Nothing at all. I just wanted to stop by in person and thank you for the gesture you made to me and my brother the other night."

Classon then walked away, leaving the money sitting on the counter.

A professional poker player can't say that he has truly arrived until his peers have granted him a nickname. The monikers, almost without fail, lack inspiration, content to comment on a player's appearance (Slim, Puggy, the Kid), previous occupation (Sailor, Cowboy, Pilot) or principal place of residence (Tahoe, Oklahoma, Miami). Teasing Brunson, Jimmy the Greek called him "Texas Doylee" for years until some addled reporter transcribed it as "Texas Dolly."

The name stuck, and for good reason. It fit. Doyle Brunson is perpetually at odds with his weight—he once won a million-dollar bet for getting himself under three hundred pounds, taking the sting out of the dozens of weight-loss bets he's lost. He has always seemed more Dolly than Doyle, in the same way that a famously hefty baseball player was more Babe than George. The similarities do not end there. If Johnny Moss was the Ty Cobb of poker, a star whose disagreeable personality limited his universal appeal, then Doyle Brunson is its Babe Ruth, the one who has had the greatest impact on the game.

Like most successful poker players, Doyle is driven by an insatiable desire to compete. As a boy growing up in Longworth, Texas, he was able to satisfy this urge playing sports. In addition to being the best schoolboy miler in the state, he was also considered one of its five best high school basketball players, good enough to earn dozens of athletic scholarships to universities around the country. He chose to attend Hardin-Simmons, a Baptist-affiliated college in nearby Abilene, where he went on to become the most valuable player in what was then called the Border Conference. The Minneapolis Lakers drafted the six-foot-three Brunson to play professional basketball, but an accident during his summer job at the U.S. Gypsum plant in Longworth—a ton of falling sheetrock crushed his right leg—ended any hoop dreams. The fracture proved so severe his leg was in a cast for two years and never fully healed—he still relies on a crutch to get around today.

Forced into a more sedentary existence, Doyle adopted poker as a means to exercise his competitive spirit, playing in the usual Saturday night games in college. He grew so proficient at the game he amassed more spending money than he knew what to do with. He graduated with a master's degree in administrative education, but, unable to find work in his field, took a job as a salesman, peddling office equipment. After getting turned down by several prospective buyers during his first day on the job, he found a profitable game of seven-card stud. Three hours later, he had earned the equivalent of a month's salary.

"My God," he told himself, "what am I doing trying to sell machines nobody wants to buy from me when I can sit down at a poker table and make ten times the money in one-sixth the time?"

He promptly quit, confident he could support himself playing poker. His education as a full-time professional began on Exchange Street in Fort Worth, a rough part of town where holdups and murders were commonplace. Successfully avoiding the many hazards intrinsic to the neighborhood, he managed to amass a bankroll large enough to allow him to play in higher-stakes games throughout Texas and as far away as Louisiana and Oklahoma. It was during one of these forays that he entered into his famous partnership with Amarillo Slim and Sailor Roberts, who were, in Doyle's estimation, "two of the finest poker hustlers I've ever met."

As much as Doyle enjoyed the financial rewards of being a road gambler, his occupation also brought him much angst. Raised by religious parents, he was often plagued by guilt and shame, especially when old acquaintances went out of their way to avoid him on the street. Every day he asked himself if this was really the kind of life he wanted to live.

In December of 1962, an alarming discovery jarred him from his contemplation: doctors had found a malignant tumor in his neck. Cancer was the diagnosis, the prognosis not good. He was told he had four months to live. Sailor Roberts, as faithful as a dog, never left his bedside. Louise, Doyle's wife of four months and a woman of great faith, prayed for a miracle. She got one. The cancer simply disappeared one day. It was a defining moment for Doyle. He not only gained a new appreciation for life, but found himself transformed from a self-described "slightly above-average player" into a poker demigod.

"After that ordeal something happened. Everything clicked. I was playing better than I had ever played in my life. My playing became almost instinctive. . . . I was reading my competitors with a devastating accuracy and I felt a self-assurance I had never known before."

In the wake of his illness he enjoyed an incredible fifty-four winning sessions in a row. More importantly, he fully embraced, at long last, the career that seemed to have chosen him.

"I had finally dispelled any doubts I had about what my profession in life was going to be. Because of pressure from my family and friends, I had thought about returning to 'legitimate' work. But now I knew I never would. I was never going to be a 'working stiff'—nor was

I ever going to have a boss. I was going to make my way through life *my* way."

The quintessential Texas road gambler, Doyle Brunson—at least in his early years—relied on a single test to measure his success at the poker table: the amount of money he earned. He never cared a fig about accolades or trophies, instead he focused with single-mindedness on whatever cash there was to be won. Why then would Doyle keep returning to the World Series year after year when only the winner took home the prize money?

It was the side action, of course, the lucrative cash games that ran around the clock at every table that wasn't being used in the tournament. The championship event itself was a sort of loss leader, a relatively inexpensive way to maintain his reputation "for being an action man."

But Doyle's competitive spirit wouldn't allow him to play the sucker, not for long. "Since I felt the need to be there anyway," he said, "I kept pondering how to win. And I noticed that Johnny Moss always seemed to do very well in the tournaments. I studied Johnny's strategy and saw that he didn't try to win early in the tournament. He just tried to exist, and to keep from losing his money. In my new strategy, I tried to avoid playing big pots until the field had been narrowed substantially. Then later, after the field had been cut to a few players, I played more aggressively, and tried to get players to jeopardize all their checks at every opportunity."

This strategy served him well in 1976 as he managed to survive the first day of competition along with fourteen others out of the original twenty-two-player field. Nine of those joining him were Texans, lending the event the same collegial feel it had always known. There were as many jokes told as hands played. Ever the ladies' man, Sailor Roberts spent half his time deflecting phone calls from his girlfriends.

"For Pete's sake," he shouted at one point, "tell her I'm playing poker!"

Johnny Moss was plagued by a similar distraction. To celebrate their fiftieth wedding anniversary, he had invited Virgie to sit near him at the table in the so-called "sweater's seat," where she could sit and agonize over his hands along with him.

The only one who seemed to be taking the game seriously was Jesse Alto. Born to Lebanese parents, Jesse entered the world in Mexico, grew up in Israel, and, after his work as a deckhand led him to the Lone Star State, settled in Texas at age nineteen. He had been playing poker ever since. While his official day job was that of a car dealer, Alto's principal passion was running the high-stakes game at the Elks Lodge in Corpus Christi.

While his opponents passed the time kibitzing, Jesse rarely spoke and often stared at the cards on the table as if trying to telekinetically change their denominations. Such concentration paid off during the 1976 championship event, as he vaulted to the chip lead and, ultimately, a heads-up match with Texas Dolly.

Known for his incredible stamina—he once played poker for a week straight—Jesse was all set to grind out a win, but he had one thing going against him: himself. He had earned a considerable reputation over the years for being a "steamer," an easily irritated player whose game crumbled whenever he got upset.

Doyle was familiar with Jesse's temper and knew his best bet was to wait for his opponent to self-destruct. "I never play the cards," Doyle once claimed. "Well, hardly ever. I play the person. After a while, you get a sixth sense on what a man is going to do. And he'll do it regardless of what he catches. One guy is getting set to tear loose, another wants to be top dog. Another is angry because he's lost a couple of close pots."

Jesse fell into the latter category. After losing a big hand and the chip lead to Doyle, he was still steaming long after he'd tossed his cards into the muck.

Doyle, recognizing this, decided to attack Jesse immediately, no matter how poor his two cards may have looked. He called a sizeable preflop raise with a very weak hand, 10♠2♠.

Holding A♠J♥, Jesse made top two pair when A♥J♠10♥ appeared on the board. He led out with a bet, but it wasn't big enough to convince Doyle to fold.

When the 2♣ showed up on fourth street, Doyle moved all in, believing his bottom two pair was the best hand. He had no idea how far behind he was until Jesse called and flipped over his cards. The only way Doyle could win the $176,000 pot was by catching a 10 or a 2. The odds were about ten-to-one in Jesse's favor.

Odds be damned. The 10♦ on fifth street gave Doyle a full house, the championship, a gold bracelet, and $220,000 in cash.

"I got lucky in a couple of key pots," he admitted afterwards. "I had the worst hand going in, but managed to outdraw the guy each time when all my chips were in the center."

Asked what his plans were now that he was the new world champion, the forty-three-year-old said, "I'm going to rest today, and then I'm going to play poker again."

As great a win as it was for Dolly, it was a horrific loss for Jesse. A man who spoke several languages fluently, he most likely was limiting himself to four-letter words as he rose from the table and left the room. As unlucky as he was temperamental, he had suffered a bad beat at the worst possible time.

BAD BEAT STORIES

Although no poker player likes to lose, all would agree that some losses are worse than others and that a bad beat is the worst of all. To qualify as a victim of a bad beat, a player must be a huge favorite to win a hand before losing to an opponent who overcomes his underdog status by making a miraculous draw.

Bad beats are the bane of every player who has ever tossed a chip into a pot. Much of the skill in poker—especially no-limit hold'em—hinges on a player putting his money into the pot when he has the best of it, those times he is an odds-on favorite to win. Few hands are invincible, however, and the vagaries of luck—a gutshot straight spiked on the river or a backdoor flush come to fruition—will taunt even the sagest players with merciless cruelty.

The only way to recover from a bad beat, it would seem, is to describe it in nauseatingly precise detail to anyone who will listen. Just ask any poker player, and he'll be glad to tell you about the time . . .

For the first seven years of its existence, the World Series of Poker, much like the rest of American culture at the time, was dominated by older white males. Inroads, however, were being made. In 1976, Walter Smiley became the first African American to win a World Series event by winning the $5,000 Seven-Card Stud tournament.

Women would have a tougher time breaking through poker's glass ceiling. When Doyle Brunson was asked if he had ever played against "a top-notch female player," he hardly gave the question any serious consideration:

"Naw, I don't believe there is such a thing."

His old partner Amarillo Slim shared the opinion, once famously vowing that he'd slit his own throat with a dull knife if a woman ever won the World Series. While he would later claim that he was referring to a *specific* woman—brusque cosmetics heiress Vera Richmond—there is plenty of evidence to suggest that Slim's views towards the distaff sex were, to be generous, a bit old-fashioned.

"Women were made to be loved and petted," he once said. "I've got an agreement with the ladies: if they agree not to play poker, I'll agree not to have any babies."

With such sexism the norm, it was hardly surprising that very few women wished to play the game. In the early 1970s Eric Drache estimated that the ratio of male to female players was 200–1.

Drache knew from firsthand experience that a woman could do everything a man could, thanks in large part to his British-born wife Jane Lovelle, a psychology major at Columbia University. Knowing that it would be as good for his home life as it would for the poker economy, Drache added a women-only event to the 1977 World Series.

"One reason we've set it up, frankly, is to encourage women to play poker," he said. "I think there are a lot who might like to play, but do not because they are afraid it'll look unfeminine. One of the things this will do is help identify some of the better women players and give them the credit they deserve."

The $100-buy-in Women's Seven-Card Stud tournament attracted 94 entrants. Jackie McDaniel, a former cop in the Las Vegas police department, won with an ace-high club flush. Jane Lovelle finished in tenth place. Her degree and intellect were evident in her evaluation of her own performance.

"I'm playing up to the Peter Principle," she said, "up to my level of incompetence."

As it turned out, Jane had underestimated her own skills. A few years later she'd win a similar event in Amarillo Slim's "Super Bowl of Poker."

Benny Binion had become one of Las Vegas's true power brokers. While he was accused, from time to time, of acting outside the law, none of the charges leveled against him managed to stick. In 1977, lawmakers attempted to implicate him in the trial of Clark County sheriff Ralph Lamb, who had been charged with accepting bribes. Witness testimony appeared to establish that Lamb had accepted money on several different occasions, including a $30,000 "loan" from Binion. Judge Roger Foley, Sr., however, dismissed the case, a surprising decision until one notes that Thomas Foley—the judge's son—was among the lawyers Benny had hired to represent him.

Perhaps the truer test of Benny's power was his apparent immunity to the insecurities that plague lesser men. That same year, Steve Wynn, the burgeoning casino mogul, told Benny about his plan to add 579 rooms to the Golden Nugget, his casino across the street. The Nugget was the Horseshoe's chief rival amongst the downtown casinos, but Benny only saw the bright side when he heard about the expansion. He placed an arm around the younger man's shoulder and grinned.

"Great," he said. "Now they can sleep in your place and gamble in mine."

Benny wasn't interested in trying to compete with the glitzier casinos. The Horseshoe would never have a health spa, fancy shops, or a pricey lounge act to entertain his customers.

"I don't want to see my money blown out the end of some guy's trumpet," he said.

Benny was happy to run his business his way. His business philosophy was, "If you wanna get rich, make little people feel like big people."

He was the first casino boss to hire limousines to pick his customers up at the airport and the first to offer free drinks to slot machine players. For those who played in the World Series he offered a free buffet that offered a famously extravagant selection: shrimp the size of crabs, crabs the size of lobsters, and fat steaks from his 100,000-acre ranch in Montana.

"Everybody gained about ten pounds that month," estimated Eric Drache.

After spotting a few "railbirds"—nonparticipants who gathered to watch the pros—sneaking their way into the buffet line, Drache immediately reported the offenders to his boss.

"Benny, tell me what you want to do on this. People that probably aren't entitled to it are doing it, how do you feel about it?"

"Well," Benny replied, "if they've got enough nerve to sneak in, I've got enough nerve to feed 'em."

As lucky as Doyle Brunson had been on the final hand of the 1976 tournament, he had demonstrated a great deal of skill to put himself in that position. He would employ that same skill throughout the 1977 tournament, playing nearly flawless poker from start to finish.

A true student of the game, Doyle had learned much sooner than his peers the tremendous value of "suited connectors," hole cards that could be used to make either a straight or a flush. As powerful as big pocket pairs look before the flop, their value frequently plummets as soon as the community cards are spread, and pushing too hard with them is often a recipe for losing a lot of chips. Suited connectors, by contrast—hands like 9♠8♠ or 8♥7♥—offer what poker players call *implied* value. You are less likely to make a winning hand with them, but the times that you do, you're liable to take down an enormous pot. Doyle began to play these types of hands more frequently, even calling large raises with them before the flop, knowing that he could simply toss his cards away if the flop proved unfavorable. If, however, his hand connected with the flop, he knew that he'd have a chance of breaking his unsuspecting opponent.

This very situation occurred shortly after five o'clock on the third day of the tournament when the blinds were $300 and $600 and the ante $200. After Buck Buchanan of Killeen, Texas limped in from early position, Gary "Bones" Berland, a soft-spoken ex-dealer from Gardena, California, raised to $3,500. Doyle called, as did Milo "Sioux Falls Slew" Jacobson, a retired restaurateur who drank martinis for breakfast and sipped Canadian Club while he played. When the action got around to the big blind, Ed "Junior" Whited of Austin, Texas moved all in with his entire $11,300.

With his thick sideburns and hair slicked back in a pompadour, Junior bore a vague resemblance to Elvis Presley in his later years, somehow bloated and compressed at the same time, but Junior was made out of far rougher material than the so-called King. He was a gambler, had been since the day he was born. After buying his first pair of shoes at the age of ten, he lost them to his cousin in a craps game. If Junior was pretending to be an easy mark, setting up his family members for a big score, it worked. A year later, the eleven-year-old won a grocery store from his uncle while they were playing craps. Junior indeed.

Everyone in Junior's current company knew that he brought his passion for gambling with him to the poker table, and his huge raise did little to scare them. All but Milo called the bet.

When the flop came 5♣7♦7♠, Buck moved all in, Bones folded, and Doyle asked the dealer to count Buck's chips. Buck had pushed in $45,400. Doyle wished it had been more. He called.

The three players turned over their cards. Sure enough, Junior had been caught making a move with only a moderate hand, K♠Q♥.

Buck had a powerhouse: pocket kings. If he had only reraised Junior all in before the flop, Doyle would have certainly folded his hand and Buck would have won $26,500, a fair-size pot. Instead, he was about to lose a big one.

Holding 7♣6♣, Doyle had flopped trips, providing a perfect illustration of the effectiveness of his new strategy. When the turn and the river served up two cards of no consequence—"blanks"—Doyle bounced two players out of the tournament and added nearly $140,000 to his chip stack, putting him in excellent position to defend his title.

Between sips of whiskey, Milo Jacobson got a kick out of telling people he was the worst poker player at the Elks Lodge back in Sioux Falls. Fast-forward to 1981, when he proved just how bad he was by getting knocked out of the $1,500 No-Limit Hold'em tournament *on the very first hand of the event*. Somehow he was still alive with four players left in the 1977 tournament along with two former champions. One of them, Sailor Roberts, had the misfortune of getting dealt pocket 8s on the same hand Milo had kings. Sailor moved in before the flop with his last $17,200, and Milo called.

"Those eights weren't much of a hand," said Sailor after he failed to catch another eight, "but it was all I had."

Milo would get no farther. Bones Berland knocked him out by making a straight to beat Milo's trip 4s, setting the stage for a heads-up match between Doyle and Bones. The two men must have created an interesting spectacle sitting across the table from each other, for as large as Dolly was, Bones was just as thin.

When quizzed about the origin of his nickname, the 140-pound Bones once replied with tongue planted firmly in cheek, "I used to be skinny." Although just twenty-eight years old, he had won the $500 Seven-Card Razz tournament earlier that spring and seemed destined to win many more. In an article for *Gambling Times*, famed poker author David Sklansky rated him the fourth best no-limit hold'em player in the world.

"This kid is better than anybody when he is in stroke—especially when he is playing against fair to good opposition," wrote Sklansky. "Unfortunately, he plays too loose against players for whom he has no respect, especially in small ante games. On the other hand, he seems to be a little in awe of the 'big names.' Once he patches up these leaks, we should have our first non-Texan hold'em champion."

As much respect as Doyle had for Bones's game, he still had to be pleased with the matchup. An earlier hand between the two not only demonstrated that Doyle had an excellent "read" on Bones, but helps to illuminate the type of thinking that makes Texas Dolly one of the best players the game has ever known.

Bones, sitting "under the gun," or in the first seat to act before the flop, had raised $6,000 with A♥J♦, and Doyle, toying with him as a cat does a mouse, opted to merely call with a pair of queens in the hole. Both liked the J♥4♦3♣ flop. Bones led out for $7,000. This was all the information Doyle needed to guess the nature of his opponent's hole cards.

The raise before the flop from under the gun indicated that Bones had a powerful hand, but Doyle could eliminate two of the hands he most feared—pocket aces and pocket kings—based on previous experience. Drawing on his almost preternatural sense of recall, Doyle knew that his opponent always limped in from early position with these hands, hoping that the players behind him would do the raising for him. No, Bones probably had a jack with a big "kicker."* Pocket jacks were a somewhat daunting possibility, but Doyle would know soon enough. He opted to merely call with his overpair, not wanting to scare Bones out of the hand.

When the 10♦ fell on the turn, Bones bet $18,500 at the pot. Now Doyle *knew* Bones didn't have pocket jacks. If he had flopped a set, he would have made a smaller bet in the hopes of keeping Doyle around. Confident he had the best of it, Texas Dolly moved all in, raising $13,800 more. Finally aware that he was probably holding the second-best hand, Bones made what poker players dub a "crying call," pushing the pot to over $90,000, all of which ended up in Doyle's stack after he won the hand. More importantly, a message had been conveyed: Doyle could read Bones like a comic book.

Ironically, it wasn't a brilliant play by Doyle, but simply bad luck that ended Bones's run at the title, a hand that would leave him muttering obscenities up and down Fremont Street for what little remained of the evening. As the hour approached ten o'clock the dealer gave Bones an 8♠5♥ and Doyle a familiar-looking 10♠2♥.

"You've got to play almost every hand when you're anteing that high," Doyle said, explaining how such weak cards led to such a momentous confrontation. "At the very least, you've got to see the flop."

The flop ensured there would be action: 10♦8♠5♥. Doyle now had top pair, Bones two pair, both enticing holdings when playing heads-up. Trying to trap each other, both players checked. If Bones had any chance to beat Doyle, he lost it when he checked the flop, for the turn brought the 2♣, giving Doyle a bigger two pair. Not one to give a free card, Doyle led out with a bet. Not convinced the lowly deuce had hurt him, Bones pushed the rest of his chips into the middle.

Doyle called just as quickly. He didn't need to improve his hand, but he did, catching the 10♣ on the river. For the second year in a row he had made a full house on the river and won the championship with a 10-2. The hand would forever after have special significance in

---

*The "kicker" is the unpaired card, a higher kicker determining the winner when both players have made the same pair or pairs.

the poker community, where it is known far and wide as a "Doyle Brunson."

"I didn't come here to lose," said Doyle, "but neither did the other guys. It's just the way the cards flop at times, I guess."

The first player to win back-to-back championships without the benefit of a popular vote, Texas Dolly proved that he was the greatest poker player on the planet, as he controlled the action from start to finish.

"I didn't make a single mistake the whole three days," he said. "I never jeopardized my stack unnecessarily, I read my opponents right every time, I threw away strong hands when I sensed I was beaten, and my chips never went down; they just built and built all the way."

In the hubbub that followed, Jack Binion was asked when the prize pool would reach $1 million. He responded with understandable enthusiasm. "The way this is going, it could be next year. We've had more signups for the final round this year than we had in the whole tournament when it first started."

As the reigning king of poker, Doyle milked his newfound cachet to satisfy a personal dream. Using the $340,000 he had earned for winning the 1977 World Series as seed money, he endeavored to produce the most comprehensive book ever written about poker. To ensure that all facets of the game were covered, he convinced some of the top players of the day to reveal the secrets to winning the games they were best at. Mike "the Mad Genius of Poker" Caro wrote the section on draw poker, David "Chip" Reese on seven-card stud, Joey Hawthorne lowball, David Sklansky high-low split, and Bobby Baldwin limit Texas hold'em. Doyle saved no-limit hold'em for himself.

Distrustful of the publishing industry, he started his own publishing company, spending a hefty sum of money just to get the book into print. The result, originally titled *How I Made over $1,000,000 Playing Poker*, failed, like so many other great works, to immediately capture the fancy of the general public. The $100 price tag—$250 for the special edition—didn't help.

Those who were willing to take a chance on the expensive tome, however, often recouped their investment after just a few poker sessions. The glossary in the back canonized poker terms that captured the imaginations of millions of new players. *Bad beats. Crying calls. The turn. The river. The nuts.* There were almost fifty pages of statistical charts, revealing to the world at large such secrets as the chances of hitting a gutshot straight with three cards to come in seven-card stud (about 23 percent) or the odds of being dealt a five-card full house (693–1). Most of the book's value, however, came from the battle-tested strategies within.

Buoyed by a change of title, *Super/System: A Course in Power Poker* eventually overcame the initially wretched sales to earn recognition as the greatest book ever written on the game, earning devotees from around the world.

Despite *Super/System*'s success, Brunson—poker's very own Prometheus—quickly came to regret his decision to write the book. In revealing his most effective strategies, he unwittingly supplied his competition with the tools they needed to beat him.

"In the old days, if a guy came along and tried playing my aggressive game, I would just moved up a gear and play right back over him. But now they've read the book, they recognize what I'm doing, they think I'm bluffing and call me. It's hampered my style. I used to be able to wreck a game without holding any cards at all, because I never got called. Now I need the cards."

In particular, other players began to recognize the value of small pairs and suited connectors. "They never used to play cards like that," he said. "When they raised, they always had big cards. So if you came in with small cards for a relatively small amount of money and beat those big hands, you could just break them. It was only a question of time until you did it. It was so easy it was like stealing. But now they've all read my book and they're smarter."

Since the book's publication, Doyle has won enough World Series events—nine and counting—to make him the all-time leader in that category, along with Johnny Chan and Phil Hellmuth, Jr., not to mention tens of millions of dollars in cash games. But he has yet to win another world championship.

"If I had to do it again," he later confessed. "I wouldn't write that book."

4

WHIZ KIDS

In 1975, Doyle Brunson remarked that he could not name a top poker player who came from a wealthy family or one who was younger than thirty. "These young fellows, they're all fierce limit players," he said. "But most of them haven't had the experience at no-limit to be good at it yet, and maybe some just don't have the heart for it."

Just a year later, twenty-five-year-old Bobby Baldwin, playing in the main event of the World Series for the first time, sat atop the leader board at the end of the first day. Although Baldwin was the first player knocked out the final day, another relative youngster, thirty-year-old Tommy Hufnagle from Schwenksville, Pennsylvania, finished third. Texas Dolly found himself forced to reconsider his position, albeit begrudgingly.

"You got good moves," he told Tommy, "for a Yankee boy."

Such stellar performances on the part of Bobby and Tommy sent an emphatic message to the older players: these "whiz kids" could play.

"These younger players used to be soft as butter for us," said Amarillo Slim, "but not anymore."

While the old Texas road gamblers depended mostly on their intuition and experience at the table, the whiz kids used a scientific approach to aid them in their decision making, relying on a keen understanding of the mathematics and percentages involved in the game.

"A new breed of poker player has come to town—the young, scientific, analytical type," declared David Sklansky, whose numerous books on poker have contributed as much as anything to the creation of the species. "With few exceptions, these players are now the best as well as the most successful poker players in the world."

Unlike their aging counterparts, the younger players tended to be specialists—some only played Texas hold'em—and they preferred to play in limit games where they could avoid potentially devastating losses to their bankrolls. Many of the old guard derided such cautious play. They felt the youngsters were taking the gamble out of the game and turning it into a "strictly business" proposition. Embracing his role as grumpy curmudgeon, Johnny Moss became the youth movement's most outspoken critic.

"There's poker players comin' up today that only have one game," he said. "You have to play all them games to be a *professional* gambler. If all that matters is the money, you take the heart out of the game."

The most noticeable difference between the generations may have been a socioeconomic one. Whereas most of the old Texas road gamblers started playing poker to escape the clutches of poverty, many of the young professionals came from relatively affluent backgrounds and started playing the game out of choice, not necessity. A few even emerged from that bastion of upper-class values, the Ivy League. David Sklansky attended the University of Pennsylvania, at least for a time. A Dartmouth graduate, Chip Reese chose poker over Stanford Law School and went on to become one of the most successful cash game players in the world.

"The world's got plenty of lawyers," said George Huber, a talented young professional from Indianapolis. "What we need is a few more gamblers."

If the whiz kids had a poster child, it was Bobby Baldwin. A native of Tulsa, Oklahoma, Bobby had learned how to play winning poker in the unlikeliest of venues—college—where he attained his knowledge in the unlikeliest of ways—reading books. While his fellow students at Oklahoma State University crammed for midterms, Bobby devoured everything that had ever been written about poker theory and strategy. The extracurricular work paid extraordinary dividends as he began to clean up in the seven-card stud games regularly played in the dorms.

"I kept the source of my improvement to myself," he writes in his memoir *Tales out of Tulsa*, "and wondered about this surprising revelation—here I was, surrounded by intelligent classmates who existed in an atmosphere of dependency upon books, and yet were obviously unaware that poker was a definite science that could not necessarily be mastered just through experimentation and time spent at the tables."

By the time he was a sophomore he had amassed a $5,000 bankroll, enough, he figured, to give Las Vegas a try. On his very first night in town, he enjoyed one of those uniquely Vegas experiences that has a way of irrevocably altering a person's life. Suffering a horrendous session at the craps table, he lost his entire bankroll as well as $425 of credit the casino had given him. With $75 left in his pocket, he proceeded to make a comeback for the ages. He bet it all on a roll of the dice—and won. He did it again—and won. He continued to push his luck until the sun came up the following morning, at which point he'd pocketed over $38,000.

Bobby wasn't finished. The hot streak he was enjoying continued at a blackjack table at the Aladdin where he played all five spots himself. Before long, hundred-dollar bills were spilling out of his pockets like straw bulging from a scarecrow. Several lucrative sessions of baccarat later, he had pushed his winnings for the weekend up to an incredible $180,000, so much money he had to use a dress box to carry it all home with him. Such a big score was all the encouragement the nineteen-year-old needed to quit school as soon as he got back to Tulsa.

Three months later, he'd lost it all, thanks to several unwise business decisions and a return trip to Vegas. He shrugged it off and took to the poker circuit full-time, completely dedicating himself to the game. It became, by his own admission, "an obsession." He consulted mathematicians and psychologists. He called Doyle Brunson and Amarillo Slim on the phone to discuss the finer points of the game.

Gradually, all the hard work began to pay off, earning him that eighth place finish in the 1976 championship. It was an auspicious start to his tournament career, but, a perfectionist to the core, he knew he could do better.

"I thought when I came here I had played as much poker as anybody," he said. "I had played several hundreds of thousands of hands. But then I come up against someone like Johnny Moss and he's played several million hands. I've got a lot to learn."

A year later, he finished seventh and won two preliminary events, the $5,000 Seven-Card Stud and the $10,000 Deuce-to-Seven tournaments. The $124,000 he earned pushed his bankroll close to a million dollars. He was at the top of his game.

THE MIND OF A CHAMPION

While there are many characteristics that make a champion, Bobby Baldwin might be best known for his ability to read his opponents, assessing the strength of their hands with whatever clues he could pull from the ether.

Baldwin once tried to dissuade Mike Akins, his adversary in a heads-up no-limit hold'em game, from pushing $5,000 into the pot.

"Mike, don't bet it. I've got a queen high, no pair, and I'm going to call you if you bet."

Mike ignored the warning, Bobby called, and, just as he had suspected, his queen high was good enough to win the pot.

Baldwin's gifts eventually proved even more lucrative away from the poker table. In the early '80s, Eric Drache, who in addition to his duties as director of the World Series was managing the poker room at the Golden Nugget, hired him as a host. It took only a month for Bobby, having caught the eye of owner Steve Wynn, to join the ranks of the executives "upstairs." Less than a year later, Baldwin was named president of the casino.

In 1978, David Sklansky took notice of the great strides Bobby had made, rating him the second best no-limit hold'em player in the world: "A player with a super quick mind, he seems to have no weaknesses. Whether it be a big bluff or a tough fold, he'll do whatever the situation calls for. Doyle [who was, of course, ranked number one] had better keep an eye on him."

Out of all the accolades being thrust upon him, he would receive none greater than Doyle Brunson asking him to write the section on limit hold'em for *Super/System*. Doyle was in effect declaring him to be the best hold'em player in the world. A former track star, Doyle should have known he was passing the baton.

As Benny receded more and more into the background, happy to observe the happenings inside the casino from a booth in the Sombrero Room, Jack assumed more and more control of the Horseshoe's operation. The son was quick to follow the example of his father, whose occasionally violent nature was almost always overshadowed by his generosity. When Jack learned that Goldie, a notorious small-time player, had convinced one of the Horseshoe's floor managers to deliver a dozen donuts and a pack of cigarettes to her house in a limousine, he did as exactly as Benny would have done and laughed off the incident.

The World Series had truly become Jack's baby. And baby was getting bigger. To accommodate the forty-two players who signed up for the main event in 1978, Jack ordered several banks of slot machines to be removed from the Horseshoe, allowing for the arrival of a handful of poker tables.

"For a change, people are replacing machines," joked Eric Drache, who more than ever looked like a cross between two icons of the day, Bruce Jenner and Jimmy Connors.

Despite his good mood, he had hoped the field would be slightly larger. In the weeks leading up to the start of the tournament, players from France, England, Italy, even Peru, contacted the casino to express their interest in participating in the World Series. To indulge the anticipated rush of Europeans, Jack inserted a new game into the tournament lineup, a variant of five-card stud that required only thirty-two cards.

"We anticipate this event alone will attract greater international participation," he said. "The game is especially popular in England and Europe, though not too well known here in the colonies."

"Well, I think that's just right neighborly of them fellows a-wantin' to come all the way over here just to sit for a spell," Benny chimed in. "The least we can do is accommodate 'em and show 'em how things are in Nevada." Turning to his son, he then asked, "Tell me, pardner. Just what in Sam Hill hell is a colony?"

Alas, the group from Britain never did show up. "I called London two times last week and had definite assurances they were going to arrive," Drache lamented as the "European poker" event was cancelled. He was quick, however, to extol the championship event's trusty base. "About seventy percent of the players will be coming from Texas. I'd be willing to put up money that a Texan wins again."

The field of entrants still managed to serve up a couple of surprises. For the first time a woman would compete for the championship, as Barbara Freer, a saloon owner from El Cajon, California, ponied up the $10,000 entry fee. "Some of these fellas told me I shouldn't be playing in this man's game," she said. "Well, honey, I'll lay you ten to one I'll do a heap better than a lot of them, even though I suppose they'll all be out to get me."

And minutes before the action got underway, comedian Gabe Kaplan, the titular star of the popular television sitcom *Welcome Back, Kotter* and a regular performer along the Las Vegas Strip, held an impromptu press conference and announced his intention to take on the professionals. "If I win, the whole thing goes to charity," he said. "If I lose, I'll just have me a good time." Despite receiving hold'em lessons from Doyle Brunson himself the day before, Gabe lasted only four hours.

"At two thousand five hundred dollars an hour, he must have been off his nut with joy," drawled Amarillo Slim.

Gabe's early departure had an upside, as it allowed him to make it on time to his scheduled performance at the Aladdin. Ironically, he had outlasted his teacher. Texas Dolly was the second player eliminated, just two hours after the tournament's two P.M. start. Holding 6-2, he flopped two pair and led out with a bet, only to be raised all in by Louis Hunsucker, a forty-four-year-old bookmaker from Houston, whose occupation would bring him many future run-ins with the law. Hunsucker had pocket aces and took the pot when a jack on the river paired the board, giving him a larger two pair.

"I played it right," said Doyle. "I just got outdrawn. Hell, it's the only way to go. Why just sit around?" He moseyed off to find a side game.

Shortly after play resumed at two P.M. the following day, both Amarillo Slim and Johnny Moss were eliminated. Adding insult to injury, Barbara Freer had outlasted both of them. She hung on until late in the day when she failed to fill an inside straight draw and exited in twenty-fourth place.

Bobby Baldwin survived the second day, and by the time the third day ended, he sat atop the leader board with $163,600. As play began at the final table on the unprecedented fourth day, Bobby held twice as many chips as his closest competitor. All five of his remaining opponents were Texans.

Thanks in large part to television producer Jerry Adler, CBS was on hand to film the tournament as part of its *Sports Spectacular* series. In return, however, the network had demanded certain concessions. At the request of their legal department, the winner-take-all payout structure that had been in place since the tournament's inception was scrapped.

CBS had recently been excoriated for covering what had been billed as a winner-take-all tennis tournament when it was later discovered that the second-place finisher had secretly been awarded prize money. It was hardly a secret that the players who reached the World Series's final table often negotiated deals, agreeing to some split of the prize money. Realizing that the practice could jeopardize their chances of getting the tournament on TV, the Binions decided to ditch the old charade in favor of a formal prize structure. This year the top five finishers would all receive a payout.

THE ART OF THE DEAL

"Any two cards can win!"

Or so goes the refrain, commonly heard at poker's lower limits, where inexperienced players will play nearly any hand that has a chance of winning (and some that don't) all the way to the river. It's an expression that will bring a smile to the face of a veteran rounder, who knows that the fluctuations of luck will, over the long haul, give way to the cold hard truths contained in the laws of probability.

Tournament poker, however, is a short-term affair. Solid play will give an experienced player an edge, but with a relatively small number of hands to determine the outcome—not to mention the inability to reach back into one's pocket to replenish a stake—luck can often win the day. One bad beat can wipe out hours of flawless play.

As a result, the players who approach a tournament's prize money are often willing to cut deals. Two evenly matched players who find themselves heads-up in a winner-take-all tournament might agree, for example, to split the purse down the middle. The vagaries of luck may determine who wins the actual title, but both players, having proven skilled enough to come this far, will get to share in the spoils.

In practice, deal making tends to get a lot more complicated, involving multiple players, the size of their stacks, even their estimated levels of skill. While few of these deals are ever made public, they are a routine part of tournament poker.

With five players set to earn prize money, the odd man out proved to be Ken "Top Hat" Smith, a chess master from Dallas who had been Bobby Fischer's second in the match against Boris Spassky in Reykjavik. He was eliminated in sixth place just an hour into the day when he lost to Crandell Addington's full house. An hour later, Louis Hunsucker filled his belly-buster straight draw to knock out Jesse Alto.* Despite the bad beat, Alto finally caught a break, albeit a small one, earning $21,000 for his fifth-place finish.

By 3:45 only Bobby Baldwin and Crandell Addington remained to compete for the world championship. It was such a perfect matchup—the best of the new breed versus a Texan from the old school—that, with the benefit of hindsight, it becomes clear that only the poker gods could have orchestrated it.

When a break was called at eight P.M., it appeared the argument had been settled and that the dominance the older Texans had enjoyed at the World Series would continue. The forty-one-year-old Crandell seemed poised to win his first title, enjoying a healthy $275,000-to-$145,000 margin over his opponent. He certainly looked the part of a champion, wearing a diamond stickpin and a mink Stetson.

As if attributing his deficit in chips to his ensemble, shabby in comparison to Crandell's usual sartorial splendor, Bobby retreated to his room to change his clothes as well as his attitude.

"I decided if Crandell was going to win the other $145,000, he was going to have to call some money," he said.

Sporting an apple-green polo shirt with the collar spread wide and an aura of supreme confidence, he returned to the table with pep in his step, only to find the CBS camera crew growing increasingly agitated over the slow play.

"Isn't there some way to speed up the action?" begged the producer Jerry Adler, who hadn't budgeted for four days of shooting. "This is getting expensive."

---

*A "belly-buster"—also known as a "gutshot"—is a straight that can only be completed by one card. Poker players greatly prefer "open-ended" or "double belly-buster" draws, straights that can be completed by either of two different cards.

"It's eight-fifteen now," replied Bobby. "I promise you, you'll all be home in bed by nine-fifteen."

He immediately set about making good on his vow, calling Crandell's $10,000 preflop raise with a plan to win much more. When the flop came queen high with two diamonds, Bobby led out for $30,000. Despite Crandell's prompt call, Bobby pushed another $65,000—two-thirds of his remaining chips—into the center after the A♦ fell on the turn.

The railbirds gasped, then grew deathly silent. It was obvious to all that the championship hinged upon this hand.

Crandell stared at the six and a half stacks of $500 chips his opponent had deposited in the middle, then at Bobby himself, searching for a clue as to the strength of his hand. After a prolonged study, Crandell threw away his hand and with it any chance he might have had of winning the championship.

Flashing a mischievous grin, Bobby raked in the $92,000 pot and tossed his cards faceup onto the center of the table where Crandell could see them: the nine and ten of hearts. Nothing. It was a bluff that would be talked about for years to come and still stands as one of the greatest in World Series history.

"People don't realize that lots of times hands are played before the players ever see a flop," T. J. Cloutier later commented. "When Baldwin called Addington's raise with a 10-9, he probably had it in his mind that, even if he didn't get a great flop to his hand, he was going to win the pot anyway. In other words, long before the flop actually came up, Baldwin had decided that he was going to make a move on this pot. When the board came with something he could represent, even though Addington had called him on the flop, he moved on it."

A consummate professional, Crandell managed to maintain his poker face, but Bobby sensed how much damage he had inflicted. If Crandell had pressed one of his hand-rolled Brazilian cigars to his forehead at that moment, it would have lit itself. "I could feel the steam," Bobby said later.

The momentum had clearly shifted—all that was left for Bobby to do was finish the job. On each of the next two hands, he checked moderately good holdings and let Crandell do the betting for him. Bobby called these hands "bluff catchers," and Crandell got caught both times, losing $30,000 on each. Crandell lost another $30,000 when he had the misfortune of making a set of 3s against Bobby's straight. In less than eight minutes, starting with the spectacular bluff, Bobby had seized total control. He now had $370,000; Crandell just $50,000.

After so much excitement, the final hand was hardly a disappointment. Looking to win a big pot, Crandell, with pocket 9s, opted to feign weakness, merely calling the big blind. Bobby seemed to play right into his hands when he raised $10,000, allowing Crandell to push in the last of his chips. This time, however, Bobby had a real hand—pocket queens. Adding to the drama of an already dramatic day, the K♣Q♠9♥ flop gave each man a set. Only the last 9 in the deck could save Crandell. When the board finished with an ace and a 10, Bobby leapt out of his chair, $210,000 richer.

Doyle Brunson applauded the new world champion. "If I couldn't have it again," he said, "then I'm glad Bobby got it. He's the class of the field."

Almost lost in the excitement was the fact that Bobby had made good on his brash promise to the television crew. It was not quite nine o'clock.

With Jack doing such a fine job running the World Series and the Horseshoe, there wasn't much left for Benny to do, other than hold court in one of the booths in the Sombrero Room every afternoon. It gave the seventy-four-year-old the time, when he wasn't regaling a crowd with stories about his days in Texas, to think about his legacy as a gambling pioneer. He found himself increasingly obsessed with the one black mark on his record, the felonious tax evasion that had sent him to Leavenworth in the '50s. In 1978, Benny made his fifth attempt at securing a presidential pardon. With the help of his friend Richard Strauss, then the Chairman of the Democratic National Committee, he offered a deal to the Carter Administration, promising to deliver a vote in the U.S. Senate on the Panama Canal treaties in return for three presidential favors.

The first was an exemption from interstate trucking regulations for a business acquaintance in Oklahoma, which quickly became unnecessary as the acquaintance in question went broke.

The second was a federal judgeship for his longtime friend and attorney Harry Claiborne. After earning a law degree from Cumberland

University in Tennessee, Claiborne moved to Nevada during World
War II and became the chief deputy district attorney of Clark County.
One of his more successful prosecutions resulted in life imprisonment for Cliff Helms, one of Benny's old sidekicks from Texas. Years
later, after Claiborne had entered private practice, Benny asked him
to become his lawyer. When Claiborne hesitated, recalling the role
he'd played in locking up one of Benny's friends, Binion stared at him
through his cold blue eyes.

"There's no goddamn law you gotta be in love with your lawyer."

The two eventually grew so close that Claiborne became something of a consigliere to Benny and the unofficial godfather to all of
his children. He used to eat lunch in the Horseshoe nearly every day.
And in 1978—thanks largely to Benny's influence—he became a federal judge.*

Benny's third request of the president was his own pardon. He
might have gotten it, if only he'd done a better job censoring himself.
Jimmy "the Weasel" Fratianno, a Mafia hit man, once testified that
Benny had hired him to kill a gambler named "Russian" Louie
Strauss. It wasn't true, but rather than simply deny it, Benny said,
"Tell them FBIs that I'm able to do my own killing without that sorry
son of a bitch."

The so-called "FBIs" heard him loud and clear, and so did those in
charge of giving presidential pardons. His application was once again
denied.

The World Series was rapidly gaining notoriety, having become a regular feature on *CBS Sports Spectacular* and *ABC's Wide World of
Sports*, television shows that presented short clips from sporting
events deemed too insubstantial to warrant full coverage. The Binions, however, were starting to suspect that the World Series of Poker
might deserve a more thorough treatment. Jack asked Jerry Adler, the

---

*Clairborne would go on to become the chief U.S. district judge for the state
of Nevada, until his career came to an abrupt end in 1983 amidst charges of
filing false tax returns and accepting a bribe from a brothel owner. He was
eventually impeached, becoming the first federal official in fifty years to be so
dishonored, and wound up spending seventeen months in prison.

man who had produced several of these clips, if he knew how to take the tournament to the next level. Adler didn't, but he knew a guy who might, a regular from his Saturday night poker game in Los Angeles.

Henri Bollinger had long been a successful Hollywood publicist—his list of clients over the years included Humphrey Bogart, David Niven, Julie Andrews, and Ernie Kovacs. Shortly after the 1978 World Series, Adler arranged a meeting between Bollinger and Jack Binion, during which the publicist offered a plan for turning poker players into stars bright enough to attract the attention of a wider audience.

"You've got the assignment," declared Jack.

One of Bollinger's first steps was to make sure that every top poker player had a colorful nickname. Bobby Baldwin, for example, became "The Owl." It didn't take too long for other players to catch on, many of whom began suggesting their own nicknames. "Poker players, particularly the guys who do it as a profession, understand that the key to it is to get invited to games," points out Bollinger, "and the only way you're going to do that is if you have a reputation and a personality."

Bollinger also began to promote the World Series like he would a movie. He issued press releases. He made casual inquiries at top newspapers and magazines to find out which reporters were regular poker players and invited them to come and watch.* He began to do what he did best—creating a "buzz."

Much of the buzz leading up to the start of the 1979 championship event surrounded the possibility of an amateur sneaking away with the title. If there was any reason for optimism, it was more a matter of numbers than skill. A record eight nonprofessionals were among the fifty-four players who had entered the championship event.

"A few amateurs have made good showings in the last couple of years," said Eric Drache, surely thinking of Milo Jacobson's third-place finish two years before. "Sooner or later an amateur is going to walk off with the prize money."

Jimmy the Greek, commentating for *CBS Sports Spectacular*, was more dismissive of their chances. When asked by his partner Frank Glieber if an amateur could win, the Greek responded bluntly, "I don't think there are many nonprofessionals in here. They're professional

---

*Bollinger went even farther in 1980, adding a "Media-Only" event to the World Series lineup.

in their own home town. But when they get here they're not quite as professional because the great professionals *are* here." He designated Bobby Baldwin, Doyle Brunson, and Crandell Addington as the favorites.

Yet somehow, with just eight players remaining, a David had snuck into the mix of poker Goliaths sitting at the final table. Hal Fowler, the owner of a public relations firm in Ventura, California, joined a group of players so powerful it left one of them in awe.

"You should have seen the final table," said Bobby Hoff. "Bobby Baldwin, Crandell Addington, George Huber, Sam Petrillo, Sam Moon, Johnny Moss. Every player at the table was a world-class player except for Hal."

Fittingly, he came armed with little more than a slingshot—of the $540,000 chips in play, he possessed a mere $2,000.

The chip leader, with $138,900, was Sam Moon, a retired farmer from Corpus Christi, Texas, who took advantage of his big stack and pocket aces to dispatch Bobby Baldwin. Bobby moved all in after flopping a set of 8s, but Moon caught a third ace on the turn. After busting out in eighth place, Bobby grabbed a microphone and joined Jimmy the Greek doing color commentary for CBS.

After a long cold streak hobbled Moon, Bobby Hoff, a venerable pro from Victoria, Texas, took over as the "table captain," the player controlling most of the action. He had enjoyed a remarkable comeback. Down to his last $1,730 at one point during the first day, he now sat behind a veritable fortress of checks totaling $225,700. Hoff's nearly magical abilities at the poker table were well known to his rivals.

"We call him the Wizard," said Doyle Brunson, perhaps inspired by Henri Bollinger's new name game, "'cause he can make whole mountains of black checks just disappear."

A scratch golfer in his youth, Hoff earned an athletic scholarship to the University of Texas, where he spent about as much time at the poker table as he did on the golf course, winning $8,000 his first semester. Three years later, he visited Las Vegas for the first time and was immediately seduced by its many temptations. He found a soul mate in Sailor Roberts, a man with whom he shared more than one addiction. The two would go on alcohol-and-cocaine-fueled binges that often lasted for several days and, in more than one instance, weeks.

"The night before a game, I would put two lines of cocaine on the bed stand," Hoff later recounted. "Then I'd put an ashtray over them so the humidity wouldn't get to them too bad. When I woke up, I'd roll over, take the two rails of cocaine, order some cognac from the bell desk, and lay there till the swelling in my wrist went down, maybe force an egg down, and then I'd go play poker."

Like Sailor, Hoff was, in his prime, considered one of the best no-limit hold'em players in the world, and the 1979 championship was his chance to show it. Armed with the big stack at the table, he began to swing it like a club.

"Conservative play is the first couple days," he declared during a break in the action. "That's when you play conservative. Conservative play is over with."

As afternoon slipped into night, Hoff continued to attack, raising $6,500 from the button. Sensing a steal, Johnny Moss, seventy-three years old and as grumpy as ever, reraised all in with A♥Q♠.

It had been a tough tournament for Johnny. His mind had been elsewhere most of the time—Virgie had been hospitalized at the Desert Springs Medical Center several days before. He had spent much of the afternoon muttering obscenities into the tiny microphone the CBS film crew had fastened to his shirt. His spirits were momentarily lifted when, an hour before the dinner break, Virgie made a surprise appearance, placing a cool towel around his neck for good luck, but the cards seemed to be conspiring against him.

Hoff called Johnny's all-in raise with A♦10♠ and, despite being a three-to-one underdog before the flop, knocked out the old man when the 10♥ fell on the river. Johnny won $27,000 for his fifth-place finish, but left the table every bit as miserable as he'd been when he'd arrived.

Twenty minutes after Hal Fowler knocked Sam Moon out in fourth place, George Huber found himself in the uncomfortable position of being the "short stack," the player possessing the fewest chips. One of the new breed of young poker professionals making their mark on the game, Huber was looking for more than just a payday.

"I don't care about second or third or fourth or fifth," he said. "I just want to win."

Earlier in the tournament he had survived an opponent's royal flush—the first in World Series history—but was now faced with a chip stack that was being rapidly eroded by the blinds and antes. Looking to pick up a lot of chips quickly or else go down trying, he found what seemed to be a perfect opportunity when Hoff raised Fowler before the flop. Huber moved all in, but he didn't have enough chips to make either of his opponents fold. Upon seeing the Q♣8♠6♦ flop, he joked that he'd made two pair, but that's all it was, a joke, and Fowler took the hand with his K♣Q♠. Huber's exit created a previously unimaginable scenario: Hal Fowler, a lowly amateur, was going to be playing heads-up for the world championship.

Hal Fowler learned to play poker through the usual routes, first as a caddy at a local golf course in Vermont, then later during a stint with the Army Air Corps. He professed an undying love for the game and offered as evidence the failure of his first three marriages.

"It's my own choosing," he said. "I tend to do my own thing. I gave my wives some time, but not all the time they wanted. I was very independent, very busy with my business on weekdays and poker on weekends. That makes me out to be the badass, but that's just the way I am. I tell it all up front. And if I had it all to do over again, I'd do it exactly the same way. I enjoy my life."

Hitting the card rooms in Gardena and Las Vegas as often as his professional life would allow, Fowler had developed an adequate competence for the game. He wasn't the most unlikely man to win the tournament, but he was close: oddsmakers at the start of the tournament had declared him a forty-to-one underdog, and that might have been generous. Now Fowler faced Bobby Hoff, the same man who had knocked him out on the second day of the previous year's main event.

"I felt real good going against Bobby," he said. "I thought that maybe it's my turn to break him this year."

Fowler took the offensive early. In their first major confrontation he bet his entire stack, $250,000, into a board that showed an ace, king, queen, and jack. When Hoff folded, Fowler revealed his cards for all to see, a deuce and a 5.

A brilliant bluff or a terrible mistake? "This guy didn't know which end was up," claims Henri Bollinger. Several observers—including Hoff—believed that Fowler was popping pills, possibly Valiums or quaaludes, throughout the heads-up match. On more than one occasion Fowler shoved the wrong amount of chips into the pot and had to be corrected. He blamed it on fatigue.

"I'm usually in bed by eleven every night," he said.

Despite his impaired faculties and relative inexperience, Fowler could do no wrong. Dealt K-J, he put all his money into the middle when a queen and a jack appeared on the board. Hoff, however, held Q-6, and was a big favorite to win the world title—until a king fell on the river.

Hoff later called it "about as tough a beat as you'll ever hear about," adding glumly, "Nobody even remembers that hand."

Just after one o'clock in the morning—well past Fowler's bedtime—another key hand arose. Trailing Hoff $204,000 to $336,000, Fowler checked a J♥9♣2♦ flop, then called when Hoff bet $20,000. A second diamond fell on the turn. Hoff upped his bet to $30,000, with Fowler calling once again. When the Q♦ arrived on the river, Fowler grabbed the last of his chips, still sitting in their racks, and shoved them into the pot, going all in for $144,000. Hoff, who had been bluffing at the pot but backdoored his way into a king-high flush, called. Fowler, who had been calling him down with an A♦8♦, had also backdoored a flush, and his was the nut. Suddenly, the amateur had a three-to-one chip lead over the stunned professional.

Entering their sixth hour of heads-up play, Hoff had scratched and clawed his way back into contention, cutting Fowler's lead to just $70,000. The two men had fallen into a familiar pattern, Hoff winning most of the little pots, but Fowler somehow managing to take down all the big ones, more often than not due to sheer dumb luck. Having watched Fowler make countless mistakes, Hoff was content to wait for his opponent to make the decisive one that would give him the championship.

As the clock struck three, Hoff found the best hand to make a strong move with, pocket aces. He made a substantial raise, and Fowler, on a rush and feeling good, called with 7♠6♦. The J♠5♥3♣ must have looked just about perfect to Hoff. With $38,000 already in the pot, he bet $40,000, roughly half of what he had left. Fowler, sucking on a cigarette, debated what to do. Most professionals would have recognized the long odds and mucked the hand without thinking twice about it. But Hal Fowler was not a professional.

"I needed a four to fill an inside straight," he later explained, "and I had a feeling it was going to fall on fourth or fifth street. I play my hunches. Sometimes when you have a hunch, it means something."

Fowler called. The 4 of spades on the turn gave him an improbable straight. Unaware of how much the seemingly innocuous card had hurt him, Hoff pushed in his last $43,000. Fowler, of course, called without any hesitation. After the 10♦ completed the board, Hoff turned over his aces, believing they were good. It was a stunning blow when he discovered they were not.

Hoff won $108,000 for coming in second, but the money hardly consoled him. Was it a coincidence that shortly after the loss he switched from snorting cocaine to shooting it with needles, a far more dangerous method of taking the drug? Quickly turning from novelty to routine, the habit lasted eight years and was the cause of the chronic hepatitis that has plagued him ever since.

"Having Hal beat me in the World Series of Poker had a big effect on my life," he said. "I had nightmares for three weeks afterward. I never realized how much I wanted to win until I got down there with a chance to win it. In my life I've been in many tough spots—I've bluffed my money many times, and I've had a huge amount of rushes. But never have the palms of my hands sweated, except for that one time at the final table. I thought I was playing for the money, but then realized that I wanted to win it. I still get emotional when I talk about it."

It was an upset of stunning proportions. An amateur from California had taken down a professional from Texas. The lamb had slaughtered the butcher. The fish had eaten the shark. David had beaten Goliath.

"Every now and then somebody will come along like the late Hal Fowler," T. J. Cloutier commented years later. "When he won the World Series in 1979 it might have been the biggest upset in the history of poker. You could've played as good as God can play and still not have beaten Hal on that day."

The story of an amateur beating the pros at their own game inspired a bevy of poker hopefuls, opening the floodgates for the massive expansion that lay ahead. It was clear that anybody could win the tournament now. You didn't have to be from Texas. You didn't even have to be a professional. All you needed was $10,000 and the nerve to take on the best in the world.

Recognizing their role as stewards of the game, the Binions founded the Poker Hall of Fame in 1979. To be admitted, a player had to have played poker against acknowledged top competition, played for high stakes, played consistently well, gained the respect of his peers, and stood the test of time. There were seven inductees the first year, including Johnny Moss and Nick "the Greek" Dandalos. The Binions erected a display inside the Horseshoe that paid tribute to these players. Admission into the Hall of Fame remains one of the greatest honors in poker, one to which all players aspire.

5

THE KID

The repercussions of the "Fowler effect" were felt far and wide. For the first time, the World Series would get a full hour of television coverage, thanks to a deal struck with a brand-new cable network called ESPN. Word that a relative novice had beaten the professionals spread quickly among the ranks of amateurs, who arrived in droves for the 1980 championship. A pair of real-life cowboys, brothers "Buffalo Butch" and "Maverick Mike" Bamrich, came straight off a Nebraska cattle ranch. And Collette Doherty, the woman who had been dubbed Ireland's first champion poker player—she had beaten her peers in a game at Dublin's aptly named "Eccentrics Club"—arrived with a large entourage of reporters and friends. "I would travel one hundred miles for a good game of poker," she once said, and here she had journeyed a good five thousand. Although she had never played Texas hold'em before and was listed as a 100–1 underdog, the woman known in her homeland as "Collect" remained confident.

"An experienced guy knows I am inexperienced," she said. "I could ruin a hand for them. It could work for me, you never know."

A member of the Irish delegation, author Raymond Smith, asked forty-seven-year-old Texas Dolly if he had any thoughts of retiring.

"Retire to what?" Doyle snapped back. "I have been retired all my life. I have done what I wanted to do since I was twenty-two years old."

Jackie Gaughan, the owner of the El Cortez Hotel and one of the true pioneers of downtown Las Vegas, seemed equally eager to see the old legends from Texas forced into early retirement, and he did so in a manner much more damning than mere words. Having taken over the bookmaking duties from Jimmy the Greek, Gaughan set up shop in the Sombrero Room, where he offered odds of 100–1 against seventy-four-year-old Johnny Moss winning the tournament, backing his conviction by accepting close to $100,000 in action.

Reports of the road gamblers' demise, however, proved greatly exaggerated. Texan Bob Hooks made quick work of Collette Doherty when she pushed in $8,000 on the strength of a 3-high full house. He showed her a 9-high full house.

"You had to go on the hand," Johnny Moss told her. "I would have bet on it too."

As the first day came to an end, Sam Moon, the tournament veteran from Corpus Christi, led the field with $40,550 in chips, while momentum seemed to be gathering for Texas Dolly, just $3,000 behind him. And in a development that must have been giving Jackie Gaughan an ulcer, Johnny Moss was very much alive and kicking with nearly $23,000, better than all but seven players.

By the end of the second day of play, an upheaval of biblical proportions had taken place: the last was now first. Gabe Kaplan, two years removed from being the punch line of a joke as well as a punching bag to the professionals, had vaulted into the lead with $203,100, nearly a third of the chips in play. He had acquired many of them when his pocket kings beat Bobby Baldwin's pocket queens on the hand that knocked Bobby from the tournament. Doyle had fallen to fifth, while Johnny Moss, with only $7,000, was just one bad play away from saying good-bye.

The player generating the most fear—ironic, given a five-foot-four-inch frame that barely carried a hundred pounds—was a brash twenty-six-year-old New Yorker by the name of Stuey Ungar, whose wildly aggressive yet masterfully controlled play had resulted in $92,500 in chips, good for second place.

"You get this feeling that he does not know quite what he is doing at times," Doyle said of the player everyone called "the Kid." "He does things naturally and they come off for him. It's almost as if he is playing by natural instincts—jungle instincts. Yes, he's like a young jungle animal when you think you have him cornered. He has the natural instincts for the right move and he seems to come up with the right move—instinctively."

The Kid could hardly disagree. "At this level you can't worry about losing. There is a lot of instinct. Sometimes when I make a play I don't know why I do it."

Stuey Ungar's natural instinct for cards—assisted by a photographic memory and an IQ of 185—was evident nearly from the day he was old enough to read them. He won his first gin rummy tournament at a resort in the Catskills when he was just ten years old. Hardly satisfied by the moderate score, he succeeded in beating the busboys out of all their tips.

Such hustling came naturally for Stuey. He was a street-wise kid from Manhattan's Lower East Side, which, thanks to numerous backroom card games and illegal sports books, was a gamblers' paradise in the 1960s. His father was very much a part of the colorful local fabric. A bookmaker by trade, Isadore "Ido" Ungar harbored dreams that his brilliant son would someday become a doctor, but for Stuey to become anything but a gambler would have been akin to Michael Jordan forsaking basketball.

Every dollar he was given at his bar mitzvah he lost betting on horses. When his father died several months later—a heart attack in the bed of his mistress—so too did the notion his son might ever study medicine. Stuey blew his entire inheritance at the track.

Not knowing what to do with this hyperactive fourteen-year-old, Stuey's mother Faye sought the advice of Hasan "Turk" Arifoglu, who ran a regular card game at the Camelot House on West Forty-fifth Street. There Stuey was appeased at last. He had found exactly what he needed, not words, but cards. Jumping right into an ongoing game filled with adults, he was in his element, chattering away, throwing big bets onto the table, and winning, always winning.

"He was like a little Chihuahua," Turk said. "It made me dizzy."

After dropping out of Seward Park High School, he started gambling full-time. By the time he was 17, he was winning thousands of dollars playing gin rummy, pinochle, the Italian card game *ziginette*, the Eastern European game *klabberjass*, whatever. It didn't matter. As long as it involved cards, Stuey would quickly master the game.

"When the cards are dealt," he said, "I just want to destroy people."

On his way to winning a $500 buy-in gin rummy tournament he never lost a single hand, easily taking the $10,000 first prize, which he promptly lost at the track. His legend quickly outgrew his diminutive frame.

"Think about fifty years from now," he boasted. "How can there be a better gin player? I can't even conceive of it."

In the world he inhabited it was only natural that Stuey would become friends with someone like Victor Romano, a sixty-year-old soldier in the Genovese crime family. Taking Stuey under his wing, Victor treated the fatherless boy like his very own son. When Stuey took an interest in Madeline Wheeler, it was from Victor that he sought advice. The older man told him to marry her, have kids, and start treating gin as a profession. Stuey, now twenty, promptly moved out of his mother's apartment and into Madeline's.

Backed by his Mafia connections, Stuey behaved as if here untouchable, and for the most part he was, until he lost $60,000 to someone who had stronger ties to the Genovese family than his own. Unable to come up with the money and fearing for his life, he fled to California where he called Victor and explained his predicament. Victor worked out a deal on Stuey's behalf—Stuey wouldn't get hurt as long as he went to Las Vegas and earned enough money to pay his debt.

Stuey did it in record time. Upon his arrival in Vegas he immediately sought out the best gin player in town, Danny Robison. In their first meeting Stuey beat him out of $100,000, allowing him to pay off his debt in New York. That was only the beginning for Stuey. When he next talked to Madeline, he had more exciting news than a debt repaid; thanks to his prowess at gin and blackjack, he now had $1 million sitting in the vault at the Dunes. He convinced her to come for a visit. She arrived with shocking news. She'd gotten engaged to a lawyer. Stuey talked her out of it and made a proposal of his own. The newlyweds were soon expecting a baby girl.

Stuey followed Victor's advice to a tee, except for the part about treating card playing like a job. After winning a $50,000 gin tournament, he couldn't resist the opportunity to correctly predict the losing player's cards on the last two hands. The news of Stuey's prodigious talents spread quickly, effectively killing any future action, even in the gambling capitol of the world. At age twenty-two Stu Ungar was finished as a professional gin rummy player.

He took up blackjack, but his irrepressible cockiness once again triggered a premature end to a potentially lucrative career. When a pit boss at Caesar's Palace accused him of counting cards after he'd won $83,000 one night, Stuey fired back with a correct inventory of the last eighteen cards left in the single-deck shoe. Impressed by the stunt, legendary casino owner Bob Stupak bet $100,000 against Stuey's $10,000 that he couldn't count down the last three decks of a six-deck shoe. Taking up the challenge, Stuey got all 156 cards right, ensuring his lifelong addition to the blacklist of every casino in town.

His second major source of income cut off, Stuey started playing poker and, as was his style, immediately jumped into the biggest games in town. He had been at it less than a year when he strutted into the Horseshoe for the 1980 World Series of Poker, just twenty-six years old and ready to take on the world.

That Stuey Ungar made the final table the first year he played in the World Series was remarkable to everyone but Stuey himself. Well, almost everyone. Terry Rogers, the legendary Irish bookmaker known as the "Red Menace" for his brightly colored hair, saw something in the Kid others did not. After watching the frail Stu shiver through the first day, thanks to his proximity to an air conditioner, Rogers declared that if Ungar were to draw a new seat—i.e., a warmer one— he'd win the title. While every other oddsmaker had listed him as a 100–1 long shot, Rogers set his own odds on him at 20–1, effectively ensuring that no one would place a bet on Ungar with him. He then proceeded to bet some of his own money on Stu to win it all.

Perhaps it was their similar backgrounds that drew Rogers to Stuey. Like Ungar, Terry Rogers was born into a family of bookmakers. By his teenage years, he was taking bets on dog races. After instantly going broke, Rogers realized that there was a science to his craft. "I have paid for enough bookmakers' funerals to realize," he said, "that amongst the most stupid of notions is the belief that there is no such thing as a poor bookmaker." He began to study the science behind laying odds, and in the 1960s revolutionized the Irish horse-racing scene, popularizing exotic bets like "chances," "forecasts," and "doubles."

Enamored by the concept and characters that made up the World Series of Poker, he founded the Eccentrics Club in Dublin to help popularize the game in his native land. Although 1980 was the first year he made his "Irish Expedition" with the club's champion and whatever fellow countrymen were mad enough to join the trip, everyone in the Horseshoe knew him by the time the final table started, for Terry was cheering so loudly for Stuey he might have been mistaken for a relative.

For Ungar the encouragement was superfluous. He began the day on a rush, winning a series of big pots and ultimately reducing the number of players to six when his pocket 9s beat Richard Clayton's A-Q. He had moved ahead of Gabe Kaplan into first place when he was faced with a stern test from an old master. Holding A-Q, Stuey opted to slowplay the A♥A♣K♣ flop in a hand that included Gabe, Doyle Brunson, and Johnny Moss. After the action was checked all the way around, Stuey fired $30,000 into the middle when the turn brought a seemingly harmless 3♥. Gabe and Johnny were quick to fold, but Doyle confounded the Kid by pushing all in with his remaining $176,000.

A-Q is not only one of the strongest hands in hold'em but also one of the most dangerous to play. Most players are happy to raise with it, but terrified when faced with a reraise, as it's a big underdog to the types of hands—pocket aces, pocket kings, A-K—that opponents are likely to reraise with. Doyle could have held either of the last two—not to mention A-3 or pocket 3s—and had Stuey dead to rights. To double up Texas Dolly at this stage in the tournament would make the veteran a near lock to win his third title, but folding three aces with a strong kicker to a weaker hand was an equally distressing scenario. Stuey counted and recounted the chips he would need to match the raise. Several tense minutes passed. The spectators craned their necks towards the action, taking in every gesture. Finally, Stuey called. An 8♦ appeared on the river, and as the crowd gasped, both men turned over their hands. Stuey's courage proved warranted as Doyle turned over . . . A-Q. Because both of them had the same hand, the large pot was divided equally between them.

Split pots can be very confusing for the players involved. On one hand, they're happy they didn't lose; on the other, they're aggravated they didn't win. The only tangible result of this hand was the murmuring of the crowd that continued to filter through the air long after it was over. As agonizing as the hand had been, it was nothing compared to what was going on in Jackie Gaughan's stomach as Johnny Moss staged an improbable comeback from his second-day low of $7,000. Johnny had arrived at the final table with $67,000, generating a buzz of excitement in the room and creating the very real possibility that Gaughan would have to pay out $1 million to those who had bet on the Grand Old Man.

"My memory of the 1980 World Series of Poker," proclaimed Terry Rogers, "will always be of the kingly courage of Jackie Gaughan, who did not shut up shop when the betting men took on the odds quoted on Johnny Moss."

While Gaughan continued to take bets on Johnny, he was also buying back as many of the betting slips as he could in an attempt to cover himself if Johnny won. Pat Callihan, winner of that year's $2,000 Draw High event, liked Johnny's chances so much that he refused to sell his $500 marker to Gaughan, even for $40,000!

Johnny's rise was perfectly timed with Gabe Kaplan's fall from the high of $212,000 he had known just an hour before. The two would tangle in a hand that did nothing to change their respective momentums. Johnny took down a $120,000 pot and eliminated Gabe when he made a diamond flush on the turn to beat Gabe's set of 4s. As they broke for the evening, Moss was still very much alive with $163,000, second only to Stuey's $395,000.

On the final day, Charles Dunwoody, an oil man and rancher from Houston, was the first player to fall, when his queens full of kings lost to Doyle's four 9s. Doyle would soon make quads again—aces this time—much to the delight of Jackie Gaughan, for the hand was against Johnny Moss, who could only show a queen-high full house.

"I am convinced," said Terry Rogers, "that if [Moss] had won the big pot . . . he would have taken complete control of the game and become an odds-on favorite to win out."

Instead, Johnny was down to his last $66,000, which he pushed in before the flop with a pair of 6s in the hole. He was a huge favorite against Stuey, who had called him with 8♥6♥, but an 8 on the flop ended Johnny's day—and saved Jackie Gaughan's bank account. After

Doyle knocked out Jay Heimowitz, a beer distributor from Monticello, New York, the final showdown was set to begin.

THE KID WALKS INTO A BAR

Carrying barely one hundred pounds on a five-four frame, paired with a pasty complexion and a mop of unkempt hair, Stuey looked more like a newspaper boy than a professional poker player. Once, after ordering a rum and Coke at the bar of a restaurant in Palm Springs, the bartender asked to see his ID.

Stuey, who was notorious for never carrying any identification on him, yelled at the man, "What are you talking about? I'm thirty-five years old!"

"Well, you might be," the bartender said, "but you look young to me, and if you don't have any ID, I can't serve you."

"You want to see some ID? I'll show you some ID." Stuey pulled two $10,000 bundles of cash out of his front pockets and slammed them on the bar. "There," he said, pointing at them. "There's my ID. Now tell me, what kind of kid carries around that kind of money?"

The bartender smiled. "You've got a good point. What'll you have?"

Before heads-up play began, Jack Binion participated in a brief publicity stunt hatched by Henri Bollinger for the benefit of the new television audience. Cameramen shot footage of Jack visiting a nearby bank, where he went through the motions of withdrawing the more than $500,000 that would go to the top two finishers. A bank employee led Jack into a vault where the bundles of hundred-dollar bills were counted, stacked, and placed into a nondescript cardboard box. Jack carried the box back to the Horseshoe with a minimum of security, as if to say "these are the kinds of stakes we play for every day," then, with little fanfare, *dumped* the contents of the box onto the poker table between the two finalists. The pantomime proved so popular that it has become a ritualized part of nearly every major poker tournament to this day.

Separated by a mountain of cash, Doyle and Stuey could not have made an odder-looking pair. One tall, the other short. One hefty, the other emaciated. One relaxed, the other manic. While Doyle was the epitome of the Texas road gambler, complete with his Stetson and languid drawl, Ungar was the perfect example of a fast-talking New Yorker. Words shot out of his mouth like gunfire. His hands twitched and shuddered. He acted like a teenager on a sugar rush.

The two men had nearly the same amount of chips, a scenario that often presages a long-drawn-out fight to the finish; but the way these two played—boldly and aggressively—the confrontation didn't figure to last long.

"I wanted to make it a shoot-out," said Stuey. "I knew he would outplay me the longer it lasted, for, make no mistake about it, Doyle Brunson is the number-one hold'em player in the world today. As far as I was concerned, someone was going to go broke quickly, and by forcing him and carrying the play to him, I hoped it would not be me."

"He was going to break me in a hurry or I was going to break him," agreed Doyle. "We both knew that as we sat down for the final session."

Fifteen minutes into heads-up play, Doyle bet $10,000 before the flop with A♥7♥. Stuey called with 5♠4♠. With roughly $17,000 in the pot, the flop came A♦7♦2♣. Hoping to trap his opponent, Doyle made a relatively small bet of $10,000. If he had bet any more, Stuey surely would have folded.

Instead, Stuey called, perhaps relying on those "jungle instincts" of his, and the turn brought him the card he most wanted to see, the 3♥. Now sitting in the catbird seat with the nut straight, the Kid fired $30,000 into the middle, goading his opponent.*

Doyle responded with what he later described as "one of the worst

---

*In most forms of poker, an ace an complete the high or low end of a straight. An ace-through-5 straight such as the one Stuey called here is called a "wheel."

plays I've ever made." With the aid of hindsight, he thought he should have simply called Stuey's bet on the turn and waited to see if the river helped him. As it turned out, it did. The 2♦ had to have been a scary-looking card to Stuey. Not only did it pair the board, potentially making Doyle a full house, it also made a diamond flush possible. Stuey would have been forced to stop betting.

But Doyle didn't call the bet. Instead, he reraised with all of his chips, believing his two pair were still good.

Stuey called and his straight held up, making him the new world champion.

"This was the greatest tournament we ever had," said Dolly, his spirits hardly dampened by the defeat.

His good mood was contagious. Terry Rogers pulled out $10,000 of the cash he had won from the bets he had placed on Stuey.

"This is from the Eccentric's Club in Dublin," he shouted. "We want to ensure that the Irish champ in Dublin next year will be the first one entered in the 1981 World Series of Poker here in Las Vegas."

Like many savants, the Kid was often overwhelmed by what most people think of as everyday existence. He didn't own a watch. He never applied for a credit card. He had never had a bank account until he moved to Las Vegas, and when he finally opened one he thought he had to go to the bank each time he wrote a check. He never had a driver's license until he purchased a brand-new Mercedes, which he promptly drove into the ground, not realizing he had to change the oil. He lived his life in hotels, and never, for even one day, toiled at what anyone would describe as a "real job."

"He was like a guy coming out of the jungle," said Jack Binion.

Shortly after his victory in 1980, Stuey went to get his first passport so he could play in a poker tournament in Ireland. The clerk told him it would take a while to process. When Stuey asked if there was any way he might speed up the process, the clerk told him that for "a few extra dollars" it could be ready in a couple of days. The clerk was merely referring to the standard processing fee for a rush job, but Stuey, thinking it was a shakedown, tried to slip the man $300.

Such obliviousness, when coupled with Stuey's insatiable desire for action, guaranteed he would never be putting any money into his bank account. He spent his poker winnings as quickly as he earned them. For him, money was simply a tool with which to gamble. The more he had, the more he bet. He went from being broke to being a millionaire and back to being broke again at least four times during his life.

"Ungar was known for gambling every single dollar in his pocket on a daily basis—and then some," write Nolan Dalla and Peter Alston in *One of a Kind*, the authorized biography of the Kid. "One week he started out with $2 million. Five days later, he was broke and owed $150,000. He burned through $100 bills like they were postage stamps."

He spent an undocumented—and unimaginable to most—amount of money maintaining his burgeoning cocaine addiction. His other, no less damaging, addiction, gambling, took whatever money he had left. Stuey would bet on anything: football, basketball, horses, the temperature outside, or the chance it might rain . . . in Paris. The first time he set foot on a golf course, at the Las Vegas Country Club, he was down $80,000 to Jack Straus before he'd even made it to the first tee. He'd lost it all on the putting green.

Stuey lost so much money playing golf he could have bought his own course. Despite being so inept at the game, he still loved it because he could always find someone eager to bet against him. He rarely re-fused a wager, although he did demand certain advantages that would help compensate for his lack of size and coordination. He insisted upon wearing gloves on both hands, hitting from the ladies' tees, and teeing up his ball on every shot until he reached the green, no matter where it lay on the course. Once after hitting his ball into a creek, his opponent grinned, convinced Stuey would have to take a penalty stroke, but his smile faded when Stuey pulled out a specially designed tee nearly a foot long, stepped into the water, and teed up his ball.

Remarkably, even with all this assistance, he rarely broke a hun-dred. He reportedly lost the entire $385,000 he earned for winning the 1980 World Series on the golf course within a week of the tourna-ment's conclusion. What might inspire caution in a lesser man meant only one thing to the Kid: he would definitely be returning in 1981 to defend his title, aiming to capture the first-place money.

Although they had entered a new decade, the Binions hadn't changed all that much. Benny was still playing the role of benevolent dictator, while his sons took care of the day-to-day requirements of running a casino and his wife looked after the books. Trusting no one but herself to do it, Teddy Jane—an unforgettable sight with her dyed hair, wiry frame, and ever-present cigarette—made all the Horseshoe's bank deposits, actually carrying hundreds of thousands of dollars in cash down Fremont Street.

Their philosophy concerning limits hadn't changed a bit either. Benny was still willing to accept wagers of nearly any size. The most notorious instance occurred in 1980 when William Lee Bergstrom of Austin, Texas, asked permission to wager $777,000 at one of the Horseshoe's craps tables, literally placing a suitcase full of cash on the DON'T PASS line. Benny readily agreed to take his action and—after the woman shooting the dice crapped out in three rolls—amiably paid the man his money, even volunteering his son Ted to escort Bergstrom to his car. Over the course of the next few years, Bergstrom pressed his luck several more times, earning payouts of $590,000, $190,000, and $90,000. In November 1984, he would up his all-or-nothing wager to a million dollars and lose it on the very first roll of the dice. Three months later he committed suicide.

"But you know," Ted Binion remarked, "he was still $400,000 winner."*

When it came to their poker tournament, however, the Binions accepted change as an inevitable part of its evolution. Although the field in 1981 only increased by two, Jack Binion and Eric Drache, formalizing what had already become the norm, officially stretched the tournament's format from three days to four. It was almost as if they were trying to make it more difficult for the Kid to repeat, and the oddsmakers agreed that it would be a difficult road. One made him a 25–1 long shot; another thought even less of his chances, setting the line on him at 40–1. They had more confidence in Doyle Brunson, making him the favorite once again.

Texas Dolly, however, was reluctant to agree. "I'm not playing as well as last year," he said. "But I'll play hard and maybe something will happen. You have to get a lot of breaks to come through that

---

*In the parlance of the Texas road gambler, "winner" and "loser" are often used as adjectives, not nouns, perhaps to emphasize how emphemeral such conditions were.

many players. In a freezeout, when you can't reach back and take more chips, the best player won't necessarily win. There's a lot of luck involved. I guess that's what attracts so many players."

His nemesis from the previous year felt much better about his chances. "I feel pretty good," Stuey said. "I have a lot more confidence than I did last year."

After everyone was seated, Jack Binion, now in his forties and quickly losing his hair, climbed onto a chair in the back of the room and introduced each of the seventy-five players. The first to go was Sam Nassi of Beverly Hills, eliminated just an hour and a half into the tournament. Quickly following him was Hugh Neville, the Irish representative from the Eccentric Club. Bones Berland and Johnny Moss were gone soon afterwards. More big names fell the following day: Jack Straus, Puggy Pearson, Amarillo Slim, Jesse Alto.

Johnny and Jesse and several others who had been bounced early were quick to shrug off the loss and jump into a side game. The minimum buy-in was $500, but there was easily $60,000 or $70,000 on the table.

"Look at it this way," said Las Vegan George Cronin. "Guys who get done with the big tournament aren't going home to bed. This same group of guys who put up $10,000 to get into the tournament are going to sit down and play some more. Only they don't bring out $10,000, they bring out $40,000 to $50,000."

At the start of the third day only twenty players remained. Perry Green of Anchorage, Alaska, was leading the way with $81,600. Bill Smith, part of a new wave of Texas road gamblers, jumped into second place with $72,900 after winning the largest pot of the night. He took $78,000 off Chip Reese after Chip got it all in with three jacks and Bill drew out on him, making a diamond flush.

Doyle reached a high point of $47,800 during the third day, but was plagued by a toothache and, worse, a bad run of cards. The best hand he had seen was a pair of kings, and he had been forced to throw them away when Gene Fisher, a fellow Texan from El Paso, reraised him with what Doyle correctly assumed were a set of 9s.

"I never even had a draw to a straight or a flush," said Doyle. "Every time I won a pot, it was with the worst hand."

One of those hands was against Ken "Top Hat" Smith. Smith's nickname derived from his fondness for wearing a top hat he claimed was found in the Ford Theatre the night Abraham Lincoln was assassinated. He was equally known for the elaborate ritual he engaged in each time he won a big pot. Rising from his chair, he would doff his famous hat, and shout, "What a player!" much to the amusement and occasional annoyance of his rivals. Al Alvarez, the British writer who would later immortalize that year's World Series in his classic book *The Biggest Game in Town*, recounted one such instance on the tournament's third day.

"You're all heart, Ken," teased Doyle. "Heart and belly."

The railbirds, enjoying the banter, egged him on.

"You know what I'm gonna do?" Doyle continued. "I'm gonna raise you on two rags and bluff you right out."

"Try me," Smith said, betting into a K-Q-J flop.

"Raise!" Doyle practically shouted as he pushed all his chips into the pot.

After Smith folded, Doyle flipped over his worthless 6-5, rose to his feet, doffed his Stetson, and, mimicking his opponent, shouted, "What a player!"

Such theatrical moves only delayed the inevitable. Low on chips, Doyle was forced to move all in before the flop with a less than stellar hand, K♦2♦. He was called by the equally desperate Andy Moore, a bar owner from Sarasota, Florida who had fallen into the habit of holding up his cards for the railbirds to see during his more dramatic hands. What they saw this time was the A♠4♠. Catching an ace on the turn, Moore knocked Doyle out in eleventh place. The crowd gave him a hearty cheer, and he acknowledged them with a wave of his hand as he limped away from the table.

Some years at the World Series there are certain hands that seem to appear more often than usual, taking on an almost magical quality as they determine the fate of the players who hold them. In 1981, pocket queens assumed that mythic status, and Bobby Baldwin, the chip leader entering the final table, would be the one who would feel their power the most.

Twenty minutes after the one o'clock start, "Chicago" Sam Petrillo, who had obtained his nickname from the town where he had left his ex-wife and three children in order to become a professional poker player, moved all in with A-K. Bobby called with pocket queens and won the hand, giving him a $150,000 pot and knocking Petrillo out in ninth place. Thanks to a change in the payout structure that awarded all nine players at the final table a piece of the prize pool, Petrillo took home $15,000. Ten minutes later, Bobby was dealt pocket queens once again, and once again they worked their magic, beating Andy Moore's A-10 to end the likeable amateur's day. These two pots pushed Bobby's chip stack close to $240,000, but, as good as the ladies had been to him, they would soon treat him just as badly.

A little over an hour after Moore's exit, Perry Green raised before the flop with a pair of queens, and Bobby called with a pair of 9s in the hole. When the dealer laid a third 9 on the board, giving Bobby a nearly unbeatable set, he checked, hoping his opponent would show as much strength after the flop as he had before. Perry did, shoving $42,000 into the pot. Bobby raised it $85,000, enough to set Perry all in if he called. Perry stared at Bobby for two full minutes before he pushed in the rest of his chips. The J♥ on the turn didn't change anything, but the Q♠ on the river certainly did. The $220,000 pot made Perry the new chip leader.

"Hang in there, Bobby!" a fan yelled from the rail.

His only response was an incredulous smile. In a single hand he had gone from nearly taking a huge chip lead to desperately needing life support. From that point forward he could seem to do no right. He tried to steal three separate pots with bluffs and, much to his dismay, got called each time. Then, when he finally picked up a real hand, pocket kings, he got outdrawn by—you guessed it—pocket queens. Gene Fisher, the stoic Texan with the walrus mustache, worn-out Stetson, and scarlet United States Cavalry shirt, called Bobby's all-in preflop raise of $100,000 and caught the Q♥ on the river, eliminating the Owl in seventh place.

The departure of Bobby Baldwin, nearly everyone's pick to win the championship after Doyle got knocked out, created a vacuum at the table that Stuey Ungar was quick to fill. Until now, the Kid had been uncharacteristically quiet. He had barely survived the first day, having to go all in three times at his very first table, and was down to his last $2,000 at one point. He had enjoyed a brief rush on the second day, but would have been eliminated on several occasions if it weren't for his ability to make some extremely difficult "laydowns"—

folding strong hands. He folded a set after his opponent made a flush on the turn, then threw away pocket queens in the face of an all-in reraise before the flop when he sensed that he was up against aces or kings. These decisions had ensured his survival but not his success. At three P.M., just prior to Bobby's elimination, Stuey only possessed $35,000.

Two hours later, he would have $340,000 and be the new chip leader.

Before the start of the final day, Doyle Brunson bet Gabe Kaplan that a Texan would win the championship. Taking up the challenge, Gabe put his money on the cadre of Jewish players at the final table. With six players left, the wager was still a toss-up. Gene Fisher and the two Smiths, Ken and Bill, represented the Texas side; Stuey Ungar, Perry Green, and Jay Heimowitz stood tall for the Jews.

The Jews would take the first hit. At 4:30 P.M., Heimowitz was dealt the hot hand of the day, pocket queens. Unfortunately for him, they would lose whatever magic they once possessed. A K-J-10 flop gave Heimowitz an open-ended straight draw, an enticing enough holding to convince him to commit all of his chips on a semibluff, but Stuey had flopped a set of jacks, which held up. For the first time all day pocket queens had lost, and Heimowitz was gone in sixth place.

"In this kind of situation I try to get a rush of cards," Stuey said later. "I try also to psyche my opponents. I start raising the pots, and if big bombs are thrown at me, I throw them back just as big."

After eliminating one of his own, Stuey evened the score for the Jews when he knocked out Bill Smith on the very next hand. Those interested in seeing poker shed the dirty image it had always borne were happy to see Bill go, for the hardened road gambler was the exception to the universal opinion that drinking at the table was bad for one's game. Bill not only drank, he got drunk, teetering in his chair, raising with a slurred tongue, demanding that the cocktail waitress keep refilling his glass with whiskey. The purists could breathe easier after Stuey made a spade flush on the river to beat the road gambler's pair of 6s. Bill finished his drink, pocketed the $37,500 he'd earned for coming in fifth, and stumbled out of the room.

When the game broke for dinner at five o'clock, Stuey, as was his nature, was far more interested in finding more action than getting some food. Brimming with confidence, he wanted to bet as much money with the bookmaker Jackie Gaughan as he could on himself to win the championship.

Watching Stuey steamroll his opponents on his way to taking the chip lead left Doyle Brunson shaking his head. "That bet of mine with Gabe don't look too healthy," he said.

His chances got worse when, just a few hours later, Perry Green made four aces with A-J to knock out Top Hat Smith. As Smith was accepting his prize money from Jack Binion, one of the railbirds shouted, "What a player!" Smith acknowledged his fan by doffing his signature hat and smiling.

The Kid was very nearly the next to fall after he raised $10,000 before the flop with pocket kings and Perry called with A-Q. The flop came ace high with two diamonds, and Perry led out for $60,000. Stuey spent several minutes playing with his chips, debating what to do. He had to have hated the ace on the flop but called anyway. He was glad he did when a king fell on the turn, making him a set. He pushed in his last $90,000. It was Perry's turn to sweat a decision. If he called and won, he would have 90 percent of the chips on the table. But he called and lost—the pot as well as the chip lead he had enjoyed all too briefly.

The last Texan fell during the seventh hour of play. Down to just $50,000, Gene Fisher looked on the verge of mounting a comeback when he was dealt pocket kings and caught a third king on the flop, but Perry called his all-in bet and completed a diamond flush draw on the turn. Finishing third, the popular Fisher received a rousing round of applause from almost everyone in the gallery, the notable exception being Doyle Brunson, who dug a fistful of $100 bills from his pocket and shoved them into Gabe Kaplan's hand.

"So much for the Texans," said Gabe gleefully. "We got ourselves an all-Jewish final."

Perry Green was the first Orthodox Jewish fur trader from Alaska to play heads-up for the world championship of poker. It's hard to imagine there will ever be a second.

Green began his career buying furs from the indigenous people who live in the remote interior of the forty-ninth state. Turning these furs into coats, he sold them to an eclectic mix of celebrities that included the Reverend Oral Roberts, Ike and Tina Turner, Sam Snead, and the Bee Gees. He occasionally played cards with the villagers he traded with, but saved his A game for the rounders in Anchorage. Squaring off once a week against the local competition gave him enough confidence to sit in a $1,000 buy-in ace-to-five lowball game during his first trip to Las Vegas in 1972. Playing against a table full of professionals—including Johnny Moss—Perry could have easily lost his shirt. Instead, he took the game for over $70,000.

Despite the beating Green had handed him nine years earlier, Moss remained unimpressed by the man's game, relative to that of Stu Ungar.

"I reckon Stuey's got it made," he said. "He may not look like no Buffalo Bill, but he's one tough poker player. That boy's got alligator blood in his veins."

For the first half hour of heads-up play, Perry and Stuey cautiously traded blows, but gradually, inexorably, Stuey asserted himself as the more aggressive of the two, frequently coming over the top with a big raise, forcing Perry to fold. Tired of being bullied, the Alaskan kicked off his shoes and dug his feet into the carpet, as if bad footing were to blame for his tentativeness. Standing five foot three and weighing 250 pounds, he was built like a rock wall and could be just as unyielding as one. He gnawed on his toothpick and waited patiently for an opportunity to strike back.

One arrived at eight-thirty when Perry, enjoying a $150,000 chip advantage, entered a pot with a hand that would bring a smile to Doyle Brunson's face: 10♣2♣. It's one of poker's hidden truths that, in certain cases, a draw can be better than a made hand. One such situation seemed to arise when the J♦9♣8♣ flop gave him an open-ended straight draw and four cards to a flush. Perry believed he had fifteen outs towards improving his hand, and the odds were better than 60 percent that the next two cards would bring one of them. After Stuey led out with a $65,000 bet, Perry moved all in. What he didn't know was that the Kid, holding A♣J♣, had flopped an even bigger hand— top pair with the better flush draw. Stuey's call reduced Perry's fifteen outs to six—only a 7 or a queen that wasn't a club would save him. Neither card arrived. Stuey raked in the $560,000 pot and took a commanding lead, $600,000 to $150,000.

"It's all over," said Jack Straus. "The kid's gonna eat him up like a boarding-house pie."

It was hard to disagree. Stuey's game was perfectly attuned to wielding large stacks of chips. A run of good cards didn't hurt his cause. As the hour closed in on ten o'clock, Stuey made a large raise before the flop with A♥Q♥, and Perry called with 10♣9♦. The 8♥7♦4♥ flop gave Stuey the nut flush draw along with his two overcards and he fired a big bet at the pot. With two overcards and a draw to an open-ended straight, Perry raised, pushing all his chips into the middle of the table. Slouching sideways with his left arm dangling over the back of his chair, Stuey debated for a moment before calling. Both men flipped over their cards. Perry stared unhappily at Stuey's two hearts before turning his back to the table. Stuey squirmed nervously in his chair.

The 4♣ fell on fourth street, the Q♦ on fifth, giving Stuey a superfluous two pair and his second consecutive world championship.

"Hey!" was all Stuey could manage by way of celebration as he jumped out of his chair. "Great!"

His play had been so magnificent it had even impressed the curmudgeonly Johnny Moss, who walked over and patted Stuey on the shoulder. "I am proud of you, Kid."

Trying to articulate a similarly sentimental reply, the Kid said, "At age seventy-three, I won't be able to whip my arm up."

Jack Binion rushed in to give Stuey and Perry each a half hug, his arms around their shoulders, while the cameras captured the moment. Stuey seemed far more interested in the $375,000 in cash sitting on the table, now his.

"What are you going to do with the money?" asked TV sportscaster Curt Gowdy, shoving a microphone into the champion's face.

"Lose it," Stuey mumbled.

Gowdy pressed him, unsure that he'd heard him correctly.

"I have no idea. I might take a vacation. I know I'll pay a lot of taxes."

Neither statement was true. Stuey never took a vacation nor paid a dime of taxes his entire life. He gathered the cash in a grocery bag and immediately set about paying off some of his old gambling debts. Within minutes a large chunk of his winnings was gone.

6

THE LION HAS HIS DAY

After winning back-to-back championships at such a young age, Stuey Ungar was the odds-on favorite to win a third in 1982. That's not the way it worked out. He didn't make it past the second day, blaming the added strain of having a bull's eye painted on his chest.

"I was expected to win," he explained. "That puts a lot of pressure on you."

The hyperaggressive approach to the game that had worked so well for him the year before had backfired on him. As effective as such a style can be in "short-handed play"—that is, playing at a less than full table—it can also be a handicap in a multiday tournament such as the World Series, where a player needs to employ extreme prudence in the early going just to survive. Never known for being cautious, Stuey, throughout his career, was just as likely to get knocked out the very first day as he was to win it all.

Possessing the same all-or-nothing style, the legendary Jack Straus, a perennial favorite to win the world championship, experienced similarly uneven results. After a promising start to his World Series career—finishing second to Johnny Moss in '71 and winning the Deuce-to-Seven Draw event two years later—his results had gotten progressively worse. In 1979 he earned the dubious distinction of being the very first person eliminated from the tournament.

The early exits hardly bothered the man. "If fortune fails to smile on you," he said, "you just shrug your shoulders and wait until next year."

One of the original Texas road gamblers, Jack had played in the World Series every year since its inception. Like Doyle Brunson, he came as much for the lucrative side action as he did for the tournament itself—getting knocked out early didn't sting so badly when he could jump right into a high-stakes cash game and win his entry fee back in a single hand. Scrutinizing his opponents from behind his thick glasses and bushy beard, Jack enjoyed a reputation as a fearless player who terrorized cash games played for sums that would make a workingman tremble. Those he regularly played against called him "Treetop," a reference to his lanky six-foot-seven-inch frame, but even if he had been two feet shorter he would have still been a towering presence at the poker table. The many tales told of him and the expression on the faces of those doing the telling attest to his indefinable greatness, not just as a player but also as a person. He was the life of every party, and for him there was no greater celebration than the World Series of Poker.

"In the Old West, they used to have trappers' rendezvous every four years," he said. "All the mountain men and people who lived in the wilderness would get together in a certain spot to swap stories, have wrestling matches and canoe races, and see their friends. This is our trappers' rendezvous, but we have it *every* year."

The ever expanding field did nothing to improve his chances of winning the world championship. In 1982, 104 players entered the main event, a dramatic 25 percent increase over the previous year. Stuey Ungar wasn't the only favorite to get knocked out sooner than anticipated. Doyle Brunson and Bobby Baldwin were also booted early.

Jack Straus nearly joined them after he moved all in on an opponent, pushing what he believed to be the last of his remaining chips into the middle, and lost the hand. He rose from his chair, prepared to seek out a side game, when he discovered a single $500 chip hidden between a napkin and the bumper.* He returned to his chair, armed with barely enough to cover the next ante.

For many poker players, the game is an obsession, blotting out any semblance of an outside life. Jack Straus was not that kind of man. He would just as soon play golf or chess or read a good book. He especially enjoyed traveling, particularly to Africa, which he visited numerous times. In an era when big-game hunting was still considered the bee's knees, he shot and killed a lion while on safari in Mozambique. He then had a favorite Italian proverb inscribed on one of the animal's stuffed paws, which he often wore around his neck. "Better one day as a lion," it read, "than a hundred years as a lamb."

It was an apt philosophy for a man who was forced to come to grips with the fleeting nature of the human condition at a young age. His father, the manager of a packing plant, spent his entire life working himself to the point of exhaustion with the idea that he would be able to enjoy the good life when he retired at sixty-five. That day never came: the elder Straus died seven years short of his goal. Understanding how short and fragile life can be, Jack vowed to make the most of his. Looking upon traditional employment as a long, slow march to one's grave, he embraced gambling as a way to make more money in less time, enough to support himself in high style. He also adopted the sort of fearlessness that is only possible when one decides to live every day as if it could be his last.

"I have only a limited amount of time on this earth," he said, "and I want to live every second of it. That's why I'm willing to play anyone in the world for any amount. It doesn't matter who they are. Once they have a hundred or two hundred thousand dollars' worth of chips

---

*There has been some confusion over the years as to how Treetop could have made an "all in" bet and still retained a chip. The answer is that it wasn't an all-in bet—Straus had merely pushed what he believed to be all of his chips into the middle. If he had verbally declared himself to be all in, or called an opponent's all-in bet, he would have had to surrender that last chip. As he had done neither, the chip still belonged to him.

in front of them, they all look the same to me. They all look like drag-
ons, and I want to slay them."

Jack's dragon slaying began at an early age. He won a car in a
poker game before he was old enough to drive. He quickly graduated
to higher-stakes games where winning a car would be considered
only a minor score. When he wasn't hosting his famed home game in
Houston, he was traveling the same circuit as Doyle, Slim, and Sailor.
They were called road gamblers for good reason. There were very few
things they wouldn't wager on, Jack in particular.

"Jack was a gambler's gambler. He would bet on anything," said
Benny Binion, perhaps thinking of the time Treetop bet $100,000 on
a high school basketball game.

Today, the word "gambler" has become synonymous with self-
destruction, interventions, and support groups, but to a man of a certain mindset in mid-twentieth-century Texas it was a compliment of
the highest order. A *gambler* wasn't some addict willing to risk everything on the spin of the wheel or the turn of a card, but a man with
the stones to put it all on the line when he saw an angle. Treetop saw
angles everywhere he looked.

"He'll bet on anything that moves," said Puggy Pearson. "Christ,
he'd bet on a cockroach race."

As long as he felt like he had a better than average chance of winning a wager, Jack would bet all the money he had in the world without
thinking twice. He had gone broke enough times to know that it wasn't
so bad, because being broke was never a permanent condition—a successful wager or two would quickly restore him to his former glory. He
understood where others did not that money was only a commodity. It
had no real value other than what it could be used for.

"If money is your god," he said, "you can forget no-limit poker because it's going to hurt too much to turn loose of it. The way I feel
about those pieces of green paper is, you can't take them with you
and they may not have much value in five year's time, but right now I
can take them and trade them in for pleasure, or to bring pleasure to
other people. If they had wanted you to hold on to money, they'd have
made it with handles on it."

Generous to a fault, Jack's capacity for giving away money was
as legendary as his ability to win it. His friends loved to tell the
story of the time the Internal Revenue Service took him to court, al-

leging he owed some $3 million in back taxes. As he waited in the back of the courtroom for his hearing to begin, he amused himself by listening to the one that was just finishing. The hapless defendant, who owed the government $35,000, begged the court for more time to pay the bill, pleading that he'd be unable able to pay his rent or feed his family.

"It's okay, your honor," Jack yelled from the back of the room. "Just stick it on my tab. It won't make that much difference."

There is obviously more to being a successful gambler than a disregard for money—Jack had the intuition and quickness of mind to insure that he was on the winning side more often than not. He also possessed a deep understanding of human nature, and he used that knowledge to give himself an edge whenever he saw an opportunity.

Any hold'em player will tell you that 7-2 offsuit is the worst possible starting hand, as they are the two lowest cards you can have that can't be used in concert to make a straight or a flush. Dealt this very hand in the midst of a rush during a no-limit session, Jack opted to ignore conventional wisdom and open with a raise. Whatever feeling of prescience he might have enjoyed when the flop came 7-3-3 quickly dissipated when his opponent raised him $5,000 with what turned out to be pocket jacks. Jack called anyway, and when a deuce appeared on the turn—pairing his second hole card but not improving his hand—he was struck by a lightning bolt of creativity. He fired $18,000 into the middle. As his opponent tried to decipher the play, Jack offered some assistance.

"I'll tell you what," he said, grinning through his beard. "You give me one of those little old twenty-five-dollar chips of yours and you can see either one of my cards, whichever you choose."

Intrigued by the offer, the man tossed over a yellow-and-green chip and pointed to one of Jack's cards. It was the deuce. The only conclusion his hapless opponent could come to was exactly the one Jack had led him to believe—the two cards had to be the same, Jack must have pocket deuces, and the turn must have improved his hand to a full house. The pocket jacks were thrown into the muck. Jack had not only tricked him into laying down the better hand but charged him $25 for the privilege to do so.

"It's just a matter of simple psychology," he said afterward.

·   ·   ·

When Jack discovered he still had one chip left in the 1982 championship, he returned to the poker table feeling as if he had a hundred of them. There was a precedent for his confidence. He had fought his way back from similarly large deficits before.

During one of his "business trips" to Las Vegas in 1970, a bad run of cards at the poker table nearly wiped out his bankroll, leaving him with only $40. Where most would have crawled home to lick their wounds, Jack strode towards a blackjack table and bet it all on a single hand. He won that first bet, then several more in quick succession, working his way back to $500. He then returned to the poker table and ran his revitalized bankroll up to $4,000. Riding his rush, he went back to the blackjack table and won another $6,000 before betting the entire $10,000 on the Kansas City Chiefs in Super Bowl IV. The Chiefs defeated the Vikings handily, and Jack cashed in his winning ticket, pocketing $20,000. In less than twenty-four hours, he had gone from near bankruptcy to relative affluence, and, amazingly, each time he'd made a bet he'd done so with all the money he had in the world.

Jack used the same all-or-nothing strategy to pull himself back from the brink of elimination in 1982. With only one chip, he didn't have a lot of room to maneuver. He would have to go all in before the blinds reached him. He picked the right hand, stealing the blinds with an inferior hand and doubling up.

"Hell, I bluffed with my last $200 bet," he boasted.

He repeated the play on the next hand, with identical results. Gathering steam, Jack used a prolonged campaign of aggression combined with a series of masterful bluffs to get himself back into contention. One of the more dramatic and rewarding hands of his comeback came against Vera Richmond, the cosmetics heiress from Beverly Hills who had eliminated Jack from the tournament the year before. She entered the 1982 tournament on a roll after winning the $1,000 Ace-to-Five Draw event, making her the first woman to win an event that included men. In the hand against Jack she flopped a set of 9s, but, holding 5-4, he caught a 4 on the flop, the turn, and the river to make quads. The $30,000 pot propelled him to the lead at the end of the second day with $90,000.

By the end of the third day, Jack had amassed $341,500, giving him a better than two-to-one chip lead over his closest opponent A. J. Meyers, a retired real estate broker from Beverly Hills. Someone asked Jack if, now that he had such a big chip lead, he'd continue to play so aggressively.

"I don't know no other way. I've only got one speed, and that's 'go get 'em.' "

When he sat down at the final table, he found himself surrounded by a pack of familiar faces: six of the nine finalists were from Texas, proving that the supremacy of poker players from the Lone Star State, although certainly waning, had yet to run its course.

Even though they were all familiar with Jack's game, his opponents seemed incapable of stopping him. He knew how to use a big stack as well as anyone in the world, entering nearly every pot with a large raise. Faced with that sort of pressure, the other players at the table fell one by one. Some started referring to the seat to his immediate right as the "electric chair," as Jack summarily executed all those who had the misfortune of sitting in it: Carl Cannon, Sailor Roberts, Buster Jackson, Dody Roach, A. J. Meyers. The nine players had been winnowed to four when Doyle—who had survived fourteen all-in attempts—moved into the electric chair. He wouldn't survive his fifteenth. With Doyle's departure, Berry Johnston inherited the ill-fated seat and, predictably, he was the next to go.

"They say it's not good to be leading," Jack said after his magnificent run at the final table, "but I'd have to say I'd rather not change places with anyone else."

The only challenger remaining was Dewey Tomko, whose survival can be linked to the fact that he had been sitting on Jack's immediate left the entire day, but that advantage had disappeared along with everyone else at the table. There would be no hiding anymore.

Playing Jack Straus heads-up for the world championship may have seemed like a daunting task, but Dewey Tomko was no stranger to perilous challenges—before becoming a professional poker player, he had been a kindergarten teacher in Florida for six years.

There was a time when he attempted to do both, teaching the children of migrant workers during the day and playing poker at night. He survived this brutal stretch by joining his students during their designated nap time.

"I developed a good rapport with their parents," Dewey recalled. "In fact, I had the parents trained. They'd tiptoe into the room and pick up their children without even waking me up. I'd wake up around eight P.M. and there wouldn't be a kid in the room. Then I'd go off to another poker game."

With a wife and child to support, Dewey relied on the steady income generated by teaching to withstand the inevitable fluctuations associated with poker. Predictably, the dual life began to wear on him. After losing $16,000 playing golf over the course of a weekend, he returned Monday morning to his $6,400-a-year job in the classroom. The dichotomy finally proved too much. He quit his teaching job that very day.

For the next ten years he played golf for high stakes while dedicating himself to improving his poker game, even going so far as to enlist the services of Chip Reese as a tutor. In 1982, he was rewarded for all his hard work, coming in second in two of the new major tournaments that had sprung from the success of the World Series, Amarillo Slim's Super Bowl of Poker and the Grand Prix at the Golden Nugget. This year's World Series was his chance to break through with a win, but now, seated in the electric chair, he would need a lot more than hard work to overcome Jack Straus.

Ten minutes into their heads-up confrontation, with the blinds at $2,000 and $4,000, Dewey opened for $100,000 with A♦4♦. Holding A♥10♣, Jack raised him another $180,000. Dewey, after deliberating for several minutes, shoved all his chips into the pot. Jack didn't take long to call. At the time it was the biggest pot in World Series history, $967,000, and its outcome would determine the championship.

Despite having the better starting hand, Treetop looked extremely nervous. "I don't know!" he said as the cards were turned over.

When the flop came 6♦5♠4♠—giving Dewey a small pair—it looked as if Treetop's magical run could be coming to an end. He shook his head and shifted uneasily in his seat.

The queen of clubs on fourth street was no help to Jack. The dealer, Brian McCandless, very slowly and dramatically placed the last card on the table.

"I didn't want to make a mistake," he later said.

It was the 10♠, giving Jack a bigger pair than Dewey's and the championship. His face betrayed the gamut of emotions coursing through him: shock, happiness, relief. He uncoiled his long body from his chair. Doyle ambled over to congratulate him.

"It was a miracle, pure luck," said Jack with typical modesty. "All my life I've been dreaming about something like this. All of a sudden I did it."

His incredible comeback from the brink of elimination inspired the widely spoken poker aphorism: "All you need is a chip and a chair."

For his victory he earned $520,000, at the time the biggest payout of any sports event in history. He pocketed a half million and gave the odd $20,000 to the dealers and the card room staff as a tip. When asked what he was going to do with the rest, he said, "I'm going to enjoy my winnings and relax for a while."

He had plans to go on an African safari in June. He also offered to buy his friend Ray Miranda an elephant.

"He's worked with elephants before in circuses," Jack explained, "and I wanted to make him happy again."

Typically solitary creatures, many poker champions celebrate alone. Not Jack. He headed straight for a party thrown in his honor at the Dunes, where Robert Goulet entertained him and over three hundred guests.

More than anything, Jack Straus had the one commodity that poker players value above all others: heart. Heart is the ability to bet all your chips and your tournament life on a stone-cold bluff. Heart is the intestinal fortitude to bet all the money you have in the world on an uncertain proposition. Heart is the capacity to keep your head when you're down to your last $500 chip.

Jack Straus had heart in spades, and that is why it is so cruelly ironic that it was the organ that finally let him down in the end. While playing no-limit Texas hold'em in a tournament at the Bicycle Casino in Los Angeles in 1988, Jack suffered a massive heart attack after making a large bet and died right there at the table. He was fifty-eight years old, the same age as his father when he passed away. According to legend, one of the players at the table peeked at Jack's hole cards, confirming that Treetop had passed on from this world in the midst of one last bluff. It was a fitting end to an epic life.

"I have no regrets about my life," Jack once said. "If I had it all to do again, I'd do it the same way."

7

SATELLITES

aving reached the age of seventy-eight, Benny Binion was starting to show some signs of mellowing. When a preacher from North Carolina lost $1,000 while playing craps at the Horseshoe, money that actually belonged to his congregation, Benny insisted the money be returned to the reverend but hapless man.

"God may forgive you, preacher," Benny told him, "but your congregation won't."

When it came to his quest to receive a presidential pardon, however, he was as determined as ever. While discussing the issue with Nevada senator Paul Laxalt, the senator suggested that a donation to the campaign treasury of the current President Ronald Reagan might help his cause.

Two days after Benny contributed $15,000, he received word that he had been denied a pardon once again. Benny responded by taking out a newspaper ad that let everyone know that Laxalt was a welsher, and he vowed, loudly and publicly, to live long enough to piss on Reagan's grave.

. . .

"No man should be fifteen-to-one, or twelve-to-one, for that matter," said Jack Straus upon hearing the line on him to repeat as champion in 1983. "I wouldn't take those odds unless I was broke and could bet on credit. There are too many people in this tournament."

The large number of entries had even greater consequences: the World Series was literally outgrowing its home, and very little was being done about it. After 232 players signed up to play in the $1,000 No-Limit Hold'em event, tournament officials were still scrambling at the last minute to borrow enough tables from several neighboring casinos to seat everyone.

Despite the popularity of the World Series, the Horseshoe had never maintained a year-round poker room. "They would try it," recalls Eric Drache, but after a month straight of fourteen- or fifteen-hour days and nights "everyone was exhausted or broke, or both. They either won enough money, where they were entitled to a vacation, or they lost enough, or were just mentally and physically beaten."

Having outgrown the temporary space provided by the old baccarat alcove, the Horseshoe's management was forced to set up extra tables wherever there was room, primarily in the new Keno area. Space was so tight the poker players occasionally had to dodge the flailing elbows of the slot machine players directly behind them. Some of the players who had signed up for one of the preliminary limit events had to start the tournament in an entirely different casino, the neighboring Golden Nugget. Adding a touch of comedy to the situation, the very same process was repeated at the start of the main event when 108 players signed up.

"We've got to do something about this," said Jack Binion.

In every other regard the man was pleased. More players meant a bigger prize pool, which meant more publicity for the Horseshoe. Tournament poker was flourishing all across the country. The late 1970s and early '80s saw the birth of a slew of high stakes tournaments: Amarillo Slim's Super Bowl of Poker, the Stardust's Stairway to the Stars, Union Plaza's Live It Up event, Bob Stupak's America's Cup Championship at Vegas World, the Golden Nugget's Grand Prix of Poker, and the latest entry, Jack Straus's World Match Play Championship at the Frontier. But the World Series of Poker would remain the undisputed world championship.

Sixteen different countries sent players to the tournament in 1983. There were nine entries from Ireland alone, including a trio from strife-ridden Belfast. Perhaps as a concession to the Europeans, Eric Drache added a new event to the lineup, $1,000 limit Omaha, a game that was growing extremely popular across the Atlantic.

"That's what we've been asking for," said Jack Binion. "If it's going to be a world championship, we have to have worldwide competition."

As Jack Straus feared, the large field made the chances of him repeating extremely difficult. He didn't make it past the first day. His stack took a big hit in a duel with Phil Matthews of Kansas City—Treetop had three queens, but Matthews showed him queens full of 10s.

"I turned a big hand against a bigger hand," said Jack. "It's a big hand, and you just can't get away from it."

Down to his last chip once again—this time only $100—he got it in with a solid hand, pocket 9s, but lost when Gabe Kaplan flopped a pair of kings.

"I guess I had one coming," Jack said. "It finally caught up with me. . . . I've been very fortunate four tournaments in a row."

Not one to delude himself, he admitted that his tendency to force the action hurt him early in tournaments. "My first day is my hardest time because the antes are cheap, and I'm a very aggressive player. . . . You get crippled so bad you can't overcome it."

Would the early exit make him change his style in the future?

Jack smiled. "I can't change. I'm too old to change."

The most significant reason for the growth of the World Series can be traced to a happy accident. Sometime in the late '70s, as the legend goes, Eric Drache trolled the side games at the Horseshoe, hoping to find a few extra players for the championship event. At that time, all of the entrants who had already paid the $10,000 fee were listed on a big board inside the casino. A long list would generate more excitement— and more entries. But many players often waited until the last minute to pay their buy-ins, making the list look feeble. Drache tried to remedy the situation by actively recruiting early entries.

"So I went over to a table about five days before the big event and asked if any of the guys wanted to pay their $10,000, just so I could have some more paid entries, start a little momentum going," Drache recalls. "Then I looked at the table and said, heck, there's just about $10,000 on the whole table." Noticing that each of the nine or ten players had about a thousand in front of them, Drache suggested they play a single-table freezeout, the winner earning an entry into the main event.

News of the first "satellite" spread quickly. Tom Bowling asked if he could run similar events in his card room at the Palace Station, and began supplying five to ten extra players to the main event each year. Several other card rooms soon followed suit.

The advent of satellites transformed the World Series into a truly *open* tournament, no longer the sole domain of those who possessed world-class skill or limitless bankrolls. The revolutionary concept worked exactly as Drache had hoped. From 1981 to 1986 the number of entrants in the championship event nearly doubled, jumping from 75 to 141.

One consequence of the satellites was that a large percentage of the newcomers were recreational players. "A decade ago probably seventy-five percent of the people at the World Series were professionals," noted Drache. "It's a lot less than that now." In fact, in 1983 less than half of the 108 entrants were full-time poker players.

While one might think the addition of so many amateurs would make winning the championship that much easier for the professionals, the opposite held true. It is often astonishingly difficult for the wolves to slay the lambs. Spectacular plays are wasted on those unfamiliar with the nuances of the game. How can you read a man when *he* doesn't even know what he's thinking? Bluffing becomes nearly impossible against a player who is not shrewd or disciplined enough to lay down his hand when it looks like he is beat.

Not even solid, straightforward play can insure success against a larger field. Get in with pocket aces against an unsuited 7-2, and you've got about a 90 percent chance of winning the hand. Most poker players are willing to risk all of their money with far worse propositions, sometimes even a coin flip. As the number of total entrants increases, so do the number of hands a player must survive to reach the final table. The odds of surviving a coin flip are fifty-fifty. The odds of surviving *three* coin flips are less than 13 percent. It was no longer enough not to get unlucky—to win, a player had to enjoy a statistical anomaly, a streak of better-than-normal success.

Further confounding the pros was the realization that not every recreational player was a chump. Many of these enthusiastic amateurs made up for their lack of experience at the table by reading every poker book in print, continuing the trend Bobby Baldwin had started in 1978.

"The astounding volume of how-to literature that is a by-product of the boom in poker's popularity has helped narrow the gap between so-called professionals and amateurs," said Drache.

It was hard enough facing off against the players you knew; now you had to worry about the players you didn't recognize. Amarillo Slim was enjoying his best showing in years until he ran into an unfamiliar face in the form of Tom McEvoy, a middle-limit player who had won his seat, like so many others, in a satellite.* Tom opened for $300 from early position. Calling with pocket 6s, Slim flopped top set, which he chose to slowplay, merely calling Tom's $600 bet.

An ace fell on the turn. Tom bet $600 once again, and once again Slim just called.

When a 9 landed on the river, Tom shoved all his chips into the pot. The move surprised Slim a little and aggravated him a lot. He thought he was ahead, and now he wasn't so sure. He showed Tom his hand, trying to get a read on the man, but he didn't call.

Tom responded to Slim's move by making one of his own. He flipped over his top card, an ace. Was there another ace beneath it? That was the only hand that could beat Slim's. Slim started to needle Tom, hoping to get *something* out of him. Tom covered his face with his hat and asked for a clock. Slim debated what to do all the way up

---

*Limit poker, that game favored by leather asses, is generally divided into three categories. Low-limit, the province of recreational players, consists of those games up to $6 and $12 blinds. Middle-limit, the-lowest stakes at which a professional has a reasonable chance of making a living, covers $10/$20 to $20/$40. High-limit poker covers the wide range of games with even bigger stakes, ranging from $30/$60 to, in several recent affairs, blinds in the hundreds of thousands.

until the clock expired, automatically folding his hand. Tom never did reveal his other card.

Never fully recovering, Slim was eliminated shortly afterwards. Bobby Baldwin asked him on camera who he thought would win. Slim predicted it would be George Huber or Dody Roach, maybe even Texas Dolly, who was still alive after winning a big pot off one of the Irish players. He never once mentioned Tom McEvoy's name.

Attesting to Slim's great forecasting abilities, Dody Roach was the chip leader after the second day with $74,300; but his success was overshadowed by that of another improbable newcomer, Larry Flynt, the controversial publisher of *Hustler* magazine. Recovering, at the time, from an assassination attempt, Flynt arrived at the tournament surrounded by a phalanx of bodyguards and two suitcases. One was full of cash. The other was full of high-quality pharmaceuticals, morphine and liquid cocaine, mitigating the pain of the injuries he'd suffered. It was impossible to determine which suitcase provoked more envy among his fellow players.

Flynt had been dead last with $1,475 at the end of the first day, but in a Treetop-like comeback he took the lead at two o'clock on the second day with $55,000 before closing the day with $41,400.

"I got lucky," he said. "I caught three flushes, two straights, three triples, and I made aces full, 10s full, and aces over jacks. I had two aces in the bucket on the hand that put me into the lead."

But the most memorable aspect to Flynt's performance that year arose from a passing comment to Doyle Brunson, who, with about thirty players left in the tournament, headed off to grab a bite to eat.

"Doyle! What'll you lay me if I make the final table?" Flynt yelled out to him. "If I bet a thousand, how much will you give me?"

Doyle eyed his stack—Flynt had only $8,000 or so in checks—and told him that he'd give him a million dollars if he made the final table. Word quickly spread, and several other bookmakers got in on the action. Before too long, Flynt stood to make *six* million dollars if he won the tournament.

By the time Doyle returned from dinner, Flynt had built his stack to $250,000. An amazing accomplishment, if only it had been on the up-and-up. Flynt had quietly been paying some of the other players twice the amount of the denomination on the tournament chips on the condition that they lose them to him.

"In reality, the only victims were going to be the bookmakers," recalls Eric Drache. The other players certainly didn't mind. "If I were one of the players who was not selling chips to him . . . and I see Larry having the chips, as opposed to some of the best players in the world, I'd rather have Larry have them, because it's more likely he'll lose them again."

Having caught wind of what Flynt was up to, the Horseshoe management notified all of the bookmakers—including Doyle—who had entered the action. All of them cancelled their wagers—except one. "If I'm dumb enough to take the bet," said the legendary Terry Rogers, "I'm dumb enough to pay it off." It was a violation of Rogers's code of ethics as a bookmaker to even think about welshing on a wager.

Ironically, Rogers was the only person to profit from the incident. Flynt ended his buying spree after he was notified that the gig was up and eventually finished twelfth, several places removed from the final table. Only Rogers still had a bet to collect.

The 1983 final table will forever be remembered for how quickly the first seven players were eliminated and how slowly the last one took to go.

12:45 P.M. George Huber, a seasoned Las Vegas pro handicapped by an extremely short stack, moved all in with his last $36,000 with A-Q. He lost to Robbie Geers's pocket 9s.

1 P.M. Tom McEvoy flopped top pair with K-10 to oust R. R. Pennington in eighth place.

1:13 P.M. McEvoy raised with pocket 6s, then called John "Austin Squatty" Jenkins when he reraised all in with A-K. The flop brought Austin Squatty an ace, but it also provided Tom with the 6 he needed for a winning set.

1:45 P.M. Doyle Brunson, whose legendary status continued to grow with each final table appearance, made a full house to bust that year's representative from the Eccentric Club, Donnacha O'Dea.

1:55 P.M. Robbie Geers tried to set a trap by slowplaying pocket kings, giving Rod Peate a cheap look at the flop with suited connectors. Despite flopping a set, Geers opted to continue his slowplay, encouraging Peate to move all in with a flush draw. Geers called, then was sent packing when Peate completed the flush.

2:08 P.M. Carl McKelvey, a road gambler of the old school, found pocket aces and moved all in with his short stack, $50,000. Peate called him with pocket 9s, then caught a third to eliminate his second opponent in less than fifteen minutes.

With three players left, Texas Dolly seemed a lock to win his third title as he squared off against Rod Peate and Tom McEvoy, two middle-limit players who, without the benefit of satellites, wouldn't have dreamed of entering the championship. While McEvoy was content to sit on his chips and wait for a hand, Peate decided to take the action to Doyle. Hardly intimidated, Doyle fired right back with whatever cards he happened to be holding, even reraising before the flop, in one memorable instance, with a 7-4. Even more remarkable, Texas Dolly won the hand when he paired his 7 on the flop.

Rod Peate's aggressiveness, however, would pay dividends. Finding pocket 9s, Peate raised $9,000 from the button. Undeterred by what had become a commonplace raise, Doyle called from the little blind with J♦9♦. The flop came 9-high with two diamonds. Doyle checked, Rod bet $15,000, and Doyle moved all in for $267,000 more, figuring if his top pair wasn't good, his flush draw gave him enough outs to justify the strong move. Having made top set, it was an easy call for Rod. The fifth diamond Doyle needed failed to materialize, and the two-time champion was eliminated.

"I was just trying to win a pot, Bobby," Doyle confided to the Owl. "I figured I had to win a big pot to get back in it. I couldn't be a very big underdog to any hand but a set of trips, and that's what he had."

For his third-place finish, Doyle earned $108,000, solidifying his position as the all-time leading money winner at the World Series of Poker with just under $1.2 million in lifetime earnings.

As the World Series continued to expand beyond its Texas road gambler roots and into the global consciousness in the early 1980's, many players began to covet the title of world champion even more than the impressive payday. Crandell Addington, who had finished second twice, claimed he'd pay as much as $1 million for the title. When Jay Heimowitz, who had made the final table in 1980 and 1981, was asked why he wanted to win it, he never once mentioned the money.

"It will sort of make you known forever," he said. "[Give you] respect among your peers, which is really what the player looks for."

Frank Cutrona, a professional poker player from New Jersey who had moved to Las Vegas in 1978, instantly found himself in the tournament's thrall. He begged his old friend Eric Drache to give him a job, *any* job, as long as he could be a part of it. Drache hired him to deliver chips to the table and clear ashtrays. Several years later, when the growth of the tournament warranted it, he was promoted to tournament coordinator, overseeing the play.

Cutrona made several important contributions to the tournament, including improved schedules and clearer rules, but his most enduring accomplishment may have been to create a real sense of history.

"I went to the library and I traced back the World Series of Poker when it originally started, who was there and this and that, and I put it all into a computer," recalls Cutrona. "Every year I kept track of all these records of who played and how much they had won." In doing so, Cutrona created a sense of legacy—every sport needs its statistics, its legends, its records to be broken.

"Believe me when I tell you, they wouldn't have them today if I didn't do that."

But while some might have been playing for the history books, Rod Peate and Tom McEvoy were glaring exceptions to this growing trend. When the two men starting playing heads-up at 6:30 P.M., they acted as if the difference between first prize ($540,000) and second ($216,000) actually meant something to them, and, in fact, it did. Friends away from the table, the two shared what sounded like the same hard-luck story.

Rod had moved to Las Vegas from Portland, Oregon, just over a year before with his girlfriend, two kids from a previous marriage, and $800 in his pocket, hoping to strike it rich as a professional poker player. It didn't work out quite as well as he had hoped. He was, in his own words, "stone-cold broke" several weeks before the start of the 1983 World Series, so poor he suffered immediate remorse after paying $25 to enter a supersatellite at the Bingo Palace.

"I wanted to sell my ticket," he said, "but nobody wanted to buy it from me. . . . So I backed myself into the corner and played in the satellite."

His eighth-place finish in the event was good enough to earn him a free seat in the $110 buy-in satellite that was slated to begin the day before the start of the main event at the Horseshoe. Still plagued by guilt, he tried to sell that ticket for $100, but his girlfriend persuaded him to play. He was glad she did after he won the satellite, earning a seat for himself in the world championship. Thinking he could use the money more than the seat, he tried to sell that ticket for $9,000 but quickly discovered that there was a rule prohibiting him from doing so.* Rod had no choice but to play.

Tom's story was eerily similar. In 1978 he lost his job as the office manager at a pie company in Grand Rapids, Michigan.

"Really, I was fired," he said. "It was the best thing that has ever happened to me. I was sick and tired of working for other people. I wanted to be my own boss, and poker seemed to be a way out."

After taking several preliminary trips to Las Vegas, he decided to move there and become a full-time poker professional. He and his wife Bobbie sold their house and all their furniture and set out for Vegas with their three children and three cats, hauling all of their belongings in a U-Haul trailer. Tom came armed with $5,000 in cash and a "five-year plan"—his goal was to compete in the main event of the World Series of Poker by 1984.

Although he accomplished his objective a year early, he had traveled a rough road to get there. "For the first six months we just barely got by," he admitted. He declared no income on the first tax return he filed as a "poker player" in 1980. In the years that had passed his finances had hardly improved. Two weeks prior to the start of the 1983 World Series, his bankroll had dwindled to a meager $3,000 before he enjoyed a much needed breakthrough, winning that year's $1,000 Limit Hold'em event and $117,000. While much of that prize money went to his creditors, McEvoy had enough left over to warrant a stab, via a satellite win, at the main event.

The checks Rod Peate had taken from Doyle Brunson gave him a 3–2 lead over Tom McEvoy when they began heads-up play, and he started

---

*This rule would later be amended. Today, selling one's seat into the main event after winning a satellite is common practice for many solid players who view the weaker competition these games tend to attract as easy pickings.

attacking Tom from the outset. At one point Rod expanded his lead to a 4–1 margin, but Tom was determined to slog it out. Wearing a black cowboy hat and a Western-style shirt, Tom looked like a Texas road gambler but hardly played like one. There was, in fact, no gamble at all to his game. He went into a shell, content to sip his bottled water and munch on his apples—he ate six at the table—and wait for the cards to come to him. The presence of his wife only furthered his resolve. She actually sat with him at the table, an unusual arrangement that didn't seem to bother Rod. His girlfriend was sitting at the table as well, smoking cigarettes, looking vaguely bored.

When midnight came, the two men had entered all-new territory, playing into a record fifth day of competition. Remarkably, most of the fans in the gallery hadn't left, inspired by the sight of two relatively low-stakes players vying for the world championship.

Finally, at 1:45 A.M., seven hours after they'd started playing heads-up, the end mercifully came. The blinds had increased to $8,000 and $16,000—a record that stood for years—when Tom opened for a $20,000 raise. Through his sad blue eyes, Rod stared at his opponent before reraising $40,000 with K♦J♦. Tom moved all in with pocket queens. Considering how tight Tom had been playing, Rod's call seemed hasty and ill-advised. The extremely long day had obviously taken its toll on the man.

The 6♦6♥3♣ flop was no help to him. The J♥ on the turn added hope, but the 3♠ on the river extinguished it. The first player to win both the limit and no-limit hold'em events in the same year, Tom scrambled atop his chair, pumped his fist into the air, and screamed, "All right! I did it! All right! I did it!" Slightly unnerved by the display, his wife took his hand, hoping to calm him down, but nothing could contain his euphoria. A high roller now, he tipped the dealers $25,000 and the security guards $1,000, the most extravagant gratuities the staff had ever seen.

"I'm glad to say that it was me and Rod, and not Doyle Brunson or anyone from Texas," Tom said in the heat of the moment. "I don't have anything against Texans, but they think they're the best in the world. I'm from Michigan, Rod's from Washington. . . . It may sound like bragging, but I'm high as a kite."

·   ·   ·

As spectacular as it was for two satellite winners to play for the world championship, neither man was able to parlay their remarkable showings into any sort of sustained success.

"I'm the same person," Rod said afterwards, and, in regard to his financial situation he was essentially correct. Having sold 64 percent of his winnings before the tournament had even started, he pocketed just $78,000 of the $216,000 he had earned for coming in second. "I'm just going to go back and play $10/$20 poker like I always have."

THE GAME WITHIN THE GAME

The entry fee to a major poker tournament doesn't seem like much to the winner, but for the players who fail to make the money it can cut a large chunk out of their net winnings for the year. A player who enters ten $10,000 buy-in tournaments in a year and fails to cash in any of them is $100,000 in the hole.

To offset this, players commonly seek "backers" to buy a "piece" of them. A backer treats the player like any other investment, providing some or all of a player's entry fee in exchange for an agreed upon percentage of his or her winnings.

Exactly what that percentage is depends on the reputation of the player—a player who is perceived as having a better chance of winning can generally negotiate a far more favorable deal than a complete unknown. While few are willing to admit it, many of today's top players don't ever have to touch their own bankrolls to enter a tournament like the World Series, yet still stand to keep a good portion of their winnings.

Having sold 66 percent of himself for less than $100 per percentage point, Tom McEvoy was essentially in the same boat as Rod. "I may be the world's greatest poker player," he said, "but I am definitely the world's worst businessman—my backers have made more money from my winning than I have."

Out of the $540,000 he won he got to keep less than $200,000. From the great high he experienced during his victory celebration he quickly returned to earth.

"I realize how fortunate I was to win and to make poker history as the first satellite winner," he said. "I'll probably spend the rest of my poker career trying to duplicate that win."

In that assessment he was also correct. His victory, wrote *Las Vegas Sun* reporter Ed Koch, "did not establish McEvoy as a respected, premier player, as he continued to participate in the lower-limit games, often drawing scorn from the local fraternity of veteran high-stakes Texas gamblers he so admired."

For the next fourteen years, until a string of successful finishes at the 1997 tournament, Tom often found himself in a struggle for financial survival. "In poker, you have your ups and downs," he admitted, "and it is no secret that I was broke—I had my back to the wall." In recent years, he has supplemented the income generated by his improved play writing poker books and magazine articles.

The repercussions of Tom's 1983 victory extended far beyond his personal life. Thanks in large part to the public relations efforts of Henri Bollinger, all three major television networks—ABC, NBC, and CBS—as well as a Canadian station and an independent crew, were on hand to cover the event. But McEvoy's grind-it-out style and the seemingly interminable play strained not only their patience, but their budgets, as they had to pay overtime to their crews. ABC was forced to cancel altogether a piece that had been scheduled for its popular *Nightline*. None of the networks would return the following year.

Then-professional player Mike Sexton observed that McEvoy's strategy, while helping him win the tournament, also "set poker back at least ten years."*

---

*Sexton is best known today as the lead television commentator of the World Poker Tour.

8

BRIDESMAIDS

As a publicity stunt just prior to the start of the 1984 World Series, the Binions planned to display the estimated $3 million that would be distributed in prize money over the course of the tournament, which now consisted of fourteen separate events. Only Benny's wife Teddy Jane couldn't stop doling out cash from the casino cage.

"That's enough, Mom," said her son Jack. "That's more than three million dollars now!"

"Oh heck, let's make it look real pretty," replied Teddy Jane. "Here, Jack, throw some of these bundles of five-hundred-dollar bills onto the table, too."

While his family was preparing for the arrival of hundreds of poker players from all around the world, Benny was recuperating in the Desert Springs Medical Center from a recent heart attack. As serious as his health problems were, he was not too incapacitated to address the problem that always arose this time of year, his casino's perpetual shortage of poker tables.

"Get the bar the hell out of there," he ordered from his hospital bed, "and get more tables in."

They managed to acquire seventeen in all, five more than the previous year, and more than enough to accommodate the 132 players who showed up for the championship. The extra tables guaranteed the tournament would come off without a hitch and that there would be plenty of side action as well.

"Our side games are bigger this year than ever before," Eric Drache confirmed. "The minimum buy-in is five-hundred dollars and the smallest game we have is thirty-sixty seven-card stud."

When asked about the 25 percent increase in the number of players entered in the main event, Drache got excited. "Let it keep getting larger, we'll just buy more chips," he said.

Benny would eventually make an appearance at the tournament before it was all over, assuring everyone, "I feel good. Real good."

Ever since the 1950s, game theorists have been debating whether or not a computer was capable of beating a world champion in chess. In the many challenges that ensued, the human brain always trumped artificial intelligence, until 1997 when Deep Blue, a chess-playing computer designed by IBM, defeated the reigning world champion Gary Kasparov.

Game theorists were equally interested to find out if a computer could defeat a poker champion, but the discussion never attained the same sort of fervor it enjoyed amongst chess afficionados, primarily because poker is a game of incomplete information and educated guesses. A chess-playing computer is programmed to always make the best move. In poker, the best move often looks hopelessly foolish. How can a programmer teach a computer to bluff?

In the early 1980s Bob Wilson, a computer programmer from Arizona, designed the program that would be the prototype for the successful Wilson Turbo Texas hold'em series. Before the rise of the Internet, this software had no rivals when it came to playing the game on and against a computer. Thousands of players have used this program to hone their games.

At nearly the same time as Wilson was perfecting his software, Mike Caro was creating ORAC, a computer programmed to play Texas hold'em. In 1984 ORAC "challenged" the defending champion

Tom McEvoy to a heads-up match. Taking into account the aggressive play of most professionals, Caro designed ORAC to occasionally call large preflop raises with medium-strength hands if it "thought" that was the correct move to make. On the final hand of the challenge McEvoy, holding A-9 offsuit, pushed enough chips into the middle to force the computer all in if it called. ORAC was game and showed a better hand, A-Q, but McEvoy caught a 9 on the flop to win the match.

"The fact that I drew out on the computer with the worst hand," he joked afterwards, "proves that ORAC is only human, just like the rest of us."

Perhaps having expended too much energy battling ORAC in the exhibition match, Tom McEvoy made an early exit after only two hours of play in the 1984 championship event. He wasn't the only returning champion to run into trouble. By the end of the second day, Puggy Pearson and Bobby Baldwin were the only former title holders still in the running.

In the tournament's early days, there was an assumption that each of the world's best players would get his moment in the spotlight—for them, earning the championship title was almost a rite of passage. Thanks to the advent of satellites and the increased participation of amateurs, it was no longer shocking to hear that a former world champion had been ousted on the tournament's first day, or that a relative newcomer had defeated a perennial contender—a so-called "bridesmaid"—for the championship. After all the hands had been played, the real story was likely to be who *hadn't* won the championship, instead of who had.

Jesse Alto felt like he had an excellent opportunity to escape his bridesmaid status. Of the nine men who survived to make the 1984 final table, only Jesse was making a repeat appearance, having placed second in 1976 and fifth in 1978.

When he was playing his best, Jesse was one of the greatest hold'em players in the world, but he wasn't always on top of his game. Age had done nothing to mellow his hair-trigger temper.

Alcohol was usually a contributing factor. "When he stayed away from the booze when he was playing, he won most of the time," said

T. J. Cloutier, "but if he got into the booze he might have a $100,000 bankroll with him and it would be gone in one game."

Going broke meant having to borrow money from his wife Bertha, who actually made him pay interest on the loan, explaining, or at least contributing to, his frequently foul mood.

This year, however, he had managed to keep his infamous temper in check, and a good run of cards, combined with aggressive play, had placed Jesse in the driver's seat.

Despite Jesse's edge in experience, the final table hardly lacked cardsharps. Howard "Tahoe" Andrew, a former industrial engineer for General Motors, had been playing serious poker in Reno since the 1950s, although, with only $27,000 left in tournament chips, he was going to have a hard time making a push. With $86,000 in chips, Curtis "Iron Man" Skinner was in a slightly better position, although his conservative style was somewhat of a handicap in tournaments. Given his nickname by Doyle Brunson for his aversion to using a driver on the golf course, Skinner could have just as well earned it for his tight-fisted play at the poker table.

"If Iron put all of his money into the pot, and you were not looking at the absolute nuts in the hole, you could soon do so by calling," said fellow poker professional Bob Ciaffone.

A regular participant in the World Series ever since its creation, Iron Man spent the rest of the year in Arlington, Texas, looking after his jewelry store and pawnshop. Proving just how small the poker world can be, he had once sold a .45 automatic to one of the other players sitting at the final table, Byron "Cowboy" Wolford.

As usual, Cowboy Wolford was hard to miss. Wearing a white Stetson and his signature denim overalls—a kaleidoscope of Western motifs designed and stitched together by his wife—he looked like the actual cowboy he had once been. While traveling the professional rodeo circuit in the '40s and '50s, Wolford competed against such rodeo legends as Don McLaughlin and Casey Tibbs. When he wasn't roping calves, he was playing poker, running games out of hotel rooms and horse trailers. He quit the rodeo circuit in 1960 to play poker full-time, eventually opening his own card room in Dallas, the Redman's Club, where he hosted a no-limit game frequented by such big names as Bobby Baldwin, Doyle Brunson, and T. J. Cloutier.

In his first year as a full-time professional, Cowboy walked into

Jesse Alto's card room in the Corpus Christi Elks Lodge looking for a game. One of the players at the table asked him why everybody called him Cowboy. Wolford intentionally downplayed his prowess in the saddle, telling him in an "aw shucks" kind of way that he used to rope calves on his uncle's ranch. Jesse and the others took Cowboy for a sucker and bet him he couldn't lasso a calf at the local fairgrounds in under a minute. Having once set a speed record at Madison Square Garden by roping a calf in 11.03 seconds, Cowboy gladly accepted the challenge, betting all the money he had on him at the time, $3,600. His only regret, after he won easily, was that he hadn't been able to wager more.

Years later, during another game in Corpus Christi, Jesse reached across the table and slapped Cowboy in the face, responding to a comment that, as far as Cowboy was concerned, wasn't even directed at him. The two men immediately squared off in a bloody fistfight.

"He'd get hot and win a lot of money, and then he'd run cold and get mad," said Cowboy, echoing the prevailing sentiment towards Jesse Alto. "He had a pretty bad temper."

They eventually repaired the damage done to their relationship that heated night, even going so far as to call each other friends, but in the highly individualistic world of professional poker, friendships get checked at the entrance to the card room.

After the field was whittled down to three finalists—Jesse Alto, Cowboy Wolford, and newcomer "Gentleman" Jack Keller—the stakes, as well as the attendant pressure, increased dramatically. David Chew, knocked out in fourth place, took home a relatively paltry $66,000, whereas the third-place finisher would earn $132,000, the runner-up $264,000, and the champion a handsome $660,000. Hoping to prevent the sluggish play that had marred the previous year's event, Jack Binion, in a moment of inspiration, removed some of the chips from the table and replaced them with wrapped bundles of cash, forcing the players to bet, raise, and call with the actual money for which they were competing.

"I wanted to see if it would have any impact on the players," he said.

It seemed to light a fire under chip leader Jesse Alto, who went into full attack mode, raising with nearly all of his hands. The strategy served him well, allowing him to amass nearly a million of the $1.32 million in cash on the table. It looked like this was finally going to be Jesse's year.

It would take a dramatic twist worthy of the great Greek tragedies to ensure otherwise.

The fateful hand began routinely enough. Jesse, as had become his custom, opened for a raise. Jack Keller folded, but Cowboy, tired of being pushed around and unwilling to relinquish any of the $156,000 he had remaining, decided to take a stand and called.

"He was just raising every pot, you know," Cowboy explained. "So I decided that on the next hand, I was either gonna get broke or whatever."

When the flop came A♣K♦9♣, Cowboy fired $15,000 at the pot, hoping to represent a big hand. As quickly as he had called, Jesse obviously didn't believe him.

The turn brought the K♥. Cowboy bet once again, this time $40,000. Jesse thought for a moment before deciding to match it.

As soon as the 2♠ appeared on the river, Cowboy tore the paper off the last of his wrapped bundles of cash and dropped all his remaining money into the pot, $101,000 in all. Finding his wife and child in the crowd, he gave them a sly wink.

Jesse stared at the cards on the table, considering his options. While his actual cards remain a mystery, it was obvious to all who watched him that his hand was strong—maybe very strong—but not unbeatable. Call and win, and he'd knock Cowboy out of the tournament, almost guaranteeing himself the championship. Were he to call and lose, he'd hardly be devastated, but it would take a healthy chunk out of his lead and give Cowboy, a dangerously crafty player, that much more ammunition with which to fight him.

After nearly five agonizing minutes, Jesse decided to take the most prudent route, throwing his hand facedown into the muck, perhaps enjoying a brief moment of self-congratulation for making such a difficult laydown. Cowboy, having gone from the verge of elimination to taking down a very substantial pot, couldn't restrain his joy. He tossed his utterly worthless hand, a 5 and a 3, onto the table for all to see. Cowboy had taken this pot from Jesse with a complete bluff, one that many still recall as the greatest in World Series history.

The crowd cheered rowdily for Cowboy, who couldn't help but grin. Jesse's response was a bit more dramatic. In the words of observer "Oklahoma" Johnny Hale, "Jesse came apart like a six-bit suitcase falling out of the tenth story of a Kansas City whorehouse."

On tilt, Jesse self-destructed. The next two hands, he pushed all of his chips into the pot without even looking at his hole cards. The lucky beneficiary was Jack Keller, who called and won both times. Having gone from near-cinch winner to third-place finisher in only three hands, Jesse stormed out of the Horseshoe.

"I just couldn't handle it," he later said. "[Cowboy] and I have been friends all our lives. When he ever needed anything, he would come to me for it, so for him to bluff me at this point just tore me up. I didn't object to him winning the hand, I just wish he hadn't shown it to me. If he'd just thrown his hand in the muck, things would've been all right."

Thanks to Jesse's unintended largesse, Jack Keller had plenty of chips with which to take on Cowboy. A Philadelphia native, Jack had sold his auto body shop two years earlier and moved to Las Vegas where he invested in several duplexes. He wasn't a landlord for very long, however, as his continuing poker education frequently required him to divest himself of his new holdings.

"I liked poker, having played in some kitchen games before, and I got more hooked on the game," he said. "Each time I lost big, I had to sell something so that my wife, Gloria, and two sons would live comfortably."

His luck changed when he won the earlier $5,000 Seven-Card Stud event. That was good for a $137,500 payday, but he had sold so many pieces of himself he didn't have enough to pay his way into the main event.

He had written off playing in the championship until his friend Dale Conway of Salt Lake City staked him $9,800. Oddsmakers listed him as a fifty-to-one long shot before the start of the tournament, but he had a lot of chips and he knew what to do with them. He was not the sort of player to waste his chips making "feeler" bets. When he thought he had the best of it, he shoved as many of his chips as he thought were needed to take down the pot.

On the final hand of the heads-up battle, Jack had pocket 10s, Cowboy 6♥4♥. The flop came 9♣6♠5♦. Cowboy liked his middle pair well enough to push all his chips into the middle of the table. Liking his overpair even more, Jack quickly called. The 8♠ on the turn and J♦ on the river didn't give Cowboy the help he needed. Jack took down the $370,000 pot. His wife crawled under the rail and gave him a big hug.

"I had a lot of outs on the flop, a pair and drawing to a straight if the right cards came," Cowboy said. "But Jack's luck held up."

It had only taken three hours for the final nine to be whittled to two and just forty more minutes to determine a champion, making it the quickest finish in history.

"I just got lucky," said Jack. "I played lucky all the way and I finished lucky."

For his effort he won $660,000. Sort of. For his $9,800 investment, Dale Conway had allowed Jack to keep 50 percent of himself. Jack, however, had further divided his half with two other players. He estimated his final take to be $280,000, which he planned on using to put his two sons through school.

"This was our greatest tournament," said Jack Binion. "With one hundred thirty-two entries this year, I think we might have a hundred and fifty or a hundred and sixty next year."

The 1985 championship event wound up attracting 140, one of whom was the perpetually grumpy Johnny Moss. The flock of spectators who hovered behind him—Moss had drawn a seat close to the rail—only further worsened his mood. He summoned tournament coordinator Frank Cutrona.

"Frank, get me out of this seat," he demanded.

"Johnny," Frank replied, "I can't do that until they break the tables down."

This was the wrong answer as far as Johnny was concerned. The Grand Old Man of Poker left the room, returning a few minutes later with Benny Binion in tow.

"Why didn't you move Johnny?" demanded Benny. It was against the rules, of course, a point Frank tried to convey to his boss.

"Frank, when you're told to jump, you jump!" Benny proceeded to give Frank a dressing-down in front of the entire field. Frank's wife, a fellow Horseshoe employee, knew what was going to happen next. She went upstairs to his office and packed her husband's belongings.

That night, Eric Drache, who was in New York for Jane Lovelle's graduation from Columbia, called Frank to see how everything was going.

"Fine," replied Frank. "I was fired."

"Nobody can fire you!"

"Benny did."

Eric immediately called Jack Binion, who approached his father hoping to get Frank reinstated. So did some of the players, including Perry Green and Amarillo Slim. "They knew that [the World Series] was something that I not only enjoyed, but it was part of me," recalls Frank. But the more everyone hounded Benny, the more resolute he became. Not only was Frank fired, he was barred from the Horseshoe.

While he may not have been welcome at the casino, it wasn't the end of Frank's association with the tournament. For the next few years, Jack Binion secretly employed him to do all the hiring and scheduling from behind the scenes.

As exciting as the end of a tournament can be, some of the most intense action comes when there are ten players left, all desperately hoping not to be the one who doesn't make the final table. Such was the case in 1985 after the record field of 140 had been winnowed to two tables of five players each. It took five and a half grueling hours to eliminate the tenth-place finisher, who would be shut out of the prize money.*

During that span, Texan Bill Smith moved all in three times with A-K, each time jolting the crowd from its lethargy with the possibility that *this* might be the last hand of the day. Much to their disappointment, each instance ended in a split pot.

Bill risked his tournament life for a fourth time with pocket 10s, calling an all-in raise from Gary Lundgren, who had him outchipped by $1,000. This time it was Gary who had A-K. The flop paired his

---

*The practice of awarding prize money to all nine of the finalists—rather than just the final five—began in 1981.

king, but also delivered a third 10 to Bill, once again allowing him to survive possible elimination. When Gary threw his last $1,000 chip into the middle on the very next hand, Bill quickly called, turning over pocket queens. All Gary could show was a K-8, which didn't improve, and the day finally came to an end.

Bill Smith's presence at the final table along with four others from the Lone Star State suggested that the Texas road gamblers were enjoying a brief renaissance. But after John Fallon was eliminated in ninth place, three of the Texans dropped in rapid succession. First, Mark Rose of Edna. Then, Johnny Moss of Odessa.

For some of the players it was an honor just to be sitting at the same table as Johnny Moss. Others, mostly rivals who had been belittled by the irascible man in the past, disparaged him for continuing to play poker when he was obviously past his prime. It was true that Johnny's game had slipped a notch, but it was also true that his B game was still better than the A game of most of the players in the field.

Johnny had managed to survive long enough to make his seventh final table appearance, thanks in part to some moral support Benny Binion gave him along the way. "I saw he was down a little bit," Benny said, "so I just jawed with him about how we played in the old days."

After Moss's A-10 lost to Scott Mayfield's A-J, Johnny rose from the table and hobbled from the room accompanied by a thunderous ovation. It seemed likely that Johnny, at age seventy-eight, wouldn't be making very much noise at the World Series in the future.

Jesse Alto, apparently recovered from the previous year's meltdown, was the next Texan to fall, and, as had become his habit, it would be brutal. He flopped top pair with A-7 when the board came A-9-2, but Scott Mayfield, who had pocket 3s, overcame nine-to-one odds to catch a third 3 on the turn, sending Alto home in sixth place.

Hamid Dastmalchi, a rising poker star from San Diego, California, was the next out when he made top pair on the flop with K-Q, only to lose to another rising star, Berry Johnston, who flopped a set with pocket 5s.

After Scott Mayfield fell in fourth place, it was down to Bill Smith, Berry Johnston, and yet one more player whose career was on the verge of taking off, T. J. Cloutier. Although originally from California,

T. J. was one of the last of the Texas road gamblers. After attending U.C. Berkeley on an athletic scholarship and serving in the U.S. Army, the six-foot-three Cloutier played five years of professional football as a tight end for the Montreal Allouettes and Toronto Argonauts of the Canadian Football league. The '70s found him back in California, failing at business and marriage. Escaping both, he fled to Texas, finding work as a derrick man on an oil rig. Within six months he had seen the light—he could be making a lot more money playing poker.

He spent the next several years doing what Slim, Sailor, and Doyle had done decades earlier, traveling the back roads in search of action. In 1981 he finally settled in Dallas, where he found a game so dependable he could treat it like a regular job. For the next eleven years he played from noon to five and from seven to midnight Monday through Friday.

"Players used to come from Vegas and everywhere else to play in that game," he said. "At least once a week, we had over a hundred thousand dollars on the table. When they finally broke that game it was like taking two hundred thousand dollars a year out of my pocket and just throwing it away because it wasn't coming in anymore. There were a ton of good players in Dallas. In fact, if you could beat the Dallas game, you could beat any game, including the World Series of Poker."

His confidence soaring, he entered the main event of the World Series for the first time in 1984. Just one year later, he found himself in a three-way battle for the title.

At the outset, Bill Smith had an enormous lead, $918,000 to Berry's $278,000 and T. J.'s $204,000. Repeating last year's procedure, Jack Binion brought out packages of $100 bills held together with rubber bands. Each package held $25,000, and the players used them, along with $1,000 chips, to make their bets. The sight of so much money being tossed around like confetti proved so exciting the fans couldn't get close enough to the action. While trying to see what hand he'd been dealt, T. J. had to admonish a man whose head was almost literally on his shoulder.

"Hey, just let me look at them first!"

T. J. won two sizeable pots early on, moving him up to $475,000, just $150,000 behind Bill. His next big confrontation came against Berry. T. J. got all his money into the pot before the flop with A♥J♦.

Berry called with A♣K♦. They each caught a piece of the K♣J♥4♠ flop, but Berry was still way ahead in the hand. In what would be a rare occurrence for T. J., who over the course of his career has been on the receiving end of some notoriously bad beats, he would deliver one himself, catching the J♣ on the turn.

A man who never seems to get ruffled, Berry accepted his fate with quiet resignation. He politely shook hands with both players, wishing them good luck. Before he was even done collecting the $140,000 he'd earned for coming in third, his wife JoAnn said to him:

"Honey, I'm hungry. Can we go get something to eat now?"

After losing in the manner he did, Berry would have been justified if he'd been a little testy, but the serene man only said:

"Okay, honey. We'll go eat if that's what you want to do."

The heads-up match between Bill Smith and T. J. Cloutier promised to be an entertaining one, for the two were not only intense rivals but also great friends, having played countless times together in Dallas. Like T. J., Bill was a Texas road gambler. After winning his first big pot—$2,900—in a game in Lubbock, the twenty-three-year-old Smith declared himself to be a professional, vowing he would make up every dime his father had lost at the poker tables. He moved around the state searching for games and, if the action was hot enough in one place, would occasionally put down roots. He spent some time in Houston and Corpus Christi, even venturing into Louisiana for a spell. While Bill was living in Shreveport, T. J. used to crash at his place after sessions at the Turf Club. It was Bill's wife Cleta who introduced T. J. to his future wife Joy.

"I knew everything he did," T. J. said of Bill, seeing the bright side of playing a good friend. "I knew every move, every little idiosyncrasy he had."

One of Bill's greatest idiosyncrasies was his fondness for alcohol. "There's not much to say," he once told a reporter who asked him about his personal life. "I just drink and gamble." Typically, he started with beer in the morning and switched to hard liquor in the afternoon. Most poker players would be handicapping themselves. Not Bill Smith.

"Bill was the tightest player you'd ever played in your life when he was sober," T. J. recalls, "and when he was halfway drunk, he was the best player I'd ever played with."

"You never worried about Bill when he was sober because you knew that he played A-B-C—tight—and you knew where he was all the time. The only time that you worried about him was when he was about halfway drunk, and then he'd play all the way to H. He'd make some fabulous plays, plays you couldn't believe."

It was when Bill passed the halfway point that his game fell apart. "You could always tell . . . because he started calling the flop. Say a flop came 7-4-10, he would say, 'twenty-one!' or some other remark like that. When he got up to take a walk, he would have a little hop in his step, a 'git up in his gittalong' we used to call it. And then you knew he was gone."

Unfortunately for his opponents at the final table, Bill had brought his best game with him. He was drinking beer of course, but looked composed, even classy in a jacket and tie, smoking a cigarette through a long black filter. He had been here before, having finished fifth in 1981, and wasn't about to let this opportunity slip away.

The chips T. J. had taken off Berry put him in the lead, $952,000 to Bill's $448,000. By four P.M., Bill had nearly clawed his way back to even when T. J. pushed all in before the flop with pocket 9s, a bet that Bill, with pocket kings, was delighted to call. The players' bankrolls were so evenly matched that a countdown was necessary to determine who had more money. Complicating the process was the fact that some of the $25,000 bundles of cash had been opened. It took Eric Drache and his new assistant Jack McClelland nearly five minutes to determine that T. J. had Bill covered by $178,000. The rest, $1.22 million, sat in the middle of the table. No one was more pleased to see a million-dollar pot than Benny Binion, who sat in the front row as excited as any of the spectators.

Bill's kings held up, and in just a single hand T. J. went from sitting pretty to reeling unsteadily, facing a six-to-one chip deficit.

T. J. managed to revive some of his momentum, winning several big hands to get back over $300,000, when he was confronted with Smith's opening raise to $40,000. Looking at his top card and finding an ace, T. J. moved all in. He didn't think Bill could call such a large raise, and if he did, well, T. J. had the proverbial ace in the hole. Seeing an opportunity to break his opponent, Bill called, turning over pocket 3s. With all of the money in the middle, T. J. finally looked at his other hole card and received the worst possible news—it was the 3♣. T. J. only had three outs. When the board came 5-5-9-5-K, Bill made a full house and took down the $742,000 pot and the championship.

It would be one of the few times T. J. didn't have the best hand when he got knocked out of the World Series. "My chances of winning were great," he said. "But, Lady Luck has a lot to do with pocker. She was smiling at Bill on that last hand. That's just the way it goes."

Earning $280,000, T. J. would learn from his mistakes and prove himself to be one of the finest tournament poker players in the world. A second-place finish in the 1995 $5,000 Limit Seven-Card Stud event made him the first player to ever exceed $1 million in World Series earnings *without winning the main event*. Like Jesse Alto, T. J. would become a fixture at the final table of the World Series, and, also like Jesse, he appears destined never to win.

This day belonged to Bill Smith. "Boy, this win sure feels good," he said. "I played the best poker of my life. It took that to win."

The roar from the four hundred spectators inside the Horseshoe was deafening, as Bill raised his arms in triumph. Not everyone was happy with the ascension of an unrepentant alcoholic to poker's most publicized crown. Four years earlier, one of the players entered in the championship event complained, "If Bill ends up beating all the nice guys, like Bobby [Baldwin] it's going to set the image of poker back ten years."

While his victory didn't actually tarnish the image of the event, it also did very little to brighten it. Broke at the start of this tournament, he had been forced to borrow the entry fee. What portion of the $700,000 first prize he was able to keep for himself was quickly spent. He returned to the final table the following year for what would be the last time.

The drinking got steadily worse, as did his financial problems. He barely had enough money to play in the satellites, and he quietly faded away from World Series play. "If I get drunk, go broke, and ask to borrow a hundred dollars from you," he'd later tell a friend, "do me a favor: don't let me have it. Just give me fifty."

He never lost his passion for tournament play, however, and com-

peted almost every Monday night in the $20 buy-in event at the Gold
Coast Casino until his death in 1996.

"If he hadn't been such a heavy drinker," Cowboy Wolford said
with palpable sorrow, "he probably would have been the world champion three or four times instead of just the one."

Plagued by the continuing reluctance of the television networks to
cover the event and a reigning champion whose personal life was discussed only in embarrassed whispers, the 1986 World Series experienced the smallest growth in its history, adding just a single player to
the field. A change in the structure of the payouts, which showered
prize money on more than just the top nine finishers, not only failed
to generate any additional enthusiasm but resulted in a first prize—
$570,000—that was for the first (and only) time smaller than that of
the previous year.

After getting ambushed by the two Texans the year before, Berry
Johnston returned ready to put an end to the resurgence that players
from that state were enjoying, just as fellow Oklahoman Bobby Baldwin had done in 1978. Down to $7,100 at one point, he very nearly
didn't make it past the third day. He gave himself a boost by making a
play that surprised many of those who had categorized him as a tight
player who rarely entered a pot unless he had a premium hand. Sitting on the button, he raised with K♥8♥, hoping to win the antes and
blinds without a fight. When one of his intended victims, Tommy
Grimes, fired back with a reraise that would put him all in, Berry decided to gamble.

"He raised and stood a reraise with [K♥8♥]," observed T. J.
Cloutier. "You wouldn't think he would ever do that. But he did it, and
at the time it was perfect."

Grimes turned over A-Q, giving Berry about a 40 percent chance
of winning the hand. Catching an 8, he won the pot and gained a new
element to his game, a willingness to mix it up. Berry pushed all in
three more times and won them all.

One of the more important hands of his run came against Roger
Moore of Eastman, Georgia, a frequent adversary in his regular pot-
limit Omaha game and the player he viewed as his most dangerous

opponent. Each of them had roughly $300,000 when Berry, sitting under the gun with pocket queens, opened with a standard raise of $20,000. Roger upped it to $120,000.

"There are many players who I could comfortably put on aces or kings and therefore could abandon my hand," said Berry, "but Roger isn't one of them."

Believing that Roger was trying to run over him with an inferior hand, Berry came back over the top with an all-in raise. Roger mucked his hand, giving Berry sole possession of the chip lead.

If Berry had lost any of these hands, he would have been out of the tournament. Instead, he made it to the final table where he found a pair of familiar faces waiting for him, Jesse Alto and Bill Smith.

The final six players resumed playing at ten in the morning on the fourth day of competition. Nineteen minutes later Mike Harthcock of Winter Haven, Florida, eliminated Roger Moore. Berry couldn't have been more pleased. He was even happier after he knocked Bill Smith out of the tournament by making 7s full of 6s with his K-7. Bill shrugged off the loss and started looking ahead.

"We'll do it again next year."

With four players left, Jesse Alto was in position to rid himself of the stigma that comes with having gotten so close so many times and failing; but whatever psychological handicap he had was compounded by a physical one. Suffering from extreme diabetes, the man was drained. The fact that he hadn't eaten all day long didn't help. Adding to his plight, he chose to go all in with an A-Q when Berry was holding an A-K.

Bones Berland, the runner-up to Doyle Brunson in 1977, wasn't in much better shape, having nearly died two months before from an undisclosed illness. Berry put him out of his misery by reraising him $305,000 with A-Q. Bones called with the last of his chips, but his A-8 never improved, leaving two players at the table and just one gold bracelet.

With his grey hair and thin-framed bifocals, Berry Johnston looks more like a doctor or a lawyer than one of the world's best card players. He has a reputation for being mild mannered, always keeping his emotions under control, but at the poker table he can be every bit as hard as the next guy.

A serious gambler since 1972, he dabbled in sports betting long enough and seriously enough to know that it was a dead-end street. "It left me broke for twenty years," he said, "so I gave it up." He was so broke in 1982 that the IRS put a lien on his house in Oklahoma City for back taxes. He took care of it the best way he knew how, heading to Las Vegas and winning his way into the main event of the World Series of Poker via a satellite. His third-place finish was good for $104,000, more than enough to pay off the tax man. Encouraged by his success during his first attempt to win the world championship, he moved to Las Vegas the next year to play poker full-time.

The man who sat between Berry and the title was Mike Harthcock, a citrus grower from Florida. Harthcock had some experience at the World Series, but very little of it was good. In 1984 he was the sixth person eliminated from the main event. Unable to come up with the entry fee during a down year for the Sunshine State's produce farmers, he didn't even play in 1985. He scraped together a $3,500 bankroll in 1986, which turned out to be plenty, as he won his seat in a $500 satellite at the Golden Nugget.

For Berry, playing Mike Harthcock turned out to be quite literally a dream matchup. "I had only four hours' sleep last night," he confessed. "I woke up twice. The first time I dreamed that I beat Mike for the title. That put me back to sleep real nice. Then I woke up with a startle when I dreamed that he beat me in the final hand."

Berry needn't have worried. When he sat down at the final table he had twice as many chips as his nearest competitor, a lead that only grew as he eliminated Smith, Alto, and Berland. Harthcock's disadvantage was so large that when one of the railbirds yelled, "Go get him, Mike!" the rest of the crowd erupted with laughter.

"You want to split it?" Mike asked Berry in jest.

Berry smiled. "I probably should."

On the first hand, Berry folded, giving Mike the $2,000 in antes and the $5,000 and $10,000 blinds. It wouldn't be enough to pull him back into contention. It wouldn't even be enough to see him through the next hand. After Berry raised before the flop with A♠10♥, Mike reraised $100,000. Berry's first instinct was to throw his hand away.

An exceedingly patient man, he was willing to wait for a better spot, but after considering the situation at length he finally decided to do exactly the opposite. He moved all in, leaving the tough decision—whether or not to call—up to Mike. Unlike Berry, Mike wasn't about to fold his ace, quickly calling with A♦8♦. The board failed to help either man, which was fine with Berry. He didn't need to improve his hand. His kicker was good enough to earn him his first gold bracelet and the world championship.

Asked if he was the best player in the world, Berry responded with his usual humility. "Nah, not me."

Bill Smith, who had stuck around to watch, wasn't about to let Berry's accomplishment go unrecognized, crowing, "He's the best in the world now."

Berry's wife JoAnn burst into tears as did his son Rick who, conveniently enough, got to watch his father win while on the clock. An aspiring poker pro, Rick was working as a security guard at the Horseshoe at the time.

Unlike the last several champions, Berry managed to hold on to 75 percent of himself, so he got to keep most of the $570,000 first prize. When he was asked the usual question—what he planned to do with the money—JoAnn proved to be a true poker wife when she answered for him: "He'll probably just play in a bigger game."

While he would never repeat his performance in the championship event, Berry Johnston has quietly put together one of the more spectacular careers in World Series history. He has "cashed," that is, earned prize money, in nearly forty different events—a record that still stands—and has won a preliminary event as recently as 2001, when he took first in the $1,500 Razz tournament. While many of his fellow players were coming to grips with the idea that they might never win a world championship, Berry Johnston immediately recognized the significance of his accomplishment.

"Winning the World Series of Poker title was more important to me than the money."

9

THE ORIENT EXPRESS AND THE POKER BRAT

As Benny Binion, now eighty-two, surveyed the landscape that was the 1987 World Series of Poker, it was evident that things just weren't what they used to be. Fourteen years earlier, he had boldly predicted that the tournament might someday attract more than fifty people. This year—the eighteenth in its history—152 had come to compete for the $625,000 first prize.

Ending a "dark period" in the tournament's history during which the event was boycotted by the networks, television crews returned after a three-year absence. ESPN agreed to cover what they called the final table, although, in a nod to the production costs, it was, in reality, the final six. This separation of the final table and the final televised table would continue for the next fifteen years.

In one more example of how small the poker world can be, two of the final six players had honed their games in the very same place, the Mayfair Club in New York City. Set in the basement of a nondescript East Side high-rise not far from Manhattan's Gramercy Park, the Mayfair had once enjoyed a heyday as the pre-eminent bridge club in the world. Al Roth, the legendary bridge player who invented the "Roth-Stone" bidding convention, purchased it in 1953 from another bridge legend, the colorful Harry Fishbein, for $50,000. Under Roth's stewardship, the Mayfair—a dingy yet homey place with a pool table, a chess board, and several card tables—managed to evolve with the times. It became a popular haven for backgammon players in the 1970s, as a host of new mathematical theories about how best to play helped the game to flourish. There was a brief Scrabble craze. And there was the occasional poker game, usually for very low stakes.

That all changed in 1985, when Erik Seidel—a onetime professional backgammon player—discovered Texas hold'em on a trip to Las Vegas. He brought the game back to the Mayfair, where they played with backgammon chips. As players became more comfortable with the rules and strategies, a $25/$50 limit game became an everyday occurrence, often followed by long debates over strategy. The Mayfair remained a breeding ground for some of poker's most talented stars—including Seidel, Jay Heimowitz, Steve Zolotow, Noli Francisco, Billy Horan, Jason Lester, and Howard Lederer—until 2000, when a task force headed by Mayor Rudolph Giuliani raided the club and shut it down.

The Mayfair game was enough of a happening to inspire Dan Harrington, a Philadelphia resident, to take the commuter train to New York two or three times a week. Dan had discovered poker while attending Suffolk University in his native Boston, where he occasionally sat at the same table as Harvard's most famous dropout, Bill Gates, and his buddy Paul Allen. After earning a law degree—and spending ten long years as a bankruptcy lawyer—Dan decided to quit the law. He had already proven himself a brilliant chess player, winning state championships in both Massachusetts and New Jersey, and decided to apply his gifts towards professional backgammon, until a tournament organizer failed to pay him a $27,000 first prize. In 1980 he moved to Philadelphia where he started playing the stock market and, several years later, serious poker.

In 1987 he entered the championship event of the World Series. Three days later he found himself at the final table and, with $231,000 in chips, in good position to overtake the chip leader, Johnny Chan. He had seemingly made the right move when he pushed all in with A♠Q♦ against Jim Spain's A♣6♣, until a 6 on the flop and the river ended his run. Dan's sixth-place finish was good for

$43,750 and confirmed his belief that he could be one of the best in the world.

He wasn't the only Mayfair regular to have come this far. Just twenty-three years old, Howard Lederer was not only the junior guy at the table, he was the youngest player ever to be a finalist. The son of a teacher at the renowned St. Paul's School in New Hampshire, Howard grew up in a house where board games and card games were played like blood sports. Perhaps the most competitive of the bunch, his sister Annie would wind up following Howard into the world of professional poker.

At eighteen, Howard moved to New York City, ostensibly to attend Columbia University, but he spent less time in class than he did at the Bar Point Chess Club. He briefly entertained the idea of becoming a professional chess player until he discovered the club's backroom, where far more impressive sums of money were changing hands at the poker table.

"I went broke daily when I first started playing poker in New York," he said. "I couldn't wait to play poker every night. I ran errands all day to make enough money to buy in to the game, and was broke at the end of the night—every night. I finally realized that I didn't have to play seventy hours straight."

According to one of his sisters, he was, for a time, homeless, sleeping on park benches during the day to rest up for whatever game was scheduled that night. Once he discovered the Mayfair Club, he took his game to the next level. Like Dan, he was playing in the World Series for the first time in 1987.

"It's very exciting," he said, sounding as surprised as everyone else. "I never expected to be here. I'm just going to take my shot today, see if I can make a big score."

Doyle Brunson, for one, was impressed. "Times are really changing with the poker players," he said. "It's a tribute to the guys, how they play at such an early age."

Often referred to as "the Professor" for his studious demeanor at the table, Howard more often answers to "Bub," short for "Bubba"—he was fairly chubby before he became a vegan. As steadfast as he is about not eating meat, he will always be more committed to gambling than anything else. The last time he strayed from his all-veggie diet, he did so in the name of easy money, winning a $10,000 bet simply for eating a hamburger.

"The one thing that disappointed the guy," Howard said, grinning, "was that I didn't get sick."

Having one of the low stacks at the 1987 final table with just over $150,000, Howard needed to make a move. After Bob Ciaffone of Saginaw, Michigan, limped in with pocket 9s, Howard raised $15,000 from the button with A♥6♣. Bob jumped on the opportunity presented to him and moved in. Although his sports jacket and full beard helped disguise his youth, Howard showed his inexperience by calling rather quickly. After Bob caught a 9 on the flop and the river to make quads, the second alumnus of the Mayfair Club at the table suffered the same fate as the first, getting knocked out in fifth place.

After Jim Spain's king-high diamond flush was trumped by Johnny Chan's flush to the ace, Jack Binion continued what had now become a yearly tradition, delivering the prize money in a ratty cardboard box and dumping it on the table.

"When you see a big stack of money out there," Jack said, "then it becomes reality to you."

The tactic proved its effectiveness as Bob Ciaffone went from grabbing the chip lead to suffering the agony of elimination in just a matter of hours. On his final hand he bet $200,000 after the flop came 6-7-J. Having only made middle pair with 7♠5♠, he was trying to steal the pot from Johnny Chan, but Johnny had made top pair with A♦J♦ and raised $115,000. Bob went all in and caught a 5 on the turn, making two pair, but the A♣ on the river ended his day. Eric Drache believed it was the most important hand of the day.

"When Bob Ciaffone and John Chan played with a million-one on the table," he said, "it was clear that whoever won that pot was going to become the overwhelming favorite to be the next world champion."

Johnny Chan had certainly come a long way. Born in the People's Republic of China, he arrived in the United States at the age of nine. His parents, who had renounced the Cultural Revolution at home, were quick to embrace American capitalism, opening several restaurants in Houston, Texas, where Johnny went on to study hotel management at the University of Houston. When he first visited Las Vegas in 1977, he lost all but $200 of his bankroll gambling. With the last of his money, he sat down at a poker table at the Golden Nugget where he enjoyed one of those amazing sessions that can quickly turn an ordinary player into a poker addict. A week later, he'd built his bankroll up to $20,000. Feeling invincible, he accepted when a poker shark from Texas by the name of E. W. challenged him to play heads-up. E. W. took every penny from Johnny before kindly loaning him $500 so he could get back to Houston. Undeterred by the loss, Johnny kept returning to Las Vegas, and he continued to lose at the game he had fallen head over heels in love with.

"I was terrible," he said years later. "People used to be happy to see me show up. 'Come over here, Johnny,' they'd say. 'Sit down and play.' And they would brush off a seat for me. Many times I had to go to pawnshops and hock all my jewelry. I ran up my credit cards. I would get money from home. Nowadays I tell people you have to be a sucker before you can be a winner. I was a sucker for a long time."

Broke and with nowhere else to turn, Johnny was forced to get a job. For six months he worked as a fry cook at the Fremont Hotel just down the street from the Horseshoe. His ambitions, however, were anything but culinary. As soon as he had built up a respectable enough bankroll, he returned to the poker tables, often with his white cook's apron still tied around his waist. Playing in whatever games he could afford, he frequented card rooms that most tourists had never heard of, places like the Landmark and Silver City. After several years playing this low-stakes circuit, he was struck by a very encouraging notion while watching some middle-limit Texas hold'em games at the Golden Nugget. "I thought to myself I could beat those guys, and some of them were supposed to be the best limit hold'em players in the world." In 1985 he would prove it, winning the $1,000 Limit Hold'em event at the World Series.

In the 1987 championship event Johnny was cruising along until, with five tables left, he suddenly found himself on the ropes. Dealt A-J, he raised from late position. Richard Klamian called from the big blind. When the flop came 4-3-2 with two hearts, Klamian checked and Johnny moved all in. Having flopped a straight and a nut flush draw with A♥5♥, Klamian quickly called. Johnny was in big trouble. The best he could hope for was that one of the three 5s left in the deck would come and they would split the pot, which, as luck would have it, is exactly what happened.

Given a second chance, he made the most of it, arriving at the final table as the chip leader with $461,000. His strategy for the day was "to play slow, play tight, and wait for good hands." It worked to perfection, as he made it to a heads-up match with a man he had played against many times back in Houston, Frank Henderson, a mechanical engineer who had helped design the scoreboard inside the Houston Astrodome.

Like Chan, Frank should have been eliminated long before. With twenty-four players left, he was dead last in the chip count. He had been down to his last $7,500 when it was costing $4,200 a round in blinds and antes. Looking at his top card and finding an ace, he moved all in and got two callers, Chan and Bobby Baldwin. After the flop brought two 5s and a jack, Frank discovered, just as Amarillo Slim had in 1972, that his other hole card was a 5. The $23,000 pot only delayed what seemed inevitable, and yet he managed to stave off elimination long enough to make the final table where, early in the day, he pushed his last $100,000 into the pot with A♥10♣ and caught an ace on the flop and a 10 on the river to double up. Later he moved in with K♥Q♣ against Johnny and caught a king on the river to survive once again. When Frank started playing heads-up, he only had $300,000, four times less than the $1.2 million Chan possessed. But no one was ready to count out this poker Rasputin, who seemed impossible to slay.

"They're playing for such high stakes right now," observed Eric Drache, "if Frank happens to win two pots in a row, he'll be the favorite to win; if Johnny wins one pot, he'll win it."

On the final hand Johnny raised $60,000 before the flop with A♠9♣. Studying Johnny through a pair of those plastic eyeshades optometrists give their patients after putting drops in their eyes, which he was wearing under his regular glasses, Frank decided to move all in for $240,000 more with pocket 4s. Johnny called and stood up from the table. The 5♣8♥K♦ flop didn't help him. The 10♣ on the turn worsened his plight. He was all set to sit back down and resume playing when the 9♥ fell on the river, giving him the winning pair.

"It feels like a miracle," said Johnny, smiling.

When asked what he was going to do with his prize money, his smile widened. "Oh, I'll probably go to a craps table," he laughed. "Or baccarat."

With a foreign-born player winning the title, Benny Binion had lived long enough to see his tournament become what it had always claimed to be, the *world* championship of poker. He had also survived several heart attacks. After the second one, Jack returned to the Horseshoe from his trip to the hospital and informed the poker players in language they could readily understand, "He drew out on 'em again. He's going to be okay."

Sensing that the road ahead would be much shorter than the one he'd already traveled, Benny decided to throw himself a birthday party. On November 30, 1987, eighteen thousand of his closest friends—as many people as there were in all of Las Vegas when he first came to town—packed into the Thomas & Mack Center to celebrate Benny's turning eighty-three. The drinks were on the house, as was the entertainment, including musical sets from Willie Nelson and Hank Williams, Jr. Country music star Eddie Raven paid tribute to Benny by writing him a song, *The Cowboy Looks at 90*. As a four-tiered birthday cake was carried onto the stage, the crowd broke into a boisterous chant:

"Benny! Benny! Benny!"

Grinning impishly, the host thanked everyone for coming. "I never dreamed it'd be anything like this. I'll do it all again someday. God bless you all."

Later that winter, the Binion clan had another occasion to celebrate. For $27 million Jack purchased the adjacent Mint Hotel and Casino, a twenty-four-story high-rise tower, effectively doubling the size of the Horseshoe. In addition to nearly three hundred additional guest rooms, the acquisition came with a fifteen-table poker room. For the first time in its history, the Horseshoe would begin spreading poker games full-time.

It wasn't all good news for the Binion clan, however. In January 1988, Benny's grandson, thirty-three-year-old Steven Binion Fechser was convicted of assaulting two blackjack players. Luckily for him, the district judge Thomas Foley—the same Thomas Foley who as an attorney was previously employed by the Binions—overturned the jury's verdict. During a break in the trial Teddy Jane walked up to the man prosecuting the case, Chief Deputy Attorney General John Redlein, and asked,

"Haven't I see you in the hotel?"

"I used to have lunch over at the Horseshoe fairly often," he said, "but I guess I won't be welcome after this, huh?"

"Not at all, honey," Teddy Jane assured him. "This is just business."

Among the 167 players who entered the 1988 tournament were eleven former world champions, including Johnny Moss.

It had already been a very successful World Series for the Grand Old Man, who turned 84 on May 14. After failing to make the money in any event for the last six years, he won the $1,500 Ace-to-Five Draw event, giving the $116,400 prize to Virgie in honor of their sixty-second wedding anniversary. Several days later, he finished second in the Seven-Card Stud event.

"I play every day," said Johnny, who had lived at the Golden Nugget for the last four years while maintaining several residences in Texas. "If I didn't play poker, I don't know what I would do. Poker keeps my mind active because you're always thinking."

Never one to be counted out, Moss mounted a respectable charge into the second day, but he wasn't the former champion making the most noise. That distinction belonged to the most recent one, Johnny Chan, who, with three tables left, got into twelve "classic showdowns" and, amazingly, won them all.

THE CLASSIC SHOWDOWN

Many of the major confrontations in a poker tournament occur when a player with a pocket pair goes all in against an opponent holding two overcards, say pocket queens against "Big Slick," an ace and a king. The frequency of such classic showdowns, which are essentially a fifty-fifty proposition, make Big Slick a tricky hand to play. As T. J. Cloutier writes, "We used to say that if you play Big Slick often enough in Dallas and you live in Houston, you're gonna have to walk back to Houston a few times."

The classic showdown, also called a "race" or a "coin flip," is a perfect example of poker's maddening intersection between luck and skill—the winners always seem to win them while the losers never do.

The good fortune Johnny was enjoying may have emanated from his lucky orange. On his way to winning the title the previous year he had discovered the rejuvenating effects of peeling the fruit's rind and inhaling its zesty aroma.

"Back in the eighties, you know, people smoked," he explained. "The air was real bad. I said, 'Man, I can't breathe.' So at the lunch break I got an orange. I just kept it. I then started peeling it and sniffing it. I said, 'This is great. This is like fresh air, you know.' So that was my trademark, the Orange Man."

Keeping an orange with him at the table in 1988, he made it to the final table for the second year in a row. In the year since his last appearance, his game had taken on a new dimension as he used his cachet as world champion to pick on opponents he perceived to be weak.

"No-limit is a game to trap people," he explained during a break in the action. "When you find a weak player, try to get everyone else out. Now it's between you and the weak player. You need to trap him, make him lose something. You don't have a hand—who cares? Bluff him out. He's weak. Make a play. When you sit down, you look around the table and see how many weak players there are. Who is the weakest? That's the one you go for. You try to avoid the good players until you get to the final table. That's what you've got to do to win."

Using this tactic, he entered the final day as the chip leader with $529,000, but winning another title was hardly a foregone conclusion, considering how tough his opponents were. Perennial brides-maid Jesse Alto, in his last appearance at the final table, was the first player eliminated. His six trips to the final table—more than anybody not named Brunson or Moss—remain the gold standard in World Series futility. He died in 1998, arguably the greatest poker player no one has ever heard of.

Other big names at the table were T. J. Cloutier; Ron Graham, a local player better known for his skill at Omaha; Erik Seidel, this year's representative from the Mayfair Club; and Humberto Brenes, a flamboyant newcomer from Costa Rica.

While most of the players were playing solid poker, looking to see flops cheaply and trying to outplay their opponents after that, Humberto and Ron were confounding the table with their willingness to move all in nearly every hand they played. T. J. found himself particularly victimized by the assault, as Humberto, whenever he was on the button, repeatedly stole his big blind. Holding A♠Q♠, T. J. finally took a stand and called one of Humberto's all-in moves. He was delighted when Humberto informed his friends in the audience what he had, "Nueve-seis." A 9 and a 6, making him a two-to-one underdog. But fortune often favors folly, and the flop paired both the 9 and the 6 for the animated Brenes. It was more than enough to win, but a third 9 on the river added an extra bit of cruelty.

On the very next hand, T. J. raised $50,000 with A♣10♣ in the small blind. Wearing a red visor set at a jaunty angle, Erik Seidel, finding pocket 5s in the big blind, raised enough to force T. J. all in if he called, which he did.

"Those hands play themselves," said T. J. "There's nothing you can do about it."

The 5♦ on the flop ended T. J.'s day.

Blessed with a good run of cards, Erik used them to dispatch Humberto and Ron. No one was happier about Erik's success than Johnny Chan. While Erik would go on to become one of the best players in the world, he was at that time painfully inexperienced. Just how inexperienced would soon be made glaringly clear.

A native of Manhattan, Erik Seidel had been an options trader on the American Stock Exchange until the previous October, when the stock market crash the pundits called "Black Monday" eliminated his job. Suddenly blessed with plenty of free time, he dedicated himself to his hobbies, backgammon and poker. His colleagues at the Mayfair, emboldened by their own success, encouraged Erik to give the 1988 World Series a try. After entering nine one-table satellites—and losing all of them—he opted to pony up the $10,000 entry fee. His persistence had so far been rewarded.

"It was surreal to find myself heads-up with [Johnny] at the final table," he said years later. "I remember looking at the whole scene, the lights and cameras and all those chips, and thinking, *What in the world am I doing here, playing heads-up for the world championship?* It was pretty awful to be in such a great spot and to be so unprepared for it."

As inexperienced as he was, he still had a substantial chip lead over Johnny, one large enough to convince him to reject the deal Johnny tried to broker before they began playing heads-up. Johnny proposed that the winner get $580,000 of the $700,000 first prize, raising the runner-up's payday to $400,000. Erik appeared to have made a poor decision as Johnny fought his way to the lead, but the momentum shifted back to Erik after he reraised Johnny all in before the flop with pocket 9s. Johnny called with pocket 8s, Erik's 9s held up, and the $1.2 million pot gave him a three-to-one chip lead.

After a timeout was called, Johnny fled outside where he went for a brief run down the street to clear his head. Commentators from ESPN used the break in the action to interview both players.

"I think what happens is, toward the last few days you'll see people who really become affected by the pressure and they want out," said Erik. "They will put all their chips in in a spot where they never do that ordinarily in a normal game, but the pressure becomes very intense."

Johnny seemed immune to any such stress. "No pressure—it's just a game. Couple more hands we'll even up. I just have to play the waiting game right now."

As play resumed, Johnny proceeded to chip away at Erik's lead with surgical precision. A critical hand with a devilish flop—three 6s—brought them even when Erik bluffed at the pot with a king high, only to be called by Johnny, who had an ace.

"In the beginning I felt I was okay and could play well heads up," Erik said, "but it turns out I was wrong. After winning the big hand

and he started coming back, there was a point when I thought I'm not sure I can really beat this guy."

After Johnny had pulled into a substantial lead, he and Erik would tangle in a hand that would later be immortalized by the movie *Rounders.* Chan had $1,374,000 in chips when he limped in with J♣9♣. Erik, with Q♣7♥, rapped the table, signifying a check.

The Q♠8♦10♥ flop hit them both well enough to ensure there would be plenty of action. In one more example of the merits of *not* slowplaying a big hand, Johnny led out for $40,000. Believing his top pair was good, Erik raised $50,000. Johnny could not have been any happier. Not only had he flopped the nut straight, but his opponent had obviously caught a piece of the flop as well. Feigning deep thought behind his dark sunglasses, Johnny languidly chewed his gum and stared at the pot. He placed his right elbow on the table and rested his head on his hand. He looked at his hole cards one more time, covering them with his hands as he peeked at them. He then carved a $50,000 chunk out of his chip stack and pushed it into the middle in a manner that suggested he wasn't entirely sure it was a wise decision. It was an act worthy of an Oscar.

Johnny's call gave Erik some cause for concern, enough that he opted to check when the 2♠ came on the turn. Johnny resumed his act. He leaned back in his chair, rolled his eyes towards the ceiling, and released a long sigh of frustration before checking. He was selling the notion he was weak, and Erik believed him, pushing all of his chips into the middle immediately after the 6♦ appeared on the river.

Johnny's cool demeanor disappeared in a flash as he scrambled to his feet while pushing his chips forward to call the bet. All Erik could do was sigh in frustration when he saw Johnny's cards.

"He was playing so fast and trying to bluff his money off," Johnny said after the hand. "So I sat back and lay a trap for him and, sure enough, he bluff all his money off on me." Taking down a $700,000 prize, the Orient Express became the fourth player to win back-to-back titles. Given the size of today's tournaments, he may very well prove to be the last.

Erik earned $280,000, much of which he had to share with people he had sold pieces of himself to along the way. More valuable than the money he earned, however, was what he gained in poker knowledge.

"It was the most incredible experience—to play for four days and get heads-up with Chan—just knowing that I could do it, that I could play at that level," he said. "Although I still was very raw, I had learned a lot during that whole event and didn't think that I was that far removed from the people who were considered to be the best."

Johnny Chan returned in 1989 looking to win an unprecedented third consecutive title—if only he could outlast 177 other competitors. The last man who had that opportunity, Stuey Ungar, had failed miserably. Stuey experienced a similar result in 1989, getting knocked out less than fifteen minutes after the start of the tournament.

Down to his last few chips at one point, Johnny looked like he would soon be joining Stuey on the rail, but rallied after moving all in on a flush draw against two other players. He missed the flush, but made two pair, which took the $50,000 pot. Chan's momentum swing continued in a hand against Steven Karabinas of Salonica, Greece. Having seen Karabinas go all in earlier with a small pocket pair, he knew the Greek didn't need a big hand to make such a move. So when Karabinas went all in for his last $34,400, Johnny called him with a hand he probably would have thrown away against a tighter player, pocket 10s.

"I put him on fives," Johnny claimed, and, sure enough, Karabinas turned over pocket 5s.

The gutsy call pushed Johnny to the top of the leader board, all but ensuring his presence at the final table. He arrived only $63,000 behind the chip leader, Steve Lott of Victoria, Texas.

It had taken the six finalists three long days to reach the final table, but once they got there it seemed like a contest to see who could get eliminated fastest. On the very first hand of the day Johnny limped in from under the gun. J. J. Furlong, nicknamed "Noel" because he was born on Christmas, raised, in his distinctive Irish lilt, $30,000 from the big blind.

Noel didn't consider himself a serious poker player—his highly successful carpet manufacturing business took up most of his energy. His primary hobby was betting horses, and he was known to wager insane amounts on equally insane propositions, but he had long since proven his natural gift for poker. Terry Rogers, a friend since the days they grew up a hundred yards apart in Dunlaoghaire County, taught

him how to play in 1984, encouraging him to participate in the Irish
Open he had created. The student went on to take three Open titles.

At the World Series Noel had confounded many of the professionals with his aggressive but occasionally erratic play, but not Johnny
Chan. He reraised to $100,000, forcing Noel to make a decision. Noel
appeared to be thinking, but later admitted he really wasn't.

"I was out of my class. I didn't think otherwise from the word *go*."

Noel called with pocket 4s and then pushed all in when the flop
came K♥10♦2♣. Johnny read him perfectly, calling with pocket
queens. The fabled luck of the Irish was apparent neither on the turn
nor the river, and Noel exited sixth.

He was soon joined by Lyle Berman, the businessman from Minneapolis, Minnesota, who would one day finance The World Poker
Tour. After three players limped in, Lyle raised to $30,000 with A♦K♣.
Everyone folded except Chan. Getting what seemed like the perfect
flop—K♣7♦6♣—Lyle fired $60,000 into the middle. A seemingly con-
templative Chan adjusted his sunglasses before raising all in with
both hands. After pushing his last $170,000 into the pot, Lyle shook
his head sadly when Johnny turned over pocket 7s, good for a nearly
unbeatable set. The K♥ on the turn gave Lyle a few more outs, but the
J♣ on the river sent him home in fifth place.

With four players left, Johnny raised from first position with
pocket 9s. Phil Hellmuth, Jr., a twenty-four-year-old whiz kid from
Madison, Wisconsin, called from the small blind, but Don Zewin, a
black-bearded former furniture store owner from upstate New York,
made it $100,000 from the big blind with A♦J♣. Johnny in turn raised
$80,000 more, hoping to force Phil out of the pot: a pocket pair is a
slight favorite to beat two overcards in a heads-up confrontation, but
loses a lot of its potency in a three-way pot. The strategy worked, as
Phil folded his hand.

"I had tens," Phil said, sliding the headphones of his Sony Walkman away from his ears. "Two black tens, I had."

Don caught an ace on the river to win the hand, but he wasn't as
happy as Phil. The youngster danced a little jig, enamored with himself for laying down what would have been a losing hand.

Several hands later, Phil opened for $35,000 with A♣10♣, and Don
called from the button with pocket 10s. Down to his last $83,000,
Steve Lott, believing he had found a good spot to steal some chips

from the big blind, moved all in with pocket deuces. Phil called, only to see Don move all in as well, adding another $163,000 to the pot. There was too much money on the table for Phil to fold. When Don saw what he was up against, he couldn't have been happier, as only five cards—three aces and two deuces—stood between him and the chance to triple his stack.

Delight turned quickly to sorrow when the A♠ appeared on the flop. Phil's pair would not only win him a million-dollar pot, but eliminate two opponents as well.

"I wouldn't have asked to be in better shape," said Don, echoing a lament familiar to every poker player. "It was just perfect. My luck ran out."

After the buzz that accompanies such a dramatic hand subsided, Johnny Chan found himself in a familiar position, heads-up for the title against a relative amateur. Only Phil Hellmuth, Jr., was no amateur. All you had to do was ask him.

"I'm the best all-round poker player in the world," Phil had announced earlier that year.

It was an amazing boast for two reasons. First, only four years prior he wasn't even considered the best player in his home state, and second, he might very well have been right.

Phil was attending the University of Wisconsin, where Phil Hellmuth, Sr. was an assistant dean, when he discovered the joys of poker. Until that point, college had been a nightmare from which he could not awake. During his freshman year he endured an outbreak of acne on his face and contracted a terrible case of warts on his hands. Despite standing six foot six, he was picked on by classmates and grew increasingly isolated. Forced to massage his own ego, Phil convinced himself that he would do something great one day.

"I didn't know what it would be or when it would happen," he said, "but I knew. I knew someday . . ."

After playing pickup basketball at the campus gym one night, one of the players introduced him to the $20 buy-in no-limit poker game played regularly at the Memorial Union. For Phil, it was like finding a new friend. He lost $20 that night and $30 the next, but more than made up for those losses during his third session, winning $450.

That's all it took. He was hooked. After he started beating that game regularly, he found a bigger one with a $100 buy-in, playing against doctors and lawyers. Before he knew it he had more than $20,000 in the bank, making college loans a distant memory. When his studies started to seem far less important than poker, he dropped out of school in search of bigger action.

"I started to play in larger games, taking home over one thousand a night. I didn't really have any idea how good I was; I just enjoyed playing."

Flush with success, he decided to test the waters of Las Vegas. His first night in town he took a seat next to Telly Savalas at the Dunes. They were dealing $30/$60 eight-or-better stud, a game Phil had never even played before. Seventy-two hours later, he would quit a loser.

"Mom, I lost all my money," Phil told his mother on the phone during his second trip to Vegas. "I don't even have enough to get home."

His mother sent him some money on the condition that it would never happen again.

Hellmuth's rebirth came—appropriately enough—on Easter Sunday 1988, at the Reno Hilton, where he won his first major poker tournament. One month later, he was playing in the World Series of Poker. With four tables left, Phil was enjoying the chip lead until Johnny Chan was relocated to his table. In their first confrontation Phil tried and failed to bluff the eventual champion and lost a great portion of his stack. The next time they collided, Phil went all in with pocket 10s, second best to Johnny's jacks, and Phil exited thirty-third.

Although Johnny had defeated Phil, he couldn't help but be impressed by his play. "I let my ego get out of hand when I was younger too," he said of Phil during an interview in *Esquire* magazine. "But Phil will be a world champ some day. All he has to do is tuck it in a bit."

As upset as Phil was by what he considered a premature departure in 1988, he only had to wait a year to get his shot at revenge.

In August of 1988, Phil entered the $1,000 No Limit Hold'em event at the Legends of Poker at the Bicycle Casino in Los Angeles. It was a make-or-break tournament for him. After paying the entry fee, he only had $300 left in his pocket, barely enough to get himself home should he lose. He ended up playing Erik Seidel heads-up for the title. The two men cut a deal—Erik went on to win the tournament, but Phil took most of the money.

The very next day, Phil entered the $5,000 main event and made it to the final table, where he faced a particularly formidable lineup that included Gentleman Jack Keller, T. J. Cloutier, and Johnny Chan. "Son, you're green," said Jack, attempting to persuade Hellmuth to make a deal. Phil politely declined and wound up busting them all. In just two days he had gone from stressing about bus fare to enjoying nearly a quarter-million-dollar payday.

Exploding with confidence, he offered to fly Phil, Sr., a recovering skeptic about his son's new career, to watch him play in a tournament. His father picked the 1989 World Series. Phil, Jr. tried to talk him out of it—he was afraid that his father's presence would be a distraction—but eventually caved in when Phil, Sr. appealed to his burgeoning ego: he was going to win.

Father knows best, or so it seemed, as Phil Hellmuth, Sr. gazed at his twenty-four-year-old son, his complexion still dotted with acne, facing off against Johnny Chan for the championship of the world.

The blinds were $5,000 and $10,000 and the ante $2,000 when Phil, who had about $1.1 million in chips, raised from the button with two black 9s and a huge grin. Chan, with $600,000, reraised him $130,000 with A♠7♠. The grin disappeared, but Phil's resolve had not betrayed him.

"I'm going all in," he announced, sweeping his hands forward before crossing his arms and leaning back in his chair.

The champion looked at him thoughtfully, rubbing his forehead, searching for a premonition. He was fairly certain that Phil had the better hand.

"I only had like four-hundred-some-odd-thousand left," Johnny would later explain. "If I won that pot, I had a chance to win the title. You've got to gamble sometimes."

Chan finally nodded. "All right."

The players flipped over their cards. As if there weren't enough drama, a timeout was called before the flop was dealt, while Johnny and Phil huddled together just outside the tournament area. The dealer quietly tapped a chip on the deck of cards he was holding. Nearly ten minutes passed before the players returned, having apparently struck some sort of deal.

Phil perched himself atop the back of his seat, holding his face in his hands as the dealer finally spread the flop: K♣K♦10♥. The Q♠ on the turn added four jacks to Johnny's list of outs, but the river was the harmless 6♠. Phil Hellmuth, Jr. was the new world champion, the youngest in its history.

"The minute after I'd won, my hands were up in the air," he said. "That was the best moment of my life, until I got married and had kids."

Phil waved his father past the line of security guards whose job it was to protect the million-plus dollars sitting on the table. The two men, father and son, celebrated the moment with a hug.

"Imagine," said Phil, "here was a man who hated poker; here was a man who couldn't stand the profession I'd chosen, and the first time he ever came to see me play, he saw me win the world championship of poker and $755,000 for first place, with ESPN filming the event and the place knee-deep in press."

Spending as much of his prize money on others as himself, Phil bought his father a Mercedes-Benz, contributed generously to the University of Wisconsin, and added to the college funds of his four younger siblings. For one so young, he was as gracious a champion as the World Series had ever known, but in the years that followed he would earn other, far less flattering, distinctions.

"Having such big success so early, I thought I was some sort of poker god," he admitted. "I was telling people I was the best. I was sure I was the best. I guess my ego got out of line."

He would boast about his superior play to anyone who would listen. He would berate players he considered inferior when they somehow managed to win a pot from him. He would kick over chairs and storm out of the cardroom after losing a tournament. He would fall on his back and kick his feet in the air, complaining about a bad beat, not caring that his tantrum was going to be seen on television. In a world full of nicknames he would become the "Poker Brat," the game's answer to John McEnroe.

Phil is very much aware of his own flaws. "It's all about self-esteem. I had very low self-esteem as a kid growing up, and probably a mild form of attention deficit disorder."

He remains one of the best players in the world, and has continued to shine on the game's biggest stage. Although he has yet to repeat as champion, he was—before the hyperinflated purse of 2004 rendered such a measure meaningless—the all-time money winner at the World Series, accruing an impressive $3.5 million, while making over thirty-five final tables. His nine victories at the World Series tie him with Johnny Chan and Doyle Brunson as the all-time best. And unlike some of his competitors who quickly burn out on the game, he still has lofty aspirations.

"I want to earn the right to be considered the best poker player of all time," he once said. "I want to achieve greatness by winning all of the major tournaments. In ten years, I want people to say Phil Hellmuth broke every record in poker, and no one else even comes close."

10

WHO WANTS TO BE A MILLIONAIRE?

Benny Binion was born into a world where telephones were newfangled luxuries and horses the primary and most reliable form of personal transportation. The 1990s must have sounded like the distant future, an era that, as recently as the 1970s, was depicted as a time of interplanetary travel, colonies on the Moon, laser gun battles with alien species.

Benny died quietly on Christmas Day, 1989, without having experienced interplanetary travel or a showdown with an alien. He had, however, seen his little publicity stunt, the World Series of Poker, grow into a multimillion-dollar affair. He had seen the game move from the back rooms of Texas onto an international stage. And he had seen the tournament evolve into the indisputable world championship.

"He was either the toughest gentleman I ever knew or the gentlest tough man I ever met," eulogized casino mogul Steve Wynn.

Benny's eldest son, Jack, had been the de facto boss of the Horseshoe since his father's stint in Leavenworth in the '50s. Now it was official, as Benny's will granted him nearly 50 percent ownership of the casino. The next biggest chunk, 25 percent, went to Benny's widow,

Teddy Jane, who continued to work in the casino cage almost to the day of her own death five years later. Nearly a fifth of the business was turned over to son Ted, who had served as casino manager for his entire adult life and would continue as "second boss." Benny's eldest daughter Barbara had died of a drug overdose, an apparent suicide, in 1983; his other two girls, Becky and Brenda Michael, would have to content themselves with relatively paltry 5 percent shares.

Benny Binion had escaped more than his fair share of legal entanglements, with only a few bumps and bruises, during his life. His death, however, did nothing to dissuade a U.S. Justice Department strike force on organized crime from continuing an investigation of the Horseshoe that had started in 1987. The feds were concentrating primarily on two incidents—the alleged beating, with baseball bats, of a couple of card counters who had been caught plying their trade at the Horseshoe's blackjack tables in 1985, and the 1979 slaying of a customer who had thrown a chair through one of the casino's plate-glass windows. Ted and a security guard chased the man down Fremont Street and shot and killed him, then returned to the Horseshoe where they locked themselves in the casino cage to escape the authorities. What happened next certainly seems testimony to Benny's remarkable influence as a Las Vegas power broker: the security guard, who pled guilty to manslaughter, received only probation, while Ted was merely chided for obstructing the police investigation.

It wouldn't be the last time Benny's youngest son—the one who most resembled his father—would stir up legal troubles for the Horseshoe. Ted had been hooked on heroin, on and off, since 1980. In 1987 he was arrested for possession. And the worst of his troubles were just beginning.

Surviving Benny's death wasn't the only loss the tournament faced as it entered a new decade. On November 22, 1989, Steve Wynn opened the Mirage casino on the Las Vegas Strip, heralding a new era of luxury that visiting high rollers soon grew to expect. Wynn closed the poker room at the Golden Nugget, but rehired the guys who ran it—Eric Drache and Frank Cutrona—to oversee the new state-of-the-art poker room at the Mirage.

Their day jobs at the Golden Nugget had never conflicted with the World Series of Poker—the Horseshoe, which didn't even have a poker room until the acquisition of the Mint, was only fifty feet away.

Now, however, Drache and Cutrona would be responsible for not only attracting poker's biggest bankrolls to the relatively distant Strip, but also for keeping them there. All parties involved agreed that it was best for these two men to end their association with the World Series. Jim Albrecht, who had been cardroom manager at the Mint, became the new tournament director, working hand in hand with tournament coordinator Jack McClelland.

Albrecht began his new job amidst the turmoil of a four-month-long strike by the Culinary and Bartender unions that had cut into the Horseshoe's revenues, creating losses of 10 to 50 percent depending on which side you believed. As the 1990 tournament got underway, players had to cross a picket line that stretched around block. The protestors shouted inside every time the doors were opened; some even carried signs that bore messages to specific players. In response, some of the players sported "We back Jack" buttons. Most didn't care one way or the other.

"Once you get inside the building," Jack explained in his usual straightforward manner, "you wouldn't even know anything is going on. The poker players aren't pro-labor and they're not pro-management. They're pro-action. They're going to go where the money is."

Benny's passing also seemed to close the chapter on the Texas road gamblers once and for all. The new face of poker wore a Walkman and looked barely old enough to buy a beer. Phil Hellmuth, Jr., the twenty-five-year-old defending champion, returned confident he would retain his title. On the first day of the 1990 tournament, finding pocket 9s—the same hand he won with the year before—Phil flopped a set and trapped his opponent, who held pocket queens, into risking all of his chips. Phil was a clear favorite, about eleven to one, to double his stack, but when a third queen fell it made his opponent a bigger set and ended Phil's bid to repeat as champion.

After Charles Dunwoody was eliminated in tenth place, one of the more formidable final tables in the tournament's history was set, featuring two returning champions (Stuey Ungar and Berry Johnston), one runner-up (Rod Peate) and a couple of players who would prove to be regular visitors to the final table in the coming years (John

Bonetti and Al Krux, yet another veteran of the legendary Mayfair Club). None of these men would seriously contend for the title. After Johnston and Krux fell on the same hand and Dave Crunkleton, a craggy-faced amateur from Gastonia, North Carolina, who had won his seat via a $100 satellite, knocked out Alaskan Jim Ward, three relatively anonymous newcomers were left to battle it out.

The best known—and undisputable crowd favorite—was Hans "Tuna" Lund. The native of Reno, Nevada, had earned his unforgettable nickname during a long losing streak. Poker players refer to losing players as "fish," and the immense Hans—six foot five and nearly three hundred pounds—was as big a fish as you were likely to find.

He had survived as a professional for a dozen years, thanks in large part to an early lesson imparted by his mother. By age eleven Hans had squirreled away what must have seemed like a king's ransom, $300, playing penny-ante poker with his family. He lost it all on a single hand of five-card draw, when Mom turned over four aces to trump Hans's four kings.

"I think that was the worst beat I ever took," he recalled. "I once made a queen-high straight flush and lost to a royal flush, but that was nothing compared to losing that pot against my mom. I asked her if she had cheated me, but she swore that she didn't."

Having been bankrupted before reaching his teens, the man who would one day be called Tuna developed an appreciation for money management. While many of his colleagues had pissed away their money on the excesses of the 1980s, Lund did his best to hold onto whatever he was able to earn at the table.

"They don't know what a dollar bill is. They don't know what that penny on the floor is. I respect that penny. I'm a pretty good money manager, and once I get the money, it's pretty tough to get it away from me. I'm like that bulldog—he hasn't eaten in three days and now he's got a T-bone steak that all the other dogs want. You can get it away from him, but you've got to kill him first. . . . Once I get it, I hang onto it because I've worked hard for it."

By dint of hard work, Tuna had built himself a large stack at the final table, which he used to "chop" on the blinds and antes, intentionally overbetting the pot, making it difficult for his opponents to stay in with anything but the strongest hands. With nearly a million in chips, he could also afford to take some chances, which he did when he called a $60,000 raise from Crunkleton with only 10♣9♦. The flop came 10♠9♥5♠ and Crunkleton, who held Q♣10♥, believed that his top pair was good enough to risk his last $270,000. Tuna quickly called. The 8♠ on the turn added a jack to Crunkleton's list of outs, but the 9♣ on the river completed his opponent's full house. The tournament was down to two players, and it was clear by the chanting from the gallery where the audience's sympathy lay:

"Tuna! Tuna! Tuna!"

One of the great challenges the world championship faced in the early 1990s was the slight wane in popularity no-limit Texas hold'em was experiencing, compared to the rapid growth of the limit version in California—where the game had recently become legal—and the emergence of Omaha, a variation of hold'em. In a hand of Omaha each player gets four hole cards instead of two and must use two, and only two, of these cards, in conjunction with three of the community cards to form the best five-card hand.

With more cards in play, Omaha is more of a gambler's game, which explains why Amarillo Slim excels at it. He won the $5,000 Pot-Limit Omaha event in 1985, back when the game was still something of a curiosity. By 1988 there were still just two Omaha events at the World Series, one with a $1,000 buy-in, the other $2,500, but in 1990 four of the fourteen preliminary events featured the game. Good news for Slim, who won $142,000 in the $5,000 Pot-Limit Omaha event.

Omaha was especially popular with Europeans, including Mansour Matloubi, a native of Iran who had settled in Cardiff, Wales.

Mansour "was the best pot-limit Omaha player I had ever seen," said T. J. Cloutier. "He just moved in and out with his hand so beautifully. His timing was great."

Mansour was also something of an international man of mystery. He claimed variously to have worked as both an hotelier and a restaurateur, but when a reporter asked him what his occupation was he took the Fifth: "No comment."

Because hold'em wasn't his strongest game, no one was more surprised than Mansour himself that he made the final table of the championship event in 1990. He had also arrived with very few chips and didn't appear to be much of a threat, which he readily admitted.

"When I got to the final table I thought that I had made it as far as I could."

But after Dave Crunkleton's departure, only Mansour and Tuna Lund were left. They took a short break, then sat down to play one of the most exciting hands in World Series history. Trailing Tuna $840,000 to $1.1 million, Mansour opened with a $75,000 raise with pocket 10s. Dealt A♣9♦, Tuna was happy to call and see if the flop improved his hand. As it turned out, it did. The 9♠2♣4♠ flop gave him a pair of 9s with an ace kicker. Unfortunately for Tuna, the flop helped Mansour even more, as it gave him an "overpair"—a pocket pair higher than any card on the board. Mansour pushed $100,000 into the middle. Slightly less than the size of the pot, such a bet was designed to goad Tuna into calling with a worse hand. Tuna responded with a $250,000 raise.

As quickly as the hand had started, the pace slowed to a snail's crawl. Drawing deeply on one of his ultrathin Capri cigarettes, Mansour spent nearly five minutes debating his next move. When he finally responded, he used both hands to push his remaining chips into the pot.

Now it was Tuna's turn to deliberate. If he called the bet and lost the hand, he would only have $250,000 left, giving him roughly a six-to-one disadvantage in chips, a large deficit to overcome. As unappealing as that scenario was, the converse was just as alluring. If he won the hand, he would win the world championship. In the end, that's what decided it for him. He slowly counted out the $382,000 he would need to call and pushed the chips into the middle of the table. The pot now contained $1,628,000, making it, by far, the largest in the tournament's history.

When Tuna saw Mansour's pocket 10s, he slapped his head in frustration. He was way behind in the hand. While Mansour excitedly paced back and forth, Tuna remained in his seat, resigned to his awful fate. Because of one bad decision, he had, for all intents and purposes, cost himself the world championship.

The A♠ on the turn flipped the script. Mansour kicked his chair in disgust. With two pair Tuna now had the upper hand, although the stoic giant of a man barely reacted. The crowd celebrated for him, releasing a rowdy cheer. Pulled back from certain defeat, their hero Tuna Lund was going to carry the day. Yes, there was still one card to come, but only another 10 could save Mansour, and there were only two of them remaining in the deck. Two out of forty-four. A blizzard hitting Las Vegas in July seemed more likely.

The river was the 10♠.

"Oh my god!" Mansour screamed.

Tuna slumped in his seat. For the first time all day he showed some emotion, as he tried to rub away the look of anguish frozen on his face.

Chip Reese, doing color commentary for ESPN, attempted to apply perspective to what had just transpired. "This is without question," he said, "the most incredible hand in the World Series of Poker." While it may have been played in a fairly straightforward fashion, there may never have been a better demonstration of the dramatic swings of fortune that can accompany each turn of the card.

Despite the setback, Tuna refused to roll over and die. He would battle Mansour for another four hours, at one point even wresting the chip lead away from him. Tuna had fallen all the way back to his last $300,000, however, when he decided to push all in with pocket 4s. After studying Tuna for a minute or two, Mansour called with a pair of his own, 6s. Tuna knocked the table in frustration. The crowd did its best for him, cheering loudly for a 4, but there would be no more miracles this day.

"I was surprised when I won the championship," Mansour said after becoming the first foreign national to take home the title. "I entered hoping to get a piece of the pie, and I got it all."

While his road to victory required several incredible draws, he bristled at any notion that he had merely lucked out. "[Tuna] was a better player with far more experience, but every time I went for the big pots I had the best cards. Every one of those hands that you mentioned, when the chips went in the pot, I had the best hand."

After winning $895,000 in 1990, Mansour Matloubi got sidetracked the following year by the high-stakes cash games that habitually arise during the World Series. Distracted, he lasted just a few hours in the 1991 tournament, finishing 186th out of 215, but hardly seemed upset about it.

"The side game we play is normally a twenty-thousand-dollar buy-in," he said. "In some of the side action that is played here, you can win more than winning a tournament. Last year, I won a two-hundred-thousand-dollar pot. This year, I've won a few eighty-thousand- or ninety-thousand-dollar pots."

More and more, the players were being forced to choose which to concentrate on, the actual tournament or the concomitant side games. In the midst of the 1991 $2,500 No-Limit Hold'em event, Doyle Brunson decided his time would be better spent in a high-action cash game that had just started up. "I tried to lose my money so I could get into a good side game that was going on," he said, "but I couldn't lose. Maybe this was preordained." Despite his best efforts not to, he ended up winning the tournament as well as the measly $208,000 first prize.

Doyle has always preferred to play in the biggest games available, and for the first two decades of the World Series that always meant cash games. "They're so much bigger than the tournaments. That's where the action is—the side games, not in the tournaments."

That began to change in the late 1980s and early 1990s, as super-satellites grew increasingly popular. Their rise hurt the side games in two ways. First, they took up so much room inside the casinos that there simply weren't enough tables to go around and, second, they allowed so many more players to enter the main event that the enormous prize pool began to entice more cash game players to enter the tournament. When Jack Binion announced in the middle of the 1990 tournament that the 1991 winner would be taking home $1 million, it got the attention of even the most dedicated cash game specialists.

"I used to play the side action all the time," T. J. Cloutier said. "I hardly play any of it anymore. With such big fields, you've got to concentrate on the tournament. That's where the money is."

Soon a new breed of player began to emerge, one who preferred to play in tournaments rather than cash games. One of them, Dan Harrington, cited the more beneficial risk-to-reward ratio that tournaments offer. As much as a player can win in a cash game, he can also lose just as much.

"If you can win $3 million, you can lose $3 million," he said. "Poker is a zero-sum game."

Phil Hellmuth, Jr., echoed Dan's sentiment. "I've lost a lot of money playing in the side games," he said. "If I would have just stuck to tournaments, I'd be a lot better off. I'm not a big fan of the side games. . . . When you have a side game, you can lose fifty thousand dollars to try to win fifty thousand dollars. It is a rich man's game."

Jack Binion's promise that the 1991 World Series would turn one of the players into an instant millionaire lent it a carnival-like atmosphere. As he surveyed a room that included several television personalities (Gabe Kaplan and Telly Savalas) and a former champion (Puggy Pearson) dressed as an Arab sheik, he shook his head in disbelief.

"Nobody in their wildest dreams could have dreamed that the poker tournament would have gotten this popular and it would have gotten this big."

The unfortunate by-product of such a large, excitable field was that it was starting to turn the event into even more of a crapshoot. Joining Matloubi with hasty first-day exits were fellow winners Doyle Brunson, Amarillo Slim, Phil Hellmuth, Jr., and Stuey Ungar. Finishing twenty-ninth, Bobby Baldwin was the last of the thirteen ex-champions to go.

Knocked out in nineteenth place, Tuna Lund was frustrated and angry, but he stuck around to cheer for his friend and protégé, Brad Daugherty.

Brad was working as a construction worker and welder in Payette, Idaho, when he heard that Doyle Brunson had earned $340,000 for winning the 1977 World Series of Poker. Vowing to win one himself, Brad moved to Reno the following year, where he learned how to play the game in between shifts dealing poker at John Ascuaga's Nugget in nearby Sparks. After he won a lowball tournament at the Las Vegas Hilton in 1987, fellow Reno pro Tuna Lund advised him to quit his job and play poker full-time. Brad entered the championship event of the World Series for the first time in 1990.

Just before the start of the 1991 tournament, a run of bad luck—in a particularly brutal side game—left him unable to come up with the $10,000 entry fee. But several backers came to Daugherty's rescue, including Huck Seed, a rising star who bought 40 percent of him.

Despite arriving at the final televised table with $150,000—the second smallest stack—Brad had already done his backers proud. The worst-case scenario, sixth place money, was $34,500. Improving his standing would require a big break, and he got one after chip leader Robert Veltri, a fifty-three-year-old former roofing contractor from Anaheim, California, raised $30,000 before the flop. Holding A♣K♦, Brad moved all in for $190,000. The hand seemed to be proceeding towards the usual two-player showdown, until Perry Green, the Orthodox Jewish fur trader from Alaska who finished runner-up in 1981, pushed in his last $305,000 with pocket 8s.

In tournament play it's fairly common practice for the big stacks to avoid one other, as players prefer to pick on the more desperate and less dangerous shorter stacks. Robert Veltri chose to ignore conventional wisdom and called Perry's huge raise with a hand that didn't figure to be a favorite, pocket jacks. The big beneficiary turned out to be Brad Daugherty, who tripled his initial investment when an ace hit the board. Veltri took the $230,000 side pot, for which Brad, short-stacked as he was, was ineligible. Green exited in fifth, complaining that he'd been "trapped from the rear."

"At this point," observed Chip Reese, "anyone can win."

The player enjoying the most momentum was sixty-four-year-old "Tucson" Don Holt, a former dry-cleaning business operator who was enjoying his retirement in nearby Henderson, Nevada. The roll he was enjoying may have had less to do with spectacular play than with his "lucky pants," which he'd been wearing for the last three days. On one particularly fortunate hand he raised before the flop with 8♠4♠ and took a half-million-dollar pot from Veltri when he gutshotted a straight on the turn. Riding his rush, he called an all-in bet from local favorite Don "The World's Greatest Unknown Poker Player" Williams. Holt's A♦10♦ dominated Williams's A♠9♠, and the 10♣ on the flop confirmed it: Williams's day was over.

Hand domination is no guarantee of success, however, as Robert Veltri discovered in a hand against Brad Daugherty. Holding K♣Q♠, Robert was a big favorite over Brad's K♥J♠, but the Q♥10♠9♣ flop, while giving Robert top pair, also gave Brad the nut straight. After Robert called Brad's all-in raise on the turn, he was out in third place.

As excited as Brad was to be playing heads-up for the world title, he had a lot of catching up to do. At one point he was down to $250,000, while Tucson Don had $1.9 million.

"I wasn't going to give up," said Brad. "I just wanted to pick my spots."

He picked a good one when he pushed all in after making a 10-high flush, beating Don's 9-high flush and earning him a $474,000 pot.

Soon the importance of hand domination became apparent once again. After Don raised to $40,000 with K♠10♥, Brad called with A♥10♦. How much did their kickers matter? A ton when the flop came 10♣5♦4♠. Both had made top pair, but Brad, on the strength of his ace, won the hand and the $1.15-million pot, nudging him into the lead.

Fifteen minutes later, Brad, with K♠J♠, made top pair when the flop came J♣9♥8♦. Armed only with 7♥3♥, Don moved in on a complete bluff. Brad called and was glad he did, when the board finished with a harmless 5 and an 8.

"I tried to bluff him when I shouldn't have," admitted Tucson Don. "That's the game. I had bluffed my way through much of the tournament, but I got caught on the last hand."

Brad's backers were obviously ecstatic, but no one was happier for him than his teacher Tuna Lund, who ambled over to congratulate his friend. "He kept his cool," said Tuna proudly. "He has a pretty good temper, but he kept it in check. I'm happy for him."

As promised, Jack Binion handed Brad a million dollars in cash, a nice round figure that would have pleased Benny to no end.

Like any other industry, poker tournaments are not immune to fluctuations in the economy. The year between the 1991 and 1992 World Series was a difficult one for the Nevada gaming industry, thanks to the recession that had a stranglehold on the entire nation. Several casinos were forced to file for bankruptcy as gaming revenues plummeted.

"Money was tight this year," Jim Albrecht acknowledged. "In the past, players would enter two or three satellites. If they didn't win, they paid the full entry fee. This year, many players who didn't win entry in a satellite waited until the next event."

For the first and only time in its history, the number of players entering the championship event decreased, dropping by 14 to 201. The smaller field, however, still offered plenty to talk about. There were two notable newcomers, Lakers owner Dr. Jerry Buss and Grateful Dead manager Hal Kant. And there was the surprisingly inspired play of eighty-five-year-old Johnny Moss. The Grand Old Man of Poker outlasted Phil Hellmuth, Jr., Tom McEvoy, Bill Smith, and Doyle Brunson, all of whom were eliminated the first day, before ultimately finishing sixty-fourth.

MOSS KEEPS ON TICKING

The previous fall, eighty-six-year-old Johnny Moss was being wheeled into the operating room at Sunrise Hospital and Medical Center to be outfitted with a pacemaker, when he remembered that the kickoff for the Houston Oilers–Dallas Cowboys game was in thirty minutes. He got on the phone with Jimmy Stefan, the manager of the Horseshoe's poker room, and told him he wanted to bet $500 on Houston.

Minutes after emerging from the operating room, a dazed but not confused Moss asked a woman what the final score was. She had no idea.

"Well," Johnny demanded, "call up the Fat Boy [his nickname for Stefan] and find out."

"I couldn't believe it," recalls Stefan, who was there to answer the call. "It was this woman. She says, 'Johnny wants to know the score of the Houston–Dallas game.'"

"Now that," said Jim Albrecht, "is a gambler."

Monday morning, Johnny was back playing poker at the Horseshoe.

As was becoming increasingly common, the most exciting poker of the entire tournament was played when there were seven players left, all desperately hoping to make it to the final televised table, which only had room for six. Hamid Dastmalchi, a longtime professional who moved from his native Iran to San Diego when he was seventeen, was the chip leader. Dealt pocket kings, he raised before the flop, only to be reraised by Mike Alsaadi, a professional from Las Vegas, who pushed all of his chips into the middle.

Hamid stared across the table at his opponent. Most players, especially those blessed with the chip lead, would call such a bet without thinking twice. Pocket kings, after all, are the second most powerful hand in Texas hold'em. Hamid, however, thought back to a comment Mike had made earlier about how badly he wanted to make it to final day. And Mike wasn't just reraising, he was reraising the chip leader, who was more than likely to call his bet.

"What do you think I've got?" Mike asked him.

"I know you've got two aces," Hamid replied as he threw his two kings into the muck.

It was an incredible laydown, one that only the top professionals are capable of making. Confirming the brilliance of the move, Mike showed his two aces to the crowd.

Both players made it to the televised table—Johnny Chan turned out to be the unlucky number seven—but the final day began with what could have been a flashback to 1990. After Tuna Lund knocked Dave Crunkleton out in fifth place, the crowd broke into a raucous and familiar cheer:

"Tuna! Tuna! Tuna!"

Popular sentiment was no match for the poker gods, however, who continued to inflict their wrath upon the hapless Tuna. Once the action got down to three players, Lund found himself unable to make a hand to save his (tournament) life.

He lost a $280,000 pot when Hamid Dastmalchi spiked a two-outer on the river to beat his two kings. Down to his last $175,000, Tuna moved all in from the small blind with 8♣7♠, hoping to steal Tom Jacobs's big blind, but Tom called with K♦8♦. Tuna couldn't have been in much worse shape. The 3♥5♦2♦ flop exacerbated his plight as it gave Tom a flush draw. The only way Tuna could win the hand was to catch a 7, and he did on the turn, but it was the wrong 7—the 7♦— giving Tom an unbeatable king-high flush. The Colorado native, wearing baggy shorts that would have made Crandell Addington cringe, celebrated by twirling around like a schoolgirl showing off a new dress, while he high-fived friends in the crowd.

The display was a little too much for Tuna, who, barely controlling his anger, issued a direct challenge. "Would you like to play [heads-up] for the million dollars if you win it?"

Thoroughly chastened, Tom returned to his seat, while Tuna was forced to abandon his, having once again come tantalizingly close to a title.

"The blinds and the antes got so high and I had to take a gamble," he explained. "I'm not going to be anted completely broke before I take my stand. I just made the play I felt I had to make."

"He's had two heartbreaks in a row," said Jim Albrecht. "More than the money, he wants the title. He can taste it."

Tuna would go on to win the $1,500 Ace-to-Five Draw event in 1996, but he has never gotten any closer to winning a world title.

During the ten-minute break before heads-up play began, Hamid retreated to a secluded corner of the Horseshoe where he spent most of the time in a handstand.

"It helps a lot," he explained later. "It makes the blood rush to your head. It makes you think better."

Perhaps he was also trying to forget what happened the last time he was in position to win a major tournament. With a two-to-one chip lead over Berry Johnston and T. J. Cloutier in a $5,000 no-limit hold'em tournament at the Stardust Casino, Hamid abandoned his usual aggressive style of play and went into a shell. T. J. took advantage of his timidity to win the tournament.

As Hamid prepared to return to battle heads-up for the world championship, T. J. warned him not to repeat the mistakes of the past.

"Look, Hamid, I'm out of the tournament," he said, "but if you're going to win it, you had better play your style. Don't do what you did the last time."

Hamid, having returned to a full upright position, took his seat, and several security guards delivered the $1 million first prize to the table in a simple cardboard box. It didn't take very long to determine its recipient. After Tom Jacobs raised to $20,000 with J♦7♠, Hamid called with 8♥4♣. The flop came J♥5♦7♦, giving Tom two pair. Hoping to pull some money out of the chip leader, Tom decided $30,000 was the perfect amount to get Hamid to call. Poker will sometimes punish a seemingly intelligent play, and this was one of those times. Just as Tom had hoped, Hamid called the bet.

The turn was the 6♥. Looking at a suddenly dangerous board—a cheap river card could complete a straight or one of two flush draws—Tom decided to take the pot down right then and there, pushing his remaining $531,000 into the pot as soon as Hamid checked to him. The damage, however, had already been done—as Tom stared in disbelief, Hamid, who had already completed his straight, called immediately. Wearing a red track suit, Hamid looked like he was out for a morning jog as he jumped nervously in place. The dealer placed a harmless 8♣ on the river.

The World Series's second million-dollar man, Hamid flashed two thumbs up to the crowd and to the television camera.

Earning $353,500 for coming in second, Jacobs dismissed any thoughts of what might have been.

"I did the best I could," he said. "If we played the same hand over again, I'd probably do the same thing and go broke again with it."

11

SILVER AND GOLD

The 1993 World Series of Poker was almost over before it even began.

Having finally caught wind of the huge sums of money changing hands during these poker tournaments, the Internal Revenue Service looked to collect what it believed to be its share. They issued a ruling in October 1992 requiring any casino that hosted a tournament to withhold 20 percent of the prize pool and 25 percent of any application fees from its players, severely curtailing any potential profits. In addition, every player would have to fill out a W2G form before the start of the tournament, anathema to men and women who now had to document their winnings, with no clear methodology to account for any losses. The Horseshoe planned to cancel the Hall of Fame Classic, the casino's fall poker tournament, and there was rampant speculation that the World Series of Poker would suffer the same fate.

Tournament director Jim Albrecht came to the rescue. With support from both of Nevada's senators, Harry Reid and Richard Bryan, Albrecht worked with a representative from the IRS to help broker a compromise called the "Binion's Closing Agreement," which guaranteed that, while a W2G would be issued involving any payout over $600, there would be no tax withholding on any U.S. citizen who won money in a poker tournament. It was a landmark decision, one that may have saved the tournament format from extinction. The Hall of Fame was back on, and so too the World Series.

There would be more good news that winter. In December, four days before Christmas, the group of prominent economists that made up the National Board of Economic Research's Business Cycle Dating Committee met on a conference call. The results of the meeting were made public in a press release the following day: the recession that had been dogging the American economy since the late '80s was officially over.

As the 1993 World Series got underway, Jack Binion surely didn't need an academic report to tell him what was right in front of his face. "It looks like everybody got more money this year than last year."

"More new faces, more ladies, more satellites, more of everything," observed Jim Albrecht. "'More' is the key word this year."

The number of entries to the main event jumped to 220, nearly a hundred of whom won their way in via satellites or supersatellites. A giant $200 buy-in supersatellite the night before the championship began produced ten entries alone.

When Albrecht was asked who he liked to win it all, he went with the players riding the most momentum. "If I were [betting]," he said, "I'd look at Jack Keller because he's been so consistent, and Ted Forrest and Phil Hellmuth, because they're so hot."

Hellmuth and Forrest, a twenty-eight-year-old pro from Las Vegas, had each won three preliminary events, while Keller had won one and placed in two others. As it turned out, none of them even made the money—the top twenty-seven got paid that year—although two women, for the first time in the event's history, did. Marsha Waggoner and Wendeen Eolis finished nineteenth and twentieth respectively, leaping across the gender gap and into the prize money.

Of the twenty-seven survivors who made it to the fourth day, the amateurs outnumbered the professionals. There were doctors, lawyers, corporate officers, and, in the case of Henry Orenstein, a toy inventor. The sixty-nine-year-old, who had survived a Nazi concentration camp, lasted all the way to twelfth place.*

A cotton farmer from Arizona was also in the mix. Although technically an amateur—one who derives his income primarily from means other than gambling—forty-one-year-old Jim Bechtel was hardly a babe in the woods. He had finished in the money in three previous World Series championships, including a final table appearance in 1988. But it was an amateur play—at least in the eyes of his unhappy opponent—that triggered Bechtel's run for the title.

Dealt K-10 on the button, Bechtel was first to act and made it $12,000 "to go," that is, raised to $12,000. The legendary Bobby "the Wizard" Hoff, with K-Q in the small blind, reraised with his last $46,000. Bechtel considered the implications of Hoff's move. Most professionals would have folded a K-10 in that spot, but Bechtel, perhaps sensing some weakness on Hoff's part, decided to call. Hoff was happy to see that he held the dominating hand, until Bechtel caught a 10 to knock him out of the tournament in twenty-fifth place.

Waiting for the valet to retrieve his car so he could drive back to Los Angeles, Hoff lamented to Mike Sexton, who had been playing at the same table and had gotten eliminated just after he did. "Mike, how could he call me?"

"Bobby, I honestly don't know."

When asked about the hand later, Bechtel said that he just couldn't let Hoff continue raising him and that he decided to take a stand. Or perhaps, in the back of his mind Bechtel remembered that the last amateur to win the tournament—Hal Fowler in 1979—had done so after gambling with the Wizard.

.   .   .

---

*Several years later, the septuagenarian Orenstein would invent a poker table designed to allow cameras to film a player's hole cards, helping to trigger poker's explosion at the turn of the millennium. Today, the octogenarian Orenstein runs the company that produces the Fox Network's successful *Poker Superstars* series of televised tournaments.

Bechtel had built his stack to a healthy $631,000 by the time play began at the final table; only John "Bono" Bonetti had more. The sixty-four-year-old Bonetti started the final day with $913,000, and, just as beneficial to his cause, plenty of experience, having finished in the money a remarkable four times in the previous six years.

Originally from Brooklyn, New York, Bono didn't start playing poker seriously until he moved to Houston in 1978. All the years he's lived in Texas has done little to dull his thick wiseguy accent or surly disposition. Whether you love or hate Bonetti's nearly constant grumbling in Brooklynese, his sharp and occasionally intimidating tongue has always been one of his greatest assets at the poker table. While trying to get away from him as fast as possible, many players end up going broke. A one-on-one confrontation with such a man resembles stepping into a cage with an angry tiger—not something anyone would want to do voluntarily, but that's exactly the situation Jim Bechtel found himself in on the last hand before the first break at the final table.

All the other players had already vacated their seats when the dealer placed A-10-A on the board. Bechtel checked to Bonetti, who bet $20,000. Bechtel called. The 4♥ arrived on the turn. Check, check. Almost as quickly as the 7♠ appeared on the river, Bechtel was pushing $120,000 towards the center. Bonetti called, thinking his pocket queens might be good, but Bechtel turned over A♠3♠ for the winner.

Bechtel's hot play continued after the break, as he built his stack to $1.2 million, twice as much as Bonetti. When former champion Mansour Matloubi limped in from under the gun and Glen Cozen, an amateur from Sherman Oaks, California, called from the button, Bechtel, in the small blind, fired $100,000 at a pot that contained less than a quarter of that amount.

Mansour had barely begun debating his decision when Bechtel shot up from his seat and announced he was going to the bathroom. Before he left, he made it clear that he would call if anyone raised. While he was gone, Mansour called, Glen folded, and the flop was dealt: A♦K♠8♦.

When Bechtel returned, he glanced quickly at the board and bet $300,000, more than enough to put Mansour all in. Hoping to elicit some sort of reaction from Bechtel, Mansour turned his hand faceup, revealing two black jacks. He would get nothing from the cotton farmer, who jammed his hands into his pockets and walked away from the table. Putting him on a bluff, Mansour pushed his chips into the middle, then walked away from the table as they toppled into a messy pile. Bechtel turned over A♣Q♣, the turn and river were blanks, and Mansour exited fourth.

"I should have raised the hand before the flop," Mansour later lamented, "but I wanted Glen to call."

He had no way of knowing that Glen Cozen, the chief financial officer of the Southern California Orthopedic Institute, was putting on a clinic in how to stay out of dangerous situations. With three players left, he wasn't merely a short stack—he was nearly invisible. Both Bechtel and Bonetti had over a million in chips, while Glen was down to his last $50,000. Supported by a vocal contingent of family and friends—GLEN'S ARMY, or so it said on their matching purple baseball caps—he survived an all-in showdown with Bonetti to build his stack to $95,000.

Glen barely had a chance to catch his breath before another critical situation arose. Dealt pocket 6s, Bechtel raised to $30,000 before the flop. Bonetti called with A-K. Glen had a hand he liked—a small pocket pair—in a position he loved—on the button—but was it worth risking all of his chips? He leaned back in his chair with his hands behind his head, considering his next move for nearly two minutes, finally arriving at a compromise: he would just call and see the flop.

"I don't know why I didn't go all in with my pair," he later confessed.

When the flop came K♠6♠4♦, Bonetti and Glen checked, Bechtel bet $85,000, and Bonetti raised to $180,000, leaving a very nervous Glen caught in the cross fire. Wiping his sweaty palms with a towel, he finally decided to fold his hand. Bechtel called the raise.

Watching the action on one of the television monitors inside the Horseshoe, T. J. Cloutier turned to Phil Hellmuth, Jr. and said, "Bonetti had better shut down right now."

T. J. knew Bechtel had a tendency to "play his big hands from behind," that is, allow his opponents to do the betting for him. Bechtel's "flat-call"—a call when a raise was expected—set off warning bells in his head, danger Bonetti didn't see.

When the J♠ fell on the turn, Bonetti pushed all in. Bechtel didn't take long to call. Bonetti had A♦K♣, good for top pair, but Bechtel had flopped a now unbeatable set.

Unable to blame anyone but himself, Bonetti flew out the door in a huff, while Glen smiled from ear to ear. As Jim Albrecht observed, "Glen Cozen has made more money throwing away hands than most people will make in a lifetime." The last laydown alone, the difference between second and third place, was good for an additional $210,000 in prize money.

As happy as Glen was, he didn't have enough chips to seriously threaten Bechtel. He entertained the crowd by practicing the motion of moving all in, and on the third hand of heads-up play, he followed through, risking his remaining chips on 7♦4♥. Bechtel called with a J♠6♠ and won the hand, as it happened, on the strength of his jack.

A scream of joy pierced the air, as eight-year-old Danielle Bechtel cheered for her father. She climbed onto his lap, awed by the million dollars in cash that lay on the table in front of her.

"This money will be put to good use," Bechtel vowed. "And some of it will be used to play a little more poker."

More than just a poker tournament, the 1994 World Series of Poker was a celebration. In the last five years the event had survived the passing of its creator, the legal troubles of those who managed it, and an economic recession. It had not only lasted twenty-five years, it had flourished. To commemorate the tournament's silver anniversary, Jim Albrecht suggested to Jack Binion that they award the champion his weight in silver bars in addition to the $1 million first prize. As much of a showman as his father, Jack thought it was a great idea and gave him the green light to proceed.

Dreams of silver—as well as the ever-increasing stream of satellite players—ensured a record field. Two hundred and sixty-eight players signed up to play, 48 more than the previous high. Some members of the local gambling community, speculating that Jack wasn't about to give away much more silver than he absolutely needed to, put their money on one of the female competitors—generally some of the lightest players in the field—breaking through with a historic victory. Annie Duke, who had recently learned how to play the game from her brother Howard Lederer, made an impressive showing, ultimately finishing twenty-sixth. Barbara Samuelson came even closer, exiting tenth, one hand away from the final table.

Jack had to have been rooting for the pint-size Stu Ungar to win it, but, a victim once again of his all-or-nothing style, Stuey was eliminated early on the first day. He would have been equally pleased to see eighty-seven-year-old Johnny Moss, nearly as slender in stature as he was advanced in years, take home another title, but he too was an early casualty.

Forced to sit in a chair for long stretches of time while relying on casino fare to sustain themselves, poker players tend to accrue pounds just as fast as they do chips. A large percentage of professionals resemble offensive linemen, massive and flabby and happy to stay that way. With only forty players left in the tournament, two of these behemoths collided after John Bonetti, the chip leader at the time and no small man, was relocated to Russ Hamilton's table.

A local professional, Russ had played at the Horseshoe often enough to know the ins and outs of its card room. He knew, for example, that the super tight $10/$20 game was much harder to beat than the looser $20/$40.

Russ also knew if he were fortunate enough to win the championship, he would be wise to milk the victory for all it was worth by packing on as many pounds as he could to his already hefty frame along the way. While Bonetti was acclimating to the rhythms of his new table, Russ ordered a steak dinner with extra everything.

Soon after his steak arrived, Russ called a large preflop raise from Bonetti, who had A-K. When the flop came K-Q-10, Bonetti bet the size of the pot. Russ called and asked the waitress for more steak sauce. After a low card fell on the turn, Bonetti bet again. Russ called at about the same time he discovered that his steak hadn't been cooked as much as he would have liked and sent it back. When another blank came on the river, Bonetti fired another large bet at the pot. Russ moved all in, forcing Bonetti to fold. When the steak returned from the kitchen, it was delivered to the new chip leader.

Four banana splits later, Russ found himself at the final televised table, which began, in the manner of a prize fight, with a weigh-in. Each of the six finalists stepped onto a scale counterbalanced by three hundred pounds of silver bars. Jack McClelland introduced the players as if they were boxers contending for the heavyweight title, announcing each one's name, hometown, and—the statistic that most interested Jack Binion—weight. Jack couldn't help but smile when he first laid eyes on Hugh Vincent, the chip leader with nearly $1.5 million, for Hugh, a retired CPA from Florida, was wiry and lean, perhaps from all the time he'd spent sport fishing. Jack's smile widened when he saw that Vince Burgio, a professional from West Hills, California, was in second place, as Vince is just as slender as Hugh. But when Jack saw Russ Hamilton lumbering towards the scale his face took on a pained expression, for Russ looked even larger than usual, so large that Jack made him pass through a metal detector just to make sure all the weight he carried was his own.

It wasn't. Russ was carrying $2,000 in half dollars on his person—for tipping the cocktail waitresses, he claimed. Relieved of his coin collection, he still had a difficult time stepping onto the scale. Jack McClelland actually had to assist him. Jack Binion's worst fears were realized when it was determined that the three hundred pounds of silver ingots they had been using to measure the weight of each player weren't enough. Thanks to his new diet, Russ Hamilton weighed a staggering 330 pounds.

Soon after Hugh Vincent knocked out Robert Turner, the marketing director of the Bicycle Casino in Los Angeles, in sixth place, Vince Burgio made a $30,000 raise before the flop. In between bites of the pancakes and eggs he'd ordered for breakfast, Russ glanced at his hole cards. Liking what he saw, he called from the big blind. When the flop came 6♣7♣10♣, Russ led out for $15,000. Vince just called.

The turn was the 9♣. While fiddling with his chips, contemplating his next move, Russ accidentally spilled his syrup. He decided to check, as did Vince.

The river was the Q♣. Russ asked a passing waitress for some Tabasco sauce for his eggs, then shoved $80,000 into the pot. Vince raised another $80,000, enough to put Russ all in.

Russ called instantly, leading Vince, who had the A♣ for an ace-high flush, to announce, "I must be beat."

Sure enough, Russ turned over K♣J♣, making him a straight flush, the first in the history of the World Series's final table. Having doubled his stack on the hand, he had the chips to call Al Krux when the Mayfair Club alumnus moved all in with pocket 7s. Russ had an ace and a queen and caught one of each to knock Krux out in fifth place. The win pushed his chip total to $1.05 million, just $150,000 behind Hugh Vincent.

It would be Vincent's only appearance at a World Series final table, but he would make it a memorable one. He would tangle with Vince Burgio in three major confrontations, ultimately eliminating the pro by making two pair with an ace and a 3. Even more impressive was his bluff against John Spadavecchia, a successful businessman from Miami who was proving equally adept at poker. With an A♥K♦Q♦ flop, Hugh quickly responded to Spadavecchia's $50,000 bet with a $550,000 raise that would put his opponent all in. Hugh sucked on a Pall Mall while Spadavecchia squirmed. Spadavecchia reluctantly tossed his hand away, and Hugh couldn't resist turning over what was certainly the second-best hand, pocket 10s. As Spadavecchia cursed himself, Russ waved a white towel toward the crowd, feigning surrender. This amateur had come to play.

These three men would battle for five and a half hours, so long that the prize money was dumped on the table a little earlier than usual in hopes of speeding up the action.

"What time is the dinner break?" Russ asked Jack McClelland.

"No dinner break today," Jack said.

Russ frowned. "Can we get some food brought to us?"

Informed that he could, Russ ordered hamburgers and french fries for everyone at the table. He then polished his off before the others had even taken a bite. While his two opponents were distracted by various food issues, Russ made a large preflop raise, something he hadn't done in hours. While munching on their fries, Hugh and Spadavecchia both called.

Russ made another large bet after he saw the K♣10♦6♦ flop. Spadavecchia, having sought out the waitress to ask if he could get his burger cooked a little longer, took so long his hand was declared dead. Hugh called but seemed more interested in getting some more pickles than winning the pot. On the river Russ moved all in.

"Hell!" said Hugh, scratching his scraggily goatee and turning over one of his cards, the K♠. "I can't call you."

When he turned over his weak kicker, the 3♦, it was clear why. The large pot made Russ the new chip leader.

At that moment, it was hard to tell who was more upset, Hugh Vincent or Jack Binion, whose frown had grown even more pronounced.

.   .   .

As slowly as the day had progressed, the end came rather suddenly for John Spadavecchia. When Hugh Vincent raised $100,000 from the button with 7♣6♣, Spadavecchia called from the big blind with a king and a queen, then checked when the flop came J♣7♦10♦. Hugh bet $250,000. Spadavecchia decided having two overcards and an open-ended straight draw gave him enough outs to justify pushing in all his money, another $310,000.

Hugh waved at the pot impatiently before Spadavecchia had even finished counting his chips.

"Whatever it is," he said, "I call."

It was a curious call as he only had a pair of 7s, but Hugh was an amateur who had been playing for eight hours on this, the fourth day of the tournament. Add the million dollars in cash sitting on the table, as well as the hamburger he desperately wanted to eat, and his odd decision seems a bit more understandable.

Spadavecchia had enough outs—fourteen—to make him a slight favorite, but none of them would come. He exited third, still kicking himself for that earlier laydown he had made against Hugh.

"I made one mistake," he said. "I did not call his bet and that cost me the tournament."

Five minutes later, Hugh, now back in the chip lead, called a $150,000 raise by Russ. When the flop came Q♥5♦6♥, both men checked. Russ then led out for $400,000 after an 8 appeared on the turn. Holding 10-9, Hugh raised him all in with nothing more than a gutshot straight draw. It was an ill-timed move, as Russ had flopped a set with his pocket queens. He called and made a full house when another 8 fell on the river, giving him the $1,980,000 pot, the biggest in World Series history.

The hand crippled Hugh, who must have blamed his poor play on hunger, because he could ignore his hamburger no longer. Eating with one hand and betting with the other, he limped in from the small blind with 8♣5♥, a hand he figured was best when the flop came 8♣2♠6♦. He bet $100,000. When Russ raised him all in, Hugh didn't take too long to call. Russ also had an 8, the 8♥, but he had a much better kicker, the K♠. The 10 on the turn and the jack on the river didn't give Hugh the help he needed.

Russ Hamilton was the new world champion of poker. In addition to the million-dollar first prize—all of which he kept, as he had no backers—the hefty champion earned $28,512 worth of silver bars. But he wasn't as concerned about the silver as he was the gold, that is, the gold bracelet he had earned and the respect that comes along with it.

"Winning the championship was something that I wanted more than anything else in the world because it puts you into an elite group of poker players that very few people can enter," he said. "When we got down to six players, the money was never in question. When we got down to three players and then two players, it was never the money. There was only one thing that mattered—having my picture on the wall and winning the bracelet. They can take the money, they can take the silver, but they can never take that picture off the wall."

12

FAMILY FEUD

It was clear from the start that the World Series's second twenty-five years would look very different from those that preceded it.

In September 1994, the Nevada Gaming Commission determined that Ted Binion's problems with drugs represented not just a hazard to himself, but to the gambling community at large. He surrendered his gaming license and agreed to remove himself from Horseshoe operations for the next sixteen months, after which, provided he stayed clean, he could apply for reinstatement.

Eldest son Jack was left to run the show alone. President of the Horseshoe since the early 1960s, no one was more familiar with its day-to-day operations. But the Horseshoe wasn't the only thing on his mind at the time—Jack was thinking *Horseshoes*. Thanks to recent state legislation legalizing riverboat gambling in Mississippi and Louisiana, Las Vegas was no longer the only game in town. Jack saw an opportunity to extend the family brand into new markets. In the summer of 1994, he opened a Horseshoe Casino in Bossier City, Louisiana. Gamblers could climb aboard a four-story paddlewheel boat docked, more or less permanently, on the Red River and receive the fabled Binion treatment. He would open a third Horseshoe the following summer along the banks of Tunica, Mississippi.

Early in the planning stages, Jack had offered his siblings the opportunity to invest in the new casinos. They had politely declined, a decision they would come to regret. Compounding their remorse was news from the lawyers handling their mother's estate. The inheritance from Teddy Jane would be substantially less than they had imagined, somewhere in the neighborhood, after taxes and legal fees, of $3 million.

It was only natural that Becky Binion-Behnen would turn her attention towards the single family asset still capable of laying golden eggs: the Las Vegas Horseshoe. She suspected—and would later allege in court—that her brother had long treated its corporate coffers as his own piggy bank, using it to extend personal loans, finance his new casinos and, in one notorious instance, post a $2 million bond to bail Kamel Nacif, a frequent high roller at the casino, out of jail. Becky ordered a complete audit of the Horseshoe's operations, determined to find out what exactly had been going on.

Sensing disaster, Harry Claiborne, the family's lawyer and friend, intervened, offering to mediate the dispute. "I warned them," he said, "that if they took this to the courthouse, it would be the ruin not only of the Binion family but of Binion's Horseshoe as well."

When the players arrived at the Horseshoe for the 1995 World Series, they discovered that downtown Las Vegas had adopted a very different look. Fremont Street, the first street in Las Vegas to be paved and the one that abutted the entrance to the Binions's casino, had been transformed into a pedestrian mall, permanently closed to vehicular traffic and covered with a giant canopy consisting of 12.5 million LED bulbs providing tourists with a spectacular overhead light show. The so-called Fremont Street Experience instantly transformed the area from a historical landmark to a poor man's version of the Strip, giving it the look of a sleazy Disneyland.

The World Series would experience an equally significant change: for the first time in the history of the tournament, Johnny Moss, finally giving in to the fatigue one might expect of an eighty-eight-year-old man, was not among the entrants.

"I wanted to play," he said as he rode his electric wheelchair through the cardroom before the start of the tournament, "but they are going until midnight, and I can't stay awake until twelve o'clock anymore."

He also was suffering from a debilitating case of gout—his ankle had swollen to nearly three times its normal size. But he didn't let it prevent him from sneaking in several sessions of $20/$40 limit hold'em in the Horseshoe's cardroom.

Even without Moss, the World Series remained hotter than ever. Two Chinese poker tournaments were added to the lineup—an experiment that lasted only one year—bringing the total number of events to twenty-three, not including a women-only stud tournament and the invitational for the visiting media. During the month it took to play all the events, a record $11.6 million in prize money would exchange hands. The championship event drew a record 273 players, almost half of them finding their way in through a satellite or supersatellite.

Ever since the championship abandoned the winner-take-all format in favor of spreading out the prize money, there has been a "bubble." The period of time it takes to eliminate the last few players, separating the money winners from the money donors is often the most stressful part of the tournament. In 1995 the number the players cared about most was twenty-seven. Whoever got eliminated in twenty-eighth place would get nothing.

With 28 players remaining at the end of the second day, 1984 champion Gentleman Jack Keller raised $12,000 before the flop with pocket 8s. Dan Harrington, the forty-nine-year-old Mayfair Club alumnus who had made the final table in 1987, called. Neither man bet the A-4-2 flop. When a jack fell on the turn, Dan checked and Gentleman Jack moved all in with his remaining $62,000. Dan thought long and hard before he finally called with K-J. A queen on the river was no help to Jack, and Dan took the pot with his pair of jacks, becoming the chip leader in the process with nearly $300,000.

It had been a remarkable spring for Dan. Just a week earlier, he was all set to return to his home in Downey, California, where he worked as a successful commercial real estate developer, when he decided to play in one last supersatellite. He ended up winning a seat in the main event. With several days to kill before the championship began, he entered the $2,500 No-Limit Hold'em event. He won, earning $249,000. There was now only one event left, the one that had grown so prestigious the players had given it its own nickname, "the Big One."

On the third day of the championship event Dan Harrington was in a comfortable position with $532,000, but the day belonged to Howard Goldfarb, a recreational player from Toronto. Playing in just his second World Series, the balding, bespectacled amateur knocked out the last two players of the day to take a dominating chip lead into the final table, nearly $1.2 million of the $2.73 million in play.

Overshadowing the accomplishments of both men was the fact that for the first and, to date, only time in its history, the championship table would not be an all-male revue. Barbara Enright, a former men's barber from California, started playing poker in the back room of the Toluca Lake shop where she worked. She quickly discovered that her gift for fleecing men was not limited to hair. An aggressive player unafraid to bluff, Barbara was, at the start of the 1995 World Series, the only player ever to have been crowned women's world champion twice. Still, no one had given her much of a chance in a coed tussle. When Barbara asked a friend who had once volunteered to stake her for a World Series event if he'd be willing to cover her $220 entry into a supersatellite, he politely refused.

"That cost him $57,000," she would later remark. It could have been a lot more were it not for a terrible beat.

There is no arguing that, at least in poker, size does matter. A player with a tall stack of chips can not only use large bets to bully his opponents into folding, but also has the ammunition to make marginal and even slightly unfavorable calls against players who have moved in with shorter stacks. The benefits of thinning the field often outweigh the risk of losing a few chips.

With five players remaining, such a mentality had taken hold of the table. Down to his last $92,000, 1992 champion Hamid Dastmalchi moved all in from the button with J♣10♣. Dan Harrington, with a stack second only to that of Howard Goldfarb, called from the big blind with a miserable hand, J-3 offsuit. Hamid was a big favorite—nearly three to one—to win the hand, and yet he still had to sweat through a five-card board to double up.

A few hands later, experienced pro Brent Carter completed the bet from the small blind with 6♦3♦, hoping to see a cheap flop. Barbara Enright, short-stacked in the big blind, found two 8s in the hole, good enough to raise all of her remaining chips. What perhaps would have been an easy fold earlier in the tournament became an opportunity to gamble. Carter called the bet and, despite being worse than a four-to-one underdog, paired both cards on the flop. Barbara snatched her purse off the floor, rose from her chair, and stared at the board in disbelief. She was still upset when asked about the hand years later.

"If he was willing to match my chips," she said, "he should have moved in with his hand in the first place to try to get me off the hand, to rob me—that would have been a good play."

She took home $114,180 for her fifth-place finish.

Hamid and Brent soon followed her out the door. Rapidly escalating blinds and antes forced Hamid to make a move with K-5. Dan called with A-10 and flopped a straight to eliminate the former champion. Faced with a similar bind, Brent, dealt K♠Q♠, called Howard's $60,000 preflop raise, then bluffed all his chips at a flop full of low cards. This time it was Howard who had a large enough stack to gamble with. The amateur called with an ace high, which, remarkably, was good enough to win the hand.

In a slight break from tradition, the cash wasn't brought to the table in a cardboard box but two black bags with the Horseshoe logo on them. Not that Howard would have noticed. He seemed totally oblivious to the magnitude of the opportunity presented him, at one point nonchalantly eating a sandwich while several million dollars worth of chips sat on the table. Eager to play the spoiler's role, he wore a black T-shirt with the word KRYPTONITE superimposed over a picture of Superman.

Dan Harrington began with the chip lead, roughly $1.7 million to $1 million, and proceeded to expand it to a four-to-one margin by winning two consecutive pots with decisive bets on the flop. Howard, who previously looked like he was having the time of his life, suddenly lost all his mirth. His brow furrowed, he raised $100,000 before the flop with A♥7♣. Dan called with 9♦8♦ and checked when the flop came 8♣2♣6♦. Misreading his opponent's passivity as weakness, Howard moved in for his last $617,000. Dan called with little hesitation.

"I just said this is too big a bet for this situation," he explained afterwards. "Based on prior experience playing with Howard, I figured
there was a good chance he was bluffing."

The professional had correctly read the amateur. After the turn and
river delivered two queens, Dan Harrington was crowned the new
world champion. He went on to win four of the six major tournaments
he entered in 1995, ensuring his position amongst poker's elite.

In January 1996, having discovered enough evidence in her audit to
charge her brother Jack with mismanagement, Becky filed suit against
him. The private family squabble became a public matter for the courts.

The informality with which the Horseshoe had always been run
did nothing to weaken Becky's claims. The closest her father had ever
come to organizing a chain of command was to declare, "Jack's boss.
Ted's next boss." Shareholder meetings didn't happen with any regu-
larity, and corporate minutes were concocted only when needed to
placate the Nevada Gaming Commission. It wasn't even clear if there
was an official board of directors; they just kind of agreed that Jack,
Becky, and Brenda held those titles.

Ted wasn't named in the suit, as he was still without a gaming license. The sixteen months of suspension had passed, but his appeal
for reinstatement was complicated by inconclusive drug tests and his
close relationship with Herbert "Fat Herbie" Blitzstein, an alleged
mobster from Chicago. The state's gaming commission ultimately decided to extend Ted's suspension for another year.

The judge assigned to the lawsuit against Jack quickly saw the
family feud for what it was—a mess that would take years to resolve.
Hoping to buy some time to unravel the strands, he ruled that for the
time being Jack and Becky were to run the Horseshoe together as co-
presidents.

The court's decision did nothing to settle the fight. "Decisions are
at loggerheads at all time," Jack would soon complain. "Every time I
think something is white, she thinks it's black."

The combatants shifted tactics. If Becky and Brenda comprised
two-thirds of the board of directors, they could vote to oust their
brother. Jack, who owned more Horseshoe stock than his two sisters
combined, petitioned the court in the hopes of forcing a sharehold-

ers' meeting, where he would have the chance to elect a new board of directors more to his liking.

Nearly lost in the wake of the ongoing scandal was the news that Johnny Moss had died of heart failure nine days before Christmas at the Medical Center Hospital in Odessa. He had been living in Texas ever since a mild stroke earlier that year had robbed him of his ability to play cards.

"Johnny told us many times that when he stopped playing poker he'd die," said Jim Albrecht. "Johnny's death marks the end of an era of gambling in Las Vegas."

Upon hearing of his old rival's passing, Doyle Brunson paid tribute to the man's abilities at the table. "Johnny was the ultimate poker player," he said. "What you saw with Johnny was what you got—he didn't go to movies, he didn't go to parties, he went to the poker table. . . . When I was younger, I saw him play for a week straight. Certainly there will never again be a person so devoted to the game. He probably played more hours of poker than any person who ever lived."

A conservative estimate of the number of poker hands Johnny played over the course of his life was once calculated at six million.

"He was human," said Jack McClelland. "He had his fiery temper, but he had a great desire to win and a great competitive edge. Some of the players loved him, some envied him—all of the players respected him. The World Series of Poker deck will forever be missing one king."

While the Binions' family feud hurt morale among the employees of the Horseshoe, it did nothing to dampen the enthusiasm generated by the World Series. The championship event attracted nearly three hundred players in 1996. The very last one to sign up was the intriguingly named Huckleberry Seed.

Born and raised in Montana among a brilliant family with equally twisted names—Caraway, Apple, Cotton—bright young Huck earned a scholarship to Cal Tech University. Much of his education, however, took place in the cardrooms around San Jose. He entered the big time in 1991, not with a breakthrough victory but a wise investment—the 40 percent stake he bought in the eventual winner

Brad Daugherty brought a handsome return of $400,000. With his bankroll fattened, he returned to the California card rooms where he quickly gained a reputation for terrorizing the biggest limit games he could find. According to fellow wunderkind Phil Hellmuth, Jr., that same year Huck "won a million two in ten days playing no-limit with two of the biggest gamblers in the world."

For all his brilliance, Huck has never been one to crow, tending more often to lapse into inscrutable silences. "You only see Huck Seed at the table, where he tends to be quiet," observed Jim Albrecht. "I get the feeling he's a loner, that he's not very social."

Men Nguyen couldn't be more different. A physically diminutive man, he relies on a large personality and incessant chatter to elicit clues from his opponents. Men grew up in Phan Thiet, a seaside town 150 miles from Saigon, where some of his earliest memories included American soldiers slicing ears—what they called "souvenirs"—from the heads of wounded Viet Cong. The violently oppressive Communist regime that followed the war provided equally nightmarish imagery. In 1977, Men joined the hundreds of thousands of "boat people" escaping Vietnam, living on rice and sips of water during a five-day voyage to a refugee camp in Malaysia. Six months later he was relocated to Los Angeles, where he found work as a machinist.

"Americans made me who I am today," he once said. "I love America. Without America, I would probably be dead."

During a trip to Las Vegas in 1984, Men accidentally wandered into a poker room. He proceeded to lose $1,600—and thousands more during the almost weekly trips thereafter—leading his opponents to dub him "Money Machine." Neither his flamboyant personality nor his penchant for heavy drinking at the table helped to dissuade this impression. Winning did. Men became a tireless student of the game, especially the psychology that underlies it, developing an expertise for reading his opponents.

"I came to this country with empty hands. Now, I got everything I want. All I need to do is say, 'Call, raise, call.' And people give me their money."

His game improved so quickly he began to attract a cultlike following, mostly other Vietnamese immigrants. He took them under his wing, teaching them what he had learned.* They honored him with a new nickname: "the Master."

At the poker table, however, the differences that separate Huck and Men are far outweighed by the character traits they share—both play with relentless aggression and utter fearlessness. Both also enjoyed better-than-average luck throughout the 1996 tournament, especially during its critical latter stages. With only forty players left, Huck made a $100,000 raise—about a fifth of his stack—from late position. Tom Jacobs, the same man who finished second in 1992, called the bet with a pair of 7s in the hole. The flop—a 6-4-2 rainbow—seemed perfect for his hand, leading him to bet $200,000. With an utterly blank expression, Huck quietly said, "Raise," pushing his remaining $400,000 into the center. Tom deliberated, staring at the three-quarters-of-a-million dollars in the middle, and finally called.

It was a good call. Huck turned over 6-5, for top pair with a gut-shot straight draw, a big underdog to Tom's overpair. The queen on the turn didn't help Huck, but the 6 on the river did, making him trips and, thanks to the huge pot, the new chip leader.

For Men the Master, luck would arrive in a more traditional package: pocket aces. On the second day of the tournament, he had received this bounty against Alex Brenes, who had been dealt pocket kings. Men's aces held up, earning him a $300,000 pot. Then, with only two players left on the bubble and Men sitting in the small blind, he was delighted to get them again. He was even happier when T. J. Cloutier made a $27,000 reraise before the flop with pocket 10s, allowing Men to come over the top, pushing all in. After T. J. mucked his hand, Men showed him his two red aces. Amazingly, he would get them again just a short time later, and, even better for Men, T. J. pushed all in with A♦Q♦. Men called. Exit T. J.

With both Huck Seed and Men the Master among the six who made the final television table, the action promised to be fast and loose.

---

*The most impressive graduate of Men's school is probably David "the Dragon" Pham, selected by *Card Player* magazine as the 2000 Player of the Year.

Along with John Bonetti, who began the day as chip leader, Huck and Men wreaked havoc on the table, raising with nothing, reraising all in with even less. Perpetuating his image as a wholly unpredictable player, Men was downing Heinekens like they were water.

The one player at the table who refused to play along was Dr. Bruce Van Horn, a pathologist from Ada, Oklahoma, who, in his own words, "was just kinda sitting there." He was waiting patiently for an opportunity to strike back and thought he'd found one when Bonetti came in for a $30,000 raise from the button. Suspecting another steal attempt, Van Horn decided that his Q-J in the small blind was good enough to call. Ironically, Bonetti had a real hand—pocket kings—and after his opponent checked, bet $40,000 into the Q-J-5 flop. Van Horn, having hit the jackpot with two pair, raised another $60,000. Unable to lay down the kings, Bonetti turned into a calling station, matching the bet on the flop, a $170,000 bet on the turn, and Van Horn's last $125,000 on the river. Bonetti's kings failed to improve and Van Horn raked in a $900,000 pot, crippling the one-time chip leader.

After the elimination of local dealer-turned-pro An Tran, Huck Seed shifted his game into an even higher gear, during one stretch raising before the flop eight out of ten hands. So when Men the Master, after raising with A♠K♠ from the button, was met by an all-in reraise from Huck in the big blind, Men believed he had finally caught him.

"I've got you!" yelled the Master. "I know you're bluffing. I've got you now! I call!" He shoved all his chips into the pot.

The Master was correct—Huck turned over a J-6. "Got you!" shouted Men once more for good measure before popping out of his chair.

His elation was short-lived. The flop came 4-5-7, giving Huck an open-ended straight draw. The turn was a 9.

"Blank, blank!" screamed Men as he paced behind his chair. In stark contrast, Huck remained immobile, staring vacantly at the cards on the table.

When the river produced an 8, giving Huck a straight, Men released an anguished cry. Huck allowed himself the slightest of grins. He had broken the Master. Whether drunk, on tilt, or both, Men pushed all in on three consecutive hands, the final time in response to a raise from John Bonetti. Bonetti, who had A-Q, called the reraise, forcing the Master to turn over 9-8. The better hand held up, and Men exited fourth, earning $195,000.

During the next break the three remaining players, Huck, Bonetti, and Bruce Van Horn, met with Jack McClelland in one of the Horseshoe's offices. If they made some sort of deal, it wasn't apparent in their play, which remained as cutthroat as ever. With pocket 3s, Bonetti reraised what he believed was another steal attempt from Huck Seed. Huck moved in with what turned out to be pocket jacks, knocking Bonetti down to $500,000. With $3,000 antes and the blinds at $15,000 and $30,000, Bonetti felt he needed to make a play. He moved in from the button with A-3, only to get called by Dr. Van Horn, who had A-J. Bonetti would have to content himself with third-place money, $341,000.

The win gave Van Horn a 2–1 chip lead, but the amateur was no closer to being able to read his opponent's unpredictable play. Once again finding A-J in the hole, Van Horn led out with a $90,000 raise, and, as he had so many times before, Huck pushed all in. The loose image Huck had created paid off handsomely when Van Horn called. Huck had a real hand this time, pocket queens, and they won Huck a $1,964,000 pot and gave him the lead.

Thirteen hands later, an even bigger pot would unfold. Van Horn raised $80,000 before the flop with K♣8♣, and Seed called with 9♦8♦. The 9♥8♥4♣ flop gave Seed two pair, and he bet $120,000. A skeptical Van Horn raised $210,000. Seed reraised, once again all in. Van Horn called, creating a record $2,328,000 pot. His hand would fail to improve,

"I want to go back home to Oklahoma now," said Van Horn, and he did.

As for Huck, winning the gold bracelet did little to affect his laconic demeanor.

"I don't know how I feel about being called the world champion," he said. "Sometimes players get lucky, but I know I can play really well, and I expected to win today. I was pretty confident."

Jack Binion finally won the right to a shareholders' meeting, and he used his leverage to add an ally to the board of directors, Benny's grandson Key Fechser. One of the first actions taken by the revamped board was to strip Becky Binion-Behnen of her copresidency.

Too much attention to issues other than the operation of the Horseshoe had taken a heavy toll. In 1997, the casino would register a $20 million net loss. The family's ranch in Montana, long a symbol of their prosperity, was sold. Ted, who had spent countless summers there, took the news of the sale especially hard.

The World Series, however, remained the crown jewel of the troubled empire. As the 1997 tournament was set to begin, one thousand silver coins were minted to commemorate the latest milestone—thanks to last year's record turnout, the total prize money that exchanged hands since the inception of the tournament had surpassed the $100 million mark.

"This is a significant event," proclaimed Jim Albrecht, "when you consider that it is more money than has been paid out in the four major pro golf tournaments—the Masters, PGA, British Open and U.S. Open—*combined* in their histories, some dating as far back as the late eighteen hundreds."

The World Series had grown to encompass, well, the world. At least twenty different countries were represented during the month of tournaments, and twelve of the twenty events preceding the championship were snatched by players born somewhere other than the United States, including three to Doctor Max and Maria Stern, a husband-and-wife team from Costa Rica.

The $10,000 championship event attracted 312 entries, more than the Horseshoe's poker room was equipped to handle. As a result, some of the later entries were forced to start in an adjacent "satellite" room. One of them was Stu Ungar.

It had been a hard road for the forty-three-year-old man once called "the Kid." He had won close to $10 million by the mid-1980s, only to lose most of it in some mindless fashion or another—he once lost $1 million over the course of a Thanksgiving weekend betting on football games.

"When there wasn't big action," recalls Chip Reese, "Stuey would try to create it, because that's what he craved. And the only way he could create it sometimes was to take a disadvantage. Then he'd lose his money."

Stuey's marriage to Madeline had dissolved by the end of the '80s. Compounding his misery, he hadn't won a major poker tournament since 1991. His financial situation had gotten so bad that two months before the start of the 1997 World Series Stuey was spotted playing in a $20 buy-in tournament at the Orleans Casino. He very likely wouldn't have even played in the main event of the World Series if fellow professional and good friend Billy Baxter hadn't spotted him the entry fee at the very last minute.

The lack of success at the tables did little to curb the excesses of his life. He had done so much cocaine it had eaten away the inside of his nose. He underwent reconstructive surgery to fix his damaged nostril, but was back snorting cocaine just hours after leaving the hospital.

By 1997 he resembled a corpse, his skin pasty from so much time spent indoors, his body even thinner than usual. His teeth, which were capped, seemed too big for his face. His mop of hair was ragged and flecked with grey. Whereas most players who wear sunglasses at the table do so to hide their eyes, Stuey wore round blue ones low on the bridge of his nose throughout the 1997 championship to hide the damage done to his nasal passages. Starting the tournament in the satellite room, Stuey seemed grateful for the low-key atmosphere.

"Away from all the cameras and excitement, it didn't feel like the World Series at all," he said. "More like a side game."

Stuey played as if it were the real thing, however, and was one of the nearly 170 players to survive into the second day. He was rewarded for his perseverance with a seat in the main room, where he found himself surrounded by one of the toughest tables ever assembled, including former champions Bobby Baldwin, Doyle Brunson, Phil Hellmuth, Jr., and Berry Johnston.

Befitting his temperament, Hellmuth desperately wanted to be the table captain, and after his A-K defeated Bobby Baldwin's pocket queens, he had the chips to do it. He also thought he had found a perfect target: the very frail-looking Stuey Ungar. With an aggressive barrage of raises, Phil Hellmuth tried to run over the weak-looking man two seats to his right, but the result was hardly what he expected.

"Stuey just flat out beat me," Phil later admitted. "I must have bluffed off $250,000 to him that day! I continued to try and bluff him, and he continued to call me. . . . I tried to run over him, but instead, he got his back up and just called me right on down."

The second day was supposed to continue until only twenty-seven players remained, but at one A.M. there were still four tables left.

"This is ridiculous for people of our age," complained sixty-four-year-old Doyle Brunson. "Why can't we just come back tomorrow with four tables and then play down to six players?"

"Well, I'll put it to the whole floor, and if it's unanimous we'll do that," Jack McClelland said before asking the room, "We have a player who wants to stop now and continue on tomorrow. Does anyone object?"

Ron "Carolina Express" Stanley, the 1991 $2,500 Limit Hold'em champion, voiced his disapproval. He was on a rush and wanted to keep playing, and so they did.

"Okay, fine," said Doyle, "I'm going to raise this pot."

He had about $80,000 in chips at that point, and the standard raise had been $10,000, but Doyle pushed all in.

Sitting to the left of Doyle, Stu Ungar, with $160,000 in his stack, took about ten minutes contemplating whether or not to call with his pocket 10s. Because Doyle had just said how tired he was, it was a very tough raise to read. Finally, Stuey mucked his hand, a very wise decision, as Doyle, who would ultimately finish in sixteenth place, had pocket jacks. The smart laydown all but ensured Stuey a spot at the final table.

While the eight men who joined him were all solid players, none of them were given even half the respect he was afforded. Jack McClelland joked that there was one former world champion and eight wannabes remaining. Stuey was indeed playing on a higher level than his opponents, making incredible reads time after time. When David "Champ" Roepke opened with a $35,000 raise, Ungar called with a suited K-Q. The 7-6-2 flop gave Stu no rational reason to stay in the hand, especially when Roepke moved all in, but his instincts told him otherwise. Stuey called the bet, forcing his chagrined opponent to turn over K♠J♠. The turn and river produced a 7 and an ace, Roepke was eliminated, and even Stu would have to agree with McClelland's assessment of the situation.

"No other player at the table would have called in that spot," said Stuey, sounding as amazed as everyone else.

In order to accommodate the swell of fans eager to catch a glimpse of the man now being called "the Comeback Kid," the final televised table was played outdoors for the first and only time in its history.

The canopy that covers the Fremont Street Experience protected the gallery from the sun, but not the ninety-eight-degree heat. The wind was also a factor—a pane of plexiglass was needed to keep the board in place, while several of those silver commemorative coins were called into service as weights to hold down the players' hole cards.

Those who were lucky enough to watch, whether from the bleachers or on closed-circuit television in a nearby tent, were treated to the unforgettable sight of one of poker's true masters playing at the very top of his game.

Despite his large chip lead—he started the day with over $1 million in chips, almost twice as many as his nearest competitor—Stuey had no intention of waiting for his opponents to knock each other out. He was aggressive, at one point raising seven hands in a row. He was merciless, making large raises on small pots that the others could not call with marginal hands. And he was animated, his legs pumping nervously beneath his chair, his hands constantly riffling his chips.

Most of all, his instincts were precise. His closest competitor that day would be Ron Stanley, a crowd favorite who was wearing a tuxedo and his lucky black-and-white baseball cap. Ron had managed to move within $200,000 of the lead when he limped in from the small blind with 9♦7♦. Stuey checked from the big blind. The flop came A♣9♥6♠, leading both men to check. When the 8♣ fell on the turn, Ron thought his middle pair might be good and bet $25,000. Stuey immediately raised $60,000, a bet the thoughtful Ron would finally call. He couldn't bring himself to call Stuey's subsequent $225,000 bet on the river, which had delivered the K♦, but he should have. After Ron folded, Stuey showed him Q♠10♣—a total bluff. Demoralized, Ron compounded his problems by showing what would have been the winning hand, eliciting snickers from the crowd.

It only got worse for Ron. He moved all in with pocket kings against amateur John Strzemp, the president of the Treasure Island Casino, whose pocket 10s made him a huge underdog. Australian Mel Judah, a hairdresser before becoming a professional poker player, announced that he had folded a 10, leaving only one card in the deck that could save Strzemp, the 10♦. It arrived on the turn. Strzemp joyfully punched the table. Ron closed his eyes in disbelief.

Flustered, Ron tried to bluff Strzemp out of a pot, moving all in with J♥8♦ after the flop came K♣7♣2♦, but the amateur's pocket aces made him all but unbluffable. His call derailed the "Carolina Express," knocking him out in fourth.

Mel Judah's elimination in third place, the result of another great read by Stuey, cued Jack Binion and eight large security guards to carry out a cardboard box that once held James River Chiffon facial tissues but was now filled with nearly $1.6 million in cash. The guards arranged the bundles of $100 bills on the table in the shape of a horseshoe. The distribution of the chips was less symmetrical, as Stuey led Strzemp $2.5 million to $600,000.

It would take Stuey only ten minutes to finish the job. On the sixth hand of the heads-up battle he raised $60,000 before the flop with A♥4♣. Strzemp called with A♠8♣. The flop came A♣5♦3♥, giving each a pair of aces. Strzemp bet $120,000. Stuey riffled his chips with his fingers and peered at Strzemp over the top of his sunglasses. He had to have figured Strzemp had a better kicker to his likely ace but couldn't resist the alluring possibility of making his opponent fold a better hand. If Strzemp did in fact have a bigger ace, Stuey still had outs, to split the pot or win it outright. In one swift motion he sat up straight and pushed $800,000 into the pot.

A more experienced player might have folded, but Strzemp called and flipped over his cards. The 3♦ came on the turn. With one card to come, the only way Stuey could win the hand was by catching a 4 or a 2. The 2♠ fell on the river, giving Stuey a straight. He slapped his hands together like a magician who has pulled off an elaborate trick. Just like 1980, he had made both a gutshot straight and a wheel to win the world championship.

Stuey flashed a picture of his daughter Stefanie at one of the television cameras recording the event. While visiting her in Florida before the tournament, she had jokingly threatened to disown him if he failed to win. Telling her he loved her too much to ever lose her, he guaranteed victory.

"There's nobody that can beat me playing cards," Stu told Gabe Kaplan, who was doing commentary for ESPN. "The only one that ever beat me was myself, my bad habits. But when I get to playing like I was, on stroke, this tournament, I really believe that no one can play with me on a daily basis."

Gabe responded by asking him the question that was on the mind of nearly every friend or acquaintance that Stuey had ever known: "Can I get that three hundred dollars you borrowed from me about six years ago?"

One observer estimated that the majority of Stuey's million-dollar prize had already been spoken for. The biggest chunk went to his backer Billy Baxter. But past debts were a world away from the effusive Comeback Kid.

"Four days ago nobody wanted to speak to me. Looks like things might be a little different now. Last night these three girls gave me their number and said I should call them if I won." He turned to Ben Oliver, a British freelance journalist. "You got a phone?"

Poker players will bet on pretty much anything. A few years earlier, a friendly wager arose during a game as to just how long Ungar would live. They settled on an over/under of forty years old. The smart play turned out to be the over. But not by much.

By the time the 1998 World Series rolled around, Stuey was once again flat broke. Teasing him, Mike Sexton asked him if he would play Russian roulette for a million dollars. "With five bullets!" shouted Stuey. Billy Baxter offered to stake him just as he had done the previous year. Stuey accepted, then bowed out ten minutes before the tournament, claiming he was too tired to play.

Seven months later, Stuey checked into a fifty-eight-dollar room at the Oasis Motel on a Friday night. The manager of the motel remembers, "Before I left his room, he asked if I would close the window because he was so cold. But the window wasn't open."

Sunday morning, Stuey was found dead, lying in bed, fully clothed. Although a toxicology report found traces of cocaine, methadone, and Percodan in his system, it wasn't an overdose that killed him—the drugs had merely conspired to shut down his already weakened heart.

He remains the only player to have won the World Series championship, in its current format, on three separate occasions. Over the course of his career he entered thirty-two tournaments with a buy-in of $5,000 or more, and won a staggering ten of them. It has been estimated that he earned some $30 million as a poker player. When he died, he had $800 in his pocket.

Stu Ungar's headstone at Las Vegas's Palm Valley View Memorial Park manages to sum up the feelings of nearly everyone who ever knew him:

"A great person but a greater loss."

In September 1997, at his now-annual shareholders meeting, Jack Binion removed Becky from the board, then laid her off, along with fifty other employees. Brenda was selected to take her place.

Jack had won a pyrrhic victory, as the Horseshoe was in dire financial straits. A memo he wrote two days after the meeting considered another 250 layoffs as a good starting point:

"These reductions do not include the possibility of any executive payroll reduction or the elimination of baccarat. With these cutbacks, we also have to review the way the family lives out of the Horseshoe.

"No one knows how the public is going to react to the changes. I'm sure that because of some cuts to customer service there will be some erosion of the revenues. Also it is probable that in the near future there will have to be further adjustments."

A month later, the new board of directors agreed to begin searching for an outside party to buy the Horseshoe. While private discussions were held with potential partners, one very interested party made her intentions public. Becky Binion-Behnen declared herself the most feasible person to buy the troubled casino.

"I'm a licensed member of the Binion family," she told the *Las Vegas Sun*. "I know the Binion philosophy. I want to reinstate what my parents built."

She also claimed not to understand why Jack refused to sell it to her.

13

TWO PRINCES

While Jack and Becky fought one another, Ted Binion was fighting to keep his life together. He was losing.

The longer he fought to have his gaming license reinstated, the more time he had to get himself into trouble. Ted claimed to be drug free, but alleged that his live-in girlfriend, stripper Sandy Murphy, regularly used illegal narcotics. He was arrested for threatening a gas station attendant with a loaded shotgun. The rumors about his close ties to organized crime continued to multiply, as it was discovered that he once lent $100,000 to a man reputed to have ties to the Kansas City mob. Nor did it help that, after Fat Herbie Blitzstein was executed in his home, gangland style, the homicide detective in charge of the investigation claimed to have heard "talk on the street" suggesting Ted might be a target as well.

Ted and his lawyers battled the Nevada State Gaming Commission with every tool they could find. Drug tests were disputed. A witness to Ted's alleged assault recanted his testimony. The character of the commission itself was called into question—Bill Curran, its chairman, recused himself from Ted's case, citing a conflict of interest.

"This is my life," Ted pleaded to them in 1997. "I've got no where else to go."

On March 23, 1998, the battle came to a resolute close. The commission voted unanimously to revoke Ted's license.

"I think we should send a clear message to the industry that we just don't like associating with notorious or unsavory characters," preached one of its members. "And one way or another we're going to eliminate all those types of situations." The town that had been built by notorious and unsavory characters, men like Ted's father, now had an image to uphold.

"It's not the end of the world," said Ted. But in a sense it was. He would have to divest himself of his Horseshoe stock, eliminating his ties to the place that had been the center of his universe for his entire life. Growing up, he had spent far more time in the casino than he had at his family's palatial home on Bonanza Road.

It was also bad news for Jack, whose virtual monopoly was in jeopardy. He didn't have the resources to buy out Ted's shares—the Horseshoe was expected to lose another $3.4 million that year—a fact that wasn't lost on Becky. She smelled blood.

The 1998 World Series almost began with an even bigger tragedy. Three nights after Doyle Brunson won $93,000 in the $1,500 Seven-Card Razz event, he finished tenth in the $1,500 Pot-Limit Omaha tournament. Admittedly still steaming from his elimination, he failed to notice the two masked men who had followed him and his wife Louise to their home.

The armed robbers set upon them as they were opening the door. Doyle was ordered to shut off the house's alarm system. The crafty rounder dropped to the ground, feigning a heart attack, giving the security company enough time to call the house. Louise took the call, and when asked for her password, intentionally gave an incorrect answer, hoping to signal that they were in trouble. Instead, the security company called back to tell her that she had given the wrong password. The infuriated robbers handcuffed Doyle and Louise together, threatening to kill them.

Doyle was able to placate them by giving them the $4,000 he had in his pocket—and $80,000 in Horseshoe chips he had won in the razz tournament. The robbers left, and Louise was able to slip Doyle's cell phone out of his pocket and call the police.

The poker legend sloughed off the affair as if it were just another bad beat. He predicted the thieves would have a hard time cashing the chips. "If they call me," he told the newspapers, "I'll buy them back at half price."

Not that Doyle would have any trouble replacing them. Less than a week later, he won $78,200 for a second-place finish in the $2,500 Pot-Limit Omaha event; five nights after that, he took third in the $5,000 Deuce-to-Seven Draw tournament, good for another $44,250.

"I guess Doyle is just in a tournament mood," Jack McClelland said when asked why Texas Dolly was playing in preliminary events for the first time in nearly twenty years. "Besides, Doyle lobbied hard to make these games two-day events, so he probably feels like he should be playing in a few of them."

As it turned out, Doyle's interest was fueled more by his competitive spirit. Since becoming the first player to earn $1 million at the World Series, he had been passed by several other players on the list of the tournament's all-time money winners.

"The reason I played," admitted Doyle, "is that I wanted to pass some players ahead of me on the list." The man who had once claimed to care nothing for the honors and accolades associated with the game found himself plagued by an unfamiliar feeling: concern for his legacy.

His three final table appearances in 1998, making nineteen in all, further solidified his place in the history of the game, while the $215,450 he earned elevated him to fourth among the all-time money winners.

The buzz over Doyle's hijacking was soon superseded by the news that Hollywood was coming to the championship event. Celebrities had been competing in the World Series since its inception. Chill Wills, Gabe Kaplan, Wilford Brimley, and Telly Savalas had all given it their best shot. This year, however, two names from the fabled A-list, Matt Damon and Ed Norton, would be competing for poker's highest crown.

It was designed as a publicity stunt—a promotion for the summer release of the poker movie *Rounders*—but the film's costars looked to make a good showing. Matt and Ed took private lessons from two young stars from poker's A-list: Phil Hellmuth, Jr. and Huck Seed.

Even after the lesson, the actors realized they would be overmatched. "I probably have a better chance of getting through a few rounds at Wimbledon," said Norton. "Winning is so inconceivable. It's not worth validating with speculation."

He was right. He only lasted two fun-filled hours before getting eliminated when his 9s full of 10s lost to British professional Surinder Sunar's four 10s. Ironically, he had outlasted one of his tutors, as Hellmuth had gotten knocked out earlier when another British pro, David "Devilfish" Ulliot, flopped a bigger set than his.

Damon fared slightly better, despite the dual misfortune of having cameras trained on his face all day and having to sit at the same table as Doyle Brunson. Although seating for the main event was randomly generated by a computer, the all-star pairing of Brunson and Damon at a table near the rail created a crowd six- and seven-deep most of the day.

On his final hand, Damon made a big raise from the button, only to get reraised all in by Doyle from the small blind. With the second-best hand in hold'em—pocket kings—Damon quickly called. Texas Dolly showed him pocket aces.

"It is like trying to swing at one of Roger Clemens's fastballs," Damon later said. "You might get ahold of one, but how often is that going to happen? I lost with a great hand to the best player in history. I have no complaints. I was going to lose. The only question was how."

The championship lured a record 352 entries, and the going proved tough for the men who had won it before. Only one—Gentleman Jack Keller—would finish in the money. His chance for a repeat died on the third day, when he got all in with pocket queens against Thuan "Scotty" Nguyen's A-Q. Drawing to an ace, Scotty got two on the flop to knock Keller out in twenty-second place.

Scotty Nguyen—whose surname is more or less pronounced "win"—was in the midst of a magical tournament. Every poker player dreams of flopping quads, four of a kind, then having an opponent push all in against him. Such an improbable scenario happened to Scotty on the second day of the tournament. Twice.

Perhaps the good cards he received represented karmic repayment for all the time he had spent on the other side of equation. Scotty had been a poker dealer before deciding to turn pro fourteen years earlier, fed up with the incessant complaints and insults he took from the players.

"They wanted to tell me what to do in the poker game," recalled Scotty, "and I just couldn't take it anymore, so I quit."

Like Men Nguyen (who is no relation—"Nguyen" is the Vietnamese equivalent of "Smith"), Thuan Nguyen fled his homeland in the late 1970s. The boat carrying him and his brother ran out of gas in the middle of the ocean, and they had nearly exhausted their meager supply of food when they were rescued by a Taiwanese boat and taken to a refugee camp. The boys found a sponsor and resettled in America, first in Chicago, then in California, where Thuan graduated from Orange County's Costa Mesa High School.

A year later, during his first trip to Las Vegas, Thuan approached the manager of the restaurant where he was eating and asked him for a job. The manager, unable to get his tongue around "Thuan," anointed his newest employee "Scotty," and the name stuck.

Scotty dealt poker at the Stardust and the Golden Nugget before shifting his aspirations to the receiving end of the cards. Over his fourteen-year career he had experienced the usual ups and downs, but steadily evolved into a consistent winner, eventually growing so accomplished at the game he earned a nickname befitting his regal manner, "the Prince."

In 1997, Scotty won his first World Series event, the $2,000 Omaha Hi-Lo Eight-or-Better tournament. He had entered that year's championship event flush with success, having made two final tables in previous events. The one-time refugee now sported several gold chains and flashy rings on his fingers. His thick, black hair, a source of great pride—his wife later insisted he cut it, claiming he loved it more than her—was shaped into a mullet. A renowned talker, he bantered with his opponents from behind his round, black-rimmed spectacles.

The rush Scotty enjoyed the second day carried over into the third. One out of every three players that were eliminated, as the field was narrowed from twenty-seven to five, met their fate at Scotty's hands, including two at once on the day's dramatic final hand. Just after eight o'clock, he found himself locked in a three-way pot with two Englishmen, both of whom had moved all in. Jan Lundberg had two black 10s, Ben Roberts pocket aces. Scotty, holding A♦Q♦, was a nine-to-one underdog to win the hand. No matter. The flop hit him perfectly: queen high with two diamonds.

"Don't worry about a thing, baby!" Scotty yelled.

As pleased as he was, he still needed to improve his hand. The jack of spades on fourth street didn't help him.

"Turn up a diamond!" he commanded the dealer.

The river was the 2♦, giving Scotty the winning flush and a $350,000 pot.

For the first time in World Series history, the final day would begin with five players instead of the usual six.

The most likely candidate to put an end to Scotty's run was T. J. Cloutier. The tournament veteran was in the midst of one of his finest years as a professional—he would ultimately be selected by *Card Player* magazine as the 1998 Player of the Year. This was T. J.'s third trip to the championship table, three more appearances than all of his opponents combined. He looked right at home in his black Horseshoe golf shirt (the same one worn by the Horseshoe staff) and his light brown Horseshoe jacket. With $829,000 in chips—only $355,000 less than Scotty—T. J. liked his chances.

"For me the tough part is getting there," he said. "Once I'm at the final table, I'm relaxed."

After the one-year experiment playing outside, the final table was back in the Horseshoe's special events room, where bleachers had been set up to accommodate family, friends, and the press. From a raised podium overlooking the table, Jim Albrecht joined actor Vince Van Patten providing commentary for ESPN.

If Scotty and T. J. were the favorites, Kevin McBride was the wild card. The amateur from Boca Raton, Florida, had a mustache and goatee and a habit of calling raises with less than premium hands. Only later did he realize how bad his play was.

"I didn't recognize it at the time," Kevin said, "because playing in a big-time no-limit hold'em tournament was completely new to me, but I was playing a style that was different from what these guys play. Instead of playing raise-and-release—they either go over the top of you with a big raise or they get rid of their hands—I was playing call-and-collect. . . . I was a calling station. . . . I was calling everything."

As unorthodox as his style was, it worked well for him, as he knocked out both Lee Salem and Dewey Weum by calling their all-in raises and making flushes with hands that had been big underdogs before the flop.

"Well," he said, before Dewey had even left the table, "when you're running good, you're running good."

After leaving his job as an investment consultant at the start of that year, Kevin was gripped by a thought he couldn't shake: wouldn't it be great to play in the World Series of Poker? Deciding to turn the dream into a reality, he headed straight for Las Vegas and entered six events in the Rio Hotel's Carnivale of Poker tournament. Remarkably, the amateur cashed in two of them. His confidence soaring, he entered five events at the Four Queens Classic and once again exceeded his expectations by finishing in the money in three of them. Moving on to the World Series, he managed a fifth-place finish in the $5,000 Limit Hold'em event. On the Sunday before the start of the main event, he entered the very last supersatellite at the Horseshoe and won a seat in the championship event.

Although his career as a serious poker player barely spanned four months, Kevin had faced each of his two remaining opponents before, Scotty Nguyen in a cash game at the Commerce Casino in Los Angeles, T. J. Cloutier during one of the events at the Carnivale of Poker. Kevin was so impressed by the latter's game he bought T. J.'s book on how to play no-limit hold'em immediately after playing against him in the tournament.

Now, in the biggest game on earth, the plucky amateur was giving the professionals fits. Before play at the final table began, McBride presented each of his competitors with a bottle of Moët Chandon champagne and suggested that they waste no time in enjoying it. Whether he was taunting the pros or merely enjoying the thrill of the moment, Kevin was catching the cards he needed to keep his dream alive. Twice, when T. J. was dealt pocket jacks Kevin found pocket kings, forcing the professional to fold both times. After flopping two pair to take a pot against Scotty, Kevin was feeling jaunty enough to talk a bit of trash.

"You taught me well when we played at Commerce. I'm a quick learner," boasted McBride, riding that high that only accompanies seemingly endless luck. "I played with you and I read T. J.'s book. That's all it takes. Win a supersatellite, you're here."

Four hours into the day T. J. finally found a situation that would allow him to strike back at the amateur. After Kevin raised $40,000 from the small blind with J♠9♠, T. J. raised $120,000 from the big blind with K♦Q♣.

Most would have respected T. J.'s raise and folded. Not Kevin. He did what he had been doing all along. He stroked his goatee and called. The flop came 4♠5♦7♠. T. J. pushed in his last $400,000 with what was, at the moment, the better hand. Once again, Kevin called on the come, and once again, luck was in his corner. He caught the J♦ on the turn to eliminate his third opponent of the day.

A victim of the poker gods' capriciousness, T. J. handled his departure with his typical aplomb:

"He told me that he bought my book and read it. In fact, he bought it twice. The man, he bought my book and beat me. That's poker."

Kevin McBride led Scotty Nguyen by nearly $1 million when they sat down to decide the next world champion of poker, but Kevin's energy seemed to be fading. The wisecracks got fewer and farther between. He continued to play passively, almost listlessly, checking when he should have bet, calling when he should have raised. Scotty countered with his usual attacking style, and before too long had pulled into a tie.

"Scotty's manhandling him," observed Jack Binion.

Scotty gradually pulled ahead to a four-to-one chip lead, but the amateur had not exhausted his reserve of pluck. Shortly after bluffing Scotty off a hand with an all-in bet and showing his hole cards to the audience, Kevin confounded his opponent with an even bolder move—a restroom break in the middle of a pivotal hand.

With an ace and two 4s among the five community cards, Scotty bet $200,000 on the river, only to get raised another $186,000 by Kevin, who sloppily pushed all of his chips into the middle before rising from the table.

"I have to go to the bathroom," he informed Jack McClelland. "Can I do that?"

"You're committed," Jack replied.

Kevin strode quickly from the room, eliciting a few chuckles from the gallery.

Scotty was far less amused. "Where'd he go?" He looked agitated as he paced around his chair, smoking a cigarette. "Where'd he go?"

Kevin returned to the room to a few cheers from the crowd. "What happened? What happened? You call, Scotty? You call?"

Scotty glared at him. "It's gonna be all over if I read you right, man. If I don't, we play again. I call."

Kevin turned over his hand, 5♦4♥, giving him three of a kind. Scotty revealed A♥Q♣, good for second best. Winning the nearly $1.5 million pot pulled Kevin within a half million of Scotty.

Scotty looked like he was steaming as he fired huge bets into the next hand. First, $42,000 on the flop. Another $120,000 on the turn. Then $300,000 on the river. With an ace, a king, and a possible straight on the board, Kevin finally decided that his pair of jacks stood little chance against whatever Scotty had and folded his hand.

"Ka-ching!" Scotty yelled, turning over 6-5 offsuit, a total bluff.

Kevin looked like his dog had just been run over by a car. Getting shown up in such a manner would have made most players play more aggressively, but Kevin remained remarkably composed, perhaps too much so. As they entered the seventh hour of play, his passivity would cost him when his failure to bet a pair of aces on the turn allowed Scotty to river a nut straight, good for an $800,000 pot.

The crowd grew edgy, sensing that the end was near. Scotty cracked open a bottle of Michelob. With the blinds at $25,000 and $50,000, Kevin made it $100,000 to go before the flop. Scotty called and checked after the flop came 9♥9♦8♣. Finally showing some fire, Kevin shoved $100,000 into the middle.

"How much you got left, man?" asked Scotty, with reptilian menace.

"Three fifty, maybe."

Scotty shrugged and called the bet. The turn was the 8♥. For the third time, Kevin pushed $100,000 into the middle, and for the third time Scotty called. It was a surprising display of passivity for him, unless, of course, he was setting a trap.

The 8♠ appeared on the river. Scotty immediately pushed all of his chips into the middle. As Kevin pondered his options, Scotty rose from the table, saluting him with his beer.

"You call and it's gonna be all over, baby!"

There was a full house—8s full of 9s—on the board. Unless Scotty was holding an 8 or a 9, or a big pocket pair, they would be splitting the pot.

Kevin pursed his lips, stared at the cards on the table, and finally announced, "I call. I play the board."

Scotty let out a victory whoop, turning over J♦9♣ for 9s full of 8s.

"I wouldn't have called if Scotty hadn't said, 'If you call, it's all over,'" Kevin later admitted. "I didn't believe him."

The $687,500 he earned for coming in second provided some consolation, but Kevin McBride would fade away from the poker scene as rapidly as he had entered it. To date, he has yet to return to a final table in a World Series of Poker event.

Having watched the coronation of the last several poker champions, Scotty Nguyen knew full well the significance of Jack Binion's arrival at the table. After Jack handed him the million dollars he had just won, Scotty took a chair beside him and confessed, only partly in jest,

"This is my dream to sit next to you."

It was a dream that had been filled in the nick of time. Less than a month later there would be a new sheriff in town. Faced with the possibility of losing control of Ted's stock, Jack finally acceded to his sister's relentless maneuvering and, after negotiating with Ted and Brenda to buy their shares, sold the Horseshoe to Becky, part and parcel.

Becky was elated. "I want to see the customs and the business of the Horseshoe go back to the way they were when I was being raised," she told the state regulators who approved the transfer. "It goes back to the same thing Daddy always said—good food, good whiskey, and a good gamble."

For Jack, life would go on. "Obviously, I felt [the Horseshoe] was efficient and we were doing the best we could do," he later told the press. "Under the circumstances, I can't make any comment about the Horseshoe under Becky's stewardship. Time will tell who had the best stewardship." Jack turned his attention to his riverboat casinos, eventually forming a "World Poker Open" in Tunica, Mississippi, a series of tournaments culminating in a $10,000 buy-in championship.

Ted Binion, meanwhile, had reached the end of his road. On September 18, at 4:05 P.M., the fifty-five-year-old was found dead in his home. An autopsy discovered heroin, Xanax, and Valium in his system.

The police initially seemed content to write up Ted's death as an overdose. Becky, however, pushed for a murder investigation. A new medical report theorized that Ted died from "burking," or what happens to a person when "the mouth and nose are obstructed and someone sits on the chest to prevent the diaphragm from moving up and down."

The following year Becky's efforts would bear fruit, as the police finally charged Ted's girlfriend, twenty-seven-year-old, ex-topless dancer Sandy Murphy, and her lover Rick Tabish, a two-time convicted felon from Montana, of attempted murder. Less than 36 hours after Ted's death, Tabish was discovered at Ted's ranch in nearby Pahrump—at 2 A.M.—apparently trying to excavate a buried stash of silver. He was armed with the combination to Ted's safe and a love note apparently written by Murphy. The case would quickly turn into the most spectacular trial in Las Vegas history.

14

CINDERELLA STORIES

y 1998 the Horseshoe was going the way of the Houston Astrodome and Veterans Stadium, venues cherished more for what they had once been than what they were. Poker players from around the world still traveled thousands of miles to visit it, but once they arrived they were usually disappointed. It was a dump compared to the new cardrooms that were starting to open all across town, the most spectacular of which resided in Steve Wynn's Bellagio Hotel and Casino.

As neglected as the Horseshoe seemed by comparison, it was still a major coup for Becky Binion-Behnen when she seized control of it. The real winner, however, may have been her husband Nick. Although Becky had been the public face of the successful fight for the Horseshoe, some saw a puppet master lurking in the shadows.

Nick Behnen was not allowed to run a casino. He wanted to, or at least he did in 1977 when he applied for a license from the Nevada Gaming Control Board. During the process, it was discovered that Nick failed to mention that he had once been arrested, in Detroit during the 1960s, for operating an illegal gambling establishment. Nick withdrew his application.

Even after twenty years the incident remained fresh in the minds of the Gaming Control Board, who were concerned that Nick might be using his wife as a proxy to gain control of a casino without having to go through the proper channels.

"My husband will not have any involvement in the Horseshoe Club," Becky promised the regulators as they approved the transfer of the casino into her name.

By the end of 1998 her assertion was already in doubt. A controversy arose when Bob "the Polish Maverick" Stupak, the Las Vegas legend who had been the visionary behind the Stratosphere Casino, tried to cash a very large sum of $5,000 chips that he claimed were from the Horesshoe. He was refused—Becky later cited concerns that there were a large number of counterfeit chips in circulation—leading Stupak to file a complaint with the Gaming Control Board and a lawsuit against the Horseshoe. He included Nick Behnen among the list of defendants, and alleged in his letter to the Gaming Control Board that Becky's husband was "controlling and overseeing and in charge of the Horseshoe Casino operations since Jack Binion departed."

Becky vehemently denied that Nick played any part in running the casino, and was offended by the speculation that she was anybody's pawn.

"It's almost insulting, people don't think I'm capable of doing this," she said. "I've been doing this . . . been around this almost all of my life."

Adding to any confusion as to who was running the Horseshoe was the rumor that the World Series of Poker might no longer be a part of it. Shortly after Becky assumed control, it was announced that the Horseshoe would not be hosting the Hall of Fame Classic. What's more, the people who had managed the World Series for more than a decade, Jim Albrecht and Jack McClelland, were fired.

Albrecht told the press that during his termination meeting, a Horseshoe executive told him that it was "unsettled" as to whether the casino would host a 1999 World Series of Poker.

"This is definitely not good news for poker," Albrecht said. "People closest to it love the World Series, but those who aren't don't understand what it means to those of us who love it."

Becky, however, was quick to list herself among its strident fans. "I remember when my father hosted the very first event," she responded. "I would never cancel the World Series. It will be here next May." She hired Cathi Wood to manage the Horseshoe's card room and coordinate the World Series of Poker.

One of Wood's first duties on the job was to hire a new tournament director. She didn't have to look very hard to find someone with just the right amount of experience. Her father, seventy-two-year-old Bob "Silver Eagle" Thompson, had been dealing poker since 1963 and had been a poker room manager on and off since 1973.

And so the World Series continued, but not without its share of changes. The number of events was reduced from twenty to thirteen. Some players grumbled that other corners were being cut, that the gold bracelets, no longer crafted by Neiman-Marcus, had been reduced from eighteen- to fourteen-carat gold, and that the food in the complimentary buffet had gotten worse. Both Doyle Brunson and Chip Reese quietly decided to boycott the tournament. Bob Stupak was not even allowed to enter the building.

Still, the championship event, in its thirtieth year, attracted a record 393 players. Some attributed it to increased media coverage or a Dow Jones average that had broken 11,000. The late great poker writer Andy Glazer had another theory: Kevin McBride.

"Last year, when Kevin came out of nowhere to finish second in the Series and take home three-quarters of a cool million, he birthed dreams among the poker masses everywhere. The ESPN special has run numerous times, and everyone has seen and heard the commentators saying how new Kevin was, how unorthodox his play was, etc., etc. There were probably thousands of decent players who saw this and said, 'Heck, I play better than Kevin McBride, maybe I should go to the Series.'"

There were plenty of familiar faces as well. Phil Hellmuth, Jr., Huck Seed, and Erik Seidel were on hand. So was Puggy Pearson, who, along with his wife Simin, came dressed as a nineteenth-century riverboat gambler, complete with a colorful long coat, bowtie, and six-shooter that he twirled around his finger. And "the Red Menace," Irish bookmaker Terry Rogers, was back with his contingent of countrymen. This year he had come with ten players. It would have been nine, but at the last minute Rogers called Noel Furlong, who had been planning to sit this one out, and said "I've got two first-class tickets. You have to come."

Coming off a handsome payday—a few weeks earlier he had bet $700,000 on a horse that was a seven-to-two long shot and won—the sixty-one-year-old Furlong was up for pressing his luck. He arrived with a simple strategy. "Initially," he said, "while most people are playing very tight, I play very loose in the competitions to try to get a decent amount of chips. So I'm either out very early or I'm there with a chance."

By the end of the second day, it was clear that this was an "on" year for Noel, whose attacking style had helped him grab the lead with nearly a half-million in chips. Even with his bifocals, white hair, and paunch, he has been called the "Irish Stu Ungar" because of his aggressive style. He bets or raises almost every hand.

"He's always had the aggression. He's fearless," bragged Rogers of his friend.

The third day began with him seated at the same table as a player with aggression to rival his own, Huck Seed. And as three tables collapsed into two, they were joined by Alan Goehring, a thirty-six-year-old corporate bond trader from New York City who also wasn't afraid to move his chips into the center. The other players could only watch as the three men went after each other time and time again. Small squabbles over blinds quickly escalated into life-threatening confrontations. It seemed only a matter of time before they knocked each other out.

They came close many times. On one dramatic hand, Noel made it $25,000 to go from the small blind. Alan, looking like the Terminator behind wraparound shades (a vestige of his recent laser eye surgery), called from the big blind as did Huck from the button. When the flop came 9♠5♥2♥, Noel pushed $100,000 into the middle. Alan raised another $100,000. New tournament director Bob Thompson informed the crowd that Noel was going to be facing a tough call.

"What about me?" asked Huck.

"Oh, yes," said Thompson. "Huck Seed is still in the hand."

Not to be outdone, Huck pushed all in with his last $217,000. Noel mucked his hand instantly. Alan didn't look too thrilled, but it only cost him $17,000 to make the call, and so he did. With Huck all in, the cards were turned over. Alan had been semibluffing with 4-3 offsuit, giving him an open-ended straight draw; Huck had flopped a set of deuces. When a 9 came on the turn, Huck made a full house and nearly tripled his stack.

Miraculously, all three players survived to make the final table. Of greater amazement, at least to everyone who wasn't Terry Rogers, Noel Furlong wasn't the only Irishman—he was joined by fellow Dubliners George McKeever and Padraig Parkinson. They were the only three members of the expedition to have entered the $10,000 championship.

"It's Ireland against the rest of the world," shouted one of the rail-birds.

"It always has been," Parkinson yelled back in his distinctive brogue.

With the blinds still relatively small ($10,000 and $20,000) compared to the average stack (over $500,000), all the ingredients were in place for a protracted battle, especially considering the fact that the next player to go wouldn't make the next day's televised table. But none of these players had made it this far playing conservatively.

When McKeever made it $70,000 to go with A-Q, Huck called from the button and Noel pushed all in from the big blind with pocket kings. McKeever called quickly; Huck tossed his pocket 9s into the muck. Noel's kings held up, eliminating his countryman and catapulting him into the chip lead with over $1.5 million.

The televised final table was reminiscent of 1981, when the Texans squared off against the Jews, only this time it was America versus Europe. The two remaining Irishmen, Furlong and Parkinson, were joined by Swiss businessman Chris Bigler. The American side was well-represented by the two tough Las Vegas pros, Huck Seed and Erik Seidel, and the bond trader Alan Goehring, but they were handicapped by short stacks. Only Alan, the least experienced of the bunch, had a decent amount of chips.

Huck pulled himself back into contention by doubling his stack over the course of the first six hands. His gathering momentum was hindered by his unfortunate position at the table, two seats to the left of Noel, who was using his chip lead to bully the ex-champion. Tired of getting picked on, Huck decided to take a stand. After he limped in for $20,000 and Noel raised it to $100,000, Huck came over the top of him with the rest of his chips. Holding a fairly mediocre hand, J♦8♦,

Huck was obviously hoping his big bet would make Noel fold. He had underestimated the Irishman's stubbornness. Furlong called with A♥3♥, and the A-Q-3 flop sent Huck home in sixth place.

"I don't know of any other player who would have made that call against Huck," Erik Seidel would later comment, having obviously never played at Dublin's Eccentrics Club.

Seidel was still alive, but severely short-stacked. He was still trying to recover from the previous day, when three devastating losses at the hands of Alan Goehring cost him $500,000 and the chip lead. Down to his last $224,000, Erik once again found himself engaged in a tussle with the unpredictable Goehring. With A-Q in the "cutoff" seat,* Erik made it $60,000 to go. Alan Goehring and Chris Bigler, the two blinds, both called. All three checked when the flop came 8♣6♥2♣, and again when the J♠ hit on the turn. Alan finally bet $150,000 after the 5♠ fell on the river. Chris folded, leaving it up to Erik to try to get a read on the man behind the wraparound sunglasses. He stared at him for two full minutes.

"When you're low on chips," Erik explained, "you're limited in terms of the decisions that you can make. You just have to pick a spot and go with it."

Call and lose, a completely plausible scenario as the only hand Erik could beat was a total bluff, and he'd be left with only $14,000, not even enough to pay for a round of blinds. But his instincts told him that calling was the right thing to do. Sure enough, Alan was bluffing with Q-10. Erik raked in a pot worth nearly a half million.

"That's why he's sitting there and we're sitting here," gushed poker columnist Mike Paulle.

A few hands later, Chris Bigler flopped a set of 9s, but Noel Furlong flopped the nut straight to cut the field down to four. Then, just a few hands after that, Erik Seidel came over the top of Padraig Parkinson's $60,000 raise with his remaining $400,000. Padraig quickly called with A-K and looked to have Erik's A-Q dominated. When the flop came Q-3-3, Erik walked away from the table, too nervous to watch. He was glad he didn't. A king fell on the river. After getting

---

*The "cutoff" is the seat just to the right of the button, the second-to-last player to act after the flop.

such a favorable flop, such an ending must have seemed doubly cruel, but Erik concentrated on the bright side of winning $280,000.

"Fourth was $100,000 better than I woke up with that morning," he said.

Because the last three players had about the same amount of chips—Noel Furlong had $1.5 million; Padraig Parkinson and Alan Goehring $1.2 million each—it seemed reasonable to expect them to tighten up, especially considering the big blind was still just $30,000. Not these guys. They came to gamble, and gamble they did.

It's not uncommon for players to settle into a standard opening bet, usually two and a half to three times the size of the big blind. This trio of fearless gamblers quickly got into the habit of opening for $200,000, nearly seven times the big blind. Big bets generally mean dramatic fluctuations in the size of chip stacks, and it was Alan who experienced the brunt of such volatility, quickly losing nearly a million in chips in the early going. That the title would be traveling to Ireland seemed a foregone conclusion until Alan's fortune took yet another dramatic swing. He doubled up with pocket kings against Padraig's pocket 10s, then again when *his* pocket 10s beat Noel's A-Q. Three times over the course of the next four hands, he took $200,000 or more from Noel. A big pot against Padraig pushed him above the $2 million mark.

The two Irishmen were suddenly battling for second. Padraig, plagued by a series of cold cards, raised $70,000 with what must have seemed like a monster hand at the time, Q♦10♦ in the small blind. Noel called from the big blind. The flop came 4♣2♦6♦, and with four cards to a flush and two overcards, Padraig decided to push in his last $617,000. Noel, suddenly anxious, couldn't stop bouncing his feet beneath the table as he pondered a call. He tried a balk move with his chips to see if Padraig would cringe, but Padraig didn't even blink. Noel continued to think for roughly three more minutes, an extremely long time for a player who had so often flown by the seat of his pants. He finally called, turning over A♦8♦, the nut flush draw. There would be no fifth diamond, but an ace on the turn sealed Padraig's fate. Having knocked out both his fellow countrymen, Noel now focused his attention on the American across the table from him.

They began their heads-up battle with relatively even stacks, but the roller coaster Alan had been riding began to make a sharp descent. Noel took advantage of Alan's poorly timed run of bad cards with unremitting pressure. Alan made several moves at pots, but each time Noel pushed back even harder, forcing Alan to back down. After Noel won two big hands with flushes, he had nearly a 3–1 chip lead over his opponent. Rattled, Alan asked for and received a bathroom break. Outside the casino, he stomped back and forth, struggling to regain his composure.

Desperately needing a good hand, he got one just fifteen minutes after the break: pocket 6s. Or at least it was good until the flop came Q♥Q♣5♠. Both men checked. When a 2♠ appeared on the turn, Alan suspected he had the best hand, and checked again to allow the aggressive Furlong to bluff at the pot. Sure enough, Noel fired $150,000 into the middle, enabling Alan to check-raise him $300,000 more. That's when, to borrow Crandell Addington's metaphor, the target fired back. Noel furrowed his brow for about twenty seconds and then pushed all in.

It was Alan's turn to frown. Folding here would leave him with only $400,000—he'd be nearly a nine-to-one chip underdog to the Irishman. Had Noel's hesitancy represented a difficult decision or an acting job? Deciding that in either case he was committed to the pot, Alan called.

Acting job, Noel flipped over pocket 5s, having flopped a full house. His good luck held through the river, the 8♠, making Noel Furlong the new world champion.

Even in victory, Noel maintained his typically laconic demeanor; so it was up to a beaming Terry Rogers to put the cap on the day. "Pretty good day for the Irish, isn't it?" asked a reporter.

Rogers responded with an even broader smile. "Every day is pretty good for the Irish."*

· · ·

---

*Sadly, this would be Rogers's last trip to the World Series. Six months later, after finishing an excellent meal in the Canary Islands, he would suddenly drop dead.

The Horseshoe, like the rest of the world, survived the Y2K bug. It had been a relatively peaceful winter for the casino, marked by Becky's quiet sale, to a private bidder, of her father's million-dollar display that had adorned the casino since 1964. For nearly half a century the famed money-filled horseshoe represented much of what the Binion family stood for—who else but Benny Binion would spend a million dollars on a cheap publicity stunt? Those days were over.

Springtime in Las Vegas looks a lot like winter, but this year there was a hum in the air. Ted's murder trial began, and its heady brew of sex, drugs, and gambling ensured a media frenzy. The Binion family was thrown into the national spotlight, which in part explains why the Horseshoe's new owner wasn't fully prepared when five thousand players showed up for the month-long series of tournaments. The championship event alone attracted 512 entries, a staggering 30 percent increase over the previous year.

"I don't know about the rest of the country," observed Johnny Chan, "but there sure were a lot of people wandering around the Horseshoe with ten thousand dollars in their pockets."

While Becky had increased the number of preliminary events from sixteen to twenty-five, she had done little else. The scramble to seat all the participants in the main event at tables scattered throughout the casino delayed the start by more than two hours. A second crisis was narrowly averted when the tournament chips were doled out—there were enough for 513 players, just one more than was needed. The upside to all the confusion was that, for the first time in a decade, the world champion would be getting a raise—a very generous raise—to $1.5 million.

On hand to cover the madness was Jim McManus, a forty-nine-year-old novelist and poet from Chicago hired by *Harper's Magazine* to pen an article about the growing strides that female players had been making in the tournament. Jerri Thomas and Jennifer Harman had already won preliminary events not restricted to their gender, and many more women had signed up for the main event.

Along the way, however, Jim's plans took an unexpected twist, as he became part of his own story. He had recently spent a good deal of time, under the guise of "research," honing his game using Bob Wilson's Turbo Texas Hold'em software. Having played poker his entire life, there was no way this poker lover was going to sit this one out, not when he was this close. Using the cash advance from the magazine as a bankroll, Jim entered several satellites and won a seat in the championship. After a rocky start, dropping to $2,000 on the first day, he rallied back to a little more than $30,000 and survived into the second.

This year, because of the increased number of entrants, everyone seated at one of the last five tables—the final forty-five players— would take home at least $15,000. With fifty players remaining, Jim McManus sat squarely on the bubble. He had only $38,000 in chips, whereas the average stack size was over $100,000. He thought he caught a break when one of the most aggressive players at his table— Daniel Negreanu, a rising poker star from Toronto, Canada—got knocked out with pocket aces against a set of 9s, until Daniel's replacement arrived: T. J. Cloutier.

Like Kevin McBride, and any hopeful who had heard his story, Jim McManus had read T. J.'s book. Now he was living it. After T. J. opened with a $5,000 raise from middle position, Jim, peeking at his hole cards to find A-J, called from the cutoff seat. The flop came A-9-6, and, after T. J. checked, Jim bet $20,000. T. J. didn't waste much time in executing an all-in check-raise.

So close to the prize money, and with such a vulnerable hand— T. J. was certainly representing a set, two pair, or at least an ace with a bigger kicker—the prudent play would have been for Jim to fold his hand and wait for a few other unlucky players to bust themselves out of the tournament. Jim realized, however, that in T. J.'s eyes, *he* was exactly the kind of guy that you'd try to steamroll over on the bubble. He called.

It was a bold and fortuitous decision. T. J. was forced to flip over A-10. They wound up splitting the pot when another 9 and another ace gave full houses to both men, but Jim earned something far greater than chips: the confidence that he could play with the best in the world. Recalling chapter 3 of T. J.'s book—"when everyone is trying to survive to get into the money, you can pick up a mountain of chips"—he began to play with newfound aggression. In the time it took to go from forty-six players to what Andy Glazer dubbed "The Fabulous 45," Jim built his stack from $36,100 to $276,000, propelling him from near oblivion into third place.

. . .

Not only had the author become the star of his own narrative, but one of his initial premises seemed on its way to becoming a reality. At the top of the leader board, with $283,500, stood thirty-two-year-old Kathy Liebert.

Kathy grew up on Long Island, then worked in investments at Dunn and Bradstreet long enough to realize that she wasn't cut out for the nine-to-five grind. She moved to San Diego, where she planned to start law school, until a vacation to Las Vegas introduced her to the $4/$8 hold'em game at the Dunes. Floated by a series of shrewd investments in the late '90s, Kathy set about becoming a professional. She made her first pilgrimage to the World Series in 1997, where she finished second in the $3,000 No-Limit Hold'em tournament. The following year she'd make the money in the championship event, placing seventeenth. This year she seemed intent on changing all of the stereotypes that had been inflicted upon female players.

"Many men seem to play women as though they were open books," Kathy said. She put herself in a man's shoes, perceiving herself as he might see her and adjusting accordingly. The primary modification she made was in the area of aggression.

"Her friendly, if not quite angelic, features don't keep her from maneuvering her $300,000 stack like some cute Vegas Rommel, blitzkrieging antes and blinds, setting us all in if we even *think* about drawing against her," later wrote Jim McManus, who was seated at the same table as Liebert for most of the second day.

Kathy wasn't the only woman to have crashed the party. Annie Duke had outgrown her status as the little sister of Howard Lederer, whose career continued to shoot skyward after his stunning debut in the 1987 World Series. Remarkably, in the seven years she'd been attending the World Series, Annie had finished in the money in twelve different events, five more than her brother had during the same span. Now she was in eighth place, with $187,000 in chips. Even more impressive, she was eight months pregnant at the time.

Amarillo Slim, reminded that he once threatened to cut his own throat if a woman won the championship event, posed for a photo with Kathy and Annie while holding a knife to his neck. He then returned to the gallery to watch with the rest of the spectators as the two women continued to carve their way through the field.

Ironically, Kathy Liebert's bid to become queen among kings got derailed during the marathon third day by kings and queens. First, she lost half her stack with pocket queens against K-10 when her opponent paired his king. A few hands later, she was dealt K-10 and moved all in. She was called by Mike Sexton, who held two queens. This time the queens would hold up, and just like that Kathy was eliminated from the tournament in seventeenth place.

Jim McManus, meanwhile, continued to find ways to tangle with T. J. Cloutier. With fourteen players left and just under $300,000 in checks, Jim was dealt A-K and opened with a $50,000 raise. T. J. reraised him $100,000 more from late position. Believing that the pro was again trying to intimidate the amateur, Jim called. The flop came 2♣5♥4♦. Jim checked, providing T. J. with the opportunity to fire another massive bet, this time $200,000, into the middle. Whether stubborn idiocy, inspired genius, or both, Jim called.

The turn card was the 7♦. Jim once again checked. This time, T. J. moved all in. He had Jim outchipped by around $150,000, forcing the author to make a decision for his tournament life. He thought T. J. was trying to buy the pot with an intimidating bet, and, after about twenty gut-wrenching seconds, he found the courage to trust his gut.

"I call."

The gallery buzzed with excitement, overwhelming whatever T. J. muttered as he turned over A-9.

"Jack of clubs on the river!" Bob Thompson exclaimed into his microphone as the final card hit the board. "Jim McManus wins $866,000 and becomes the new chip leader!"

"Ah'd bet on that boy," said an impressed Amarillo Slim. "He's got the heart of a cliff divah."

"T. J. taught me everything I know about this game," Jim said. "Read his book and you'll see."

Years later, T. J. would admit that Jim had made a great call. "I fired three barrels at him and he called me with no pair all three times. And he was right."

In the heat of the moment, however, the legendary pro was feeling far less magnanimous. He crushed the Salem he'd been smoking, stared at his opponent, and growled, "I didn't teach you *that*, boy."

. . .

The player generating the most buzz entering the final table had long, beautiful hair, but—to the dismay of all the vocal supporters of Howard Lederer's sister who crowded the rail—it wasn't Annie Duke.

Aside from his flowing locks, Chris Ferguson sports a full beard, creating an uncanny resemblance to a certain Son of God and earning him the nickname "Jesus." In 2000, the rail-thin thirty-seven-year-old also wore a black cowboy hat and mirrored glasses, which made him look more like a rock star than a professional poker player. But a professional he is. Crediting his father, a professor in game theory at UCLA, with teaching him the fundamentals of probability, he has thrived at the game.

"I'm really more of a poker theoretician than a player," he claims, despite having clearly proven himself as both. This championship table was the fourth he'd made during the 2000 World Series. He had already won the $2,500 Seven-Card Stud event.

With ten players left Annie moved all in with A♠9♠, but she ran into Jesus' pocket aces and got bounced from the tournament. Her tenth-place finish in the championship event was the best for a female player since Barbara Enright in 1995, and the $52,160 prize would make her the highest-earning woman in World Series history, an honor she has, as of today, yet to relinquish.

With nine players left, Jesus had about $800,000, good for third behind Jim McManus and new chip leader Jeff Shulman, the twenty-three-year-old son of *Card Player* magazine owner Barry Shulman. Only six would make the next day's televised table, leaving three more players to be eliminated before the day could end. After tournament veterans Mickey Appleman and "Captain" Tom Franklin exited with little fanfare, Jesus and Jeff tangled in several thunderous hands.

The first arose after Jeff raised $200,000 from the button. Suspecting a steal, Jesus moved all in from the big blind with pocket 6s. Jeff shrugged and called, flipping over pocket 7s, a huge favorite to win until a third 6 appeared on the flop. Despite picking up a straight and a flush draw to add to Jeff's outs, Jesus' set held up.

"Jesus makes 6-6-6," joked Jim McManus.

A few hands later, Jesus opened with a $90,000 raise. T. J. Cloutier reraised $290,000 before Jeff pushed all in with pocket kings. Jesus then put in a fourth raise, pushing all of his chips into the center.

"I'm going to get out of their way," T. J. muttered, knowing that as good as his hand was, it wasn't good enough. "All *I* had were jacks."

It turned out to be a fortunate decision for T. J., as Jesus turned over pocket aces. This time the best hand would win. Duplicating the dubious accomplishment Kathy Liebert achieved earlier, Jeff Shulman went from chip leader to the exits in only two hands.

Chris Ferguson's run gave him $2,853,000 to use in battle on the final day; his closest competitor Jim McManus only had $554,000. T. J. Cloutier was the short stack with $216,000, but unlike the others he had plenty of experience—this was his fourth visit to the championship table—and a plan.

"I'll let them knock each other out and try to get heads-up with Chris," he said. "They were all fine players, but none of them were experienced in final table play except Chris. That's why I thought they would make major errors in crucial spots—and, as it came up, that's exactly what happened. They dropped like flies."

More accurately, flies sprayed with a major dose of insecticide. Roman Abinsay made the first big move of the day, going all in with A-Q. Enjoying the luxury of being able to gamble, Jesus called with pocket 8s. When the 8s held up, Roman was out in sixth place.

Jim McManus was next to go. When Hasan Habib moved all in with A♥4♥, Jim called with A♣Q♣. Hasan was in terrible shape, until he caught a 4 on the river to win the hand. It was huge blow for Jim, knocking him down to $100,000, leading him to move all in with A-2 from under the gun. Steve Kaufman called with A-Q, and when the board didn't help him Jim's storybook run was over. Andy Glazer asked him if he felt like a rock star.

"Nah," said the man who would go on to chronicle his experience in the best-seller *Positively Fifth Street*. "If I'd made A-Q stand up, I'd be in there now and I'd be a rock star. As it is, I feel like a backup band."

Hasan Habib and Steve Kaufman soon joined him on the rail, falling to Jesus' A-K and pocket 10s respectively. Hardly an hour had passed since the first hand of the day was dealt, and they were already down to two players. T. J. Cloutier's plan had worked to perfection, although he was facing a nine-to-one chip deficit.

At the start of heads-up play, Bob Thompson announced that, given the blinds and antes, it would cost each player $51,000 to see two hands.

"Sounds like I got about nine hands left," T. J. said, grinning.

Becky Binion-Behnen reminded a reporter of the story of Treetop Straus's amazing comeback in 1982. "Expect the unexpected," she said. "Some things are just meant to be."

Six hands in, T. J. managed to double up with three 10s against Jesus' two pair. Twenty hands later, T. J. had built his stack to $1.4 million and was in position to double up again when he got all in with A-K against Jesus' A-7. The board came 2-5-2-J-J, resulting in a split pot. No worries. Just a few hands later, T. J.'s three kings against Ferguson's two pair would give him a million-dollar pot, nudging him into the lead, $2.6 million to $2.5 million.

"I was feeling good," he said. "I knew I was in control of the game."

T. J.'s mastery of Chris continued when the two got all in again, T.J.'s A♥7♥ against Ferguson's A♠2♠. However, the 3-10-Q-K-10 board resulted in yet another chopped pot, providing Jesus with some much needed salvation.

The chip lead swung back and forth, but T. J. could tell Chris was faltering. "As I started chipping away at him his hands were shaking so bad he brought his cards behind his chips to look at them so I couldn't see [them]. He was nervous. I could see that he was getting worried, and I thought there might be a chance that he was going to miscalculate the value of a hand—and he did."

Jesus had edged into a small lead, $2.8 to $2.3 million, when T. J. opened for $175,000. Finding A♠9♣, Jesus raised $600,000. T. J. quickly moved all in.

Chris removed his hat and sunglasses as he debated what to do for more than five minutes. Several times he lifted his cards as if to muck them. Finally, however, he called, a decision that has been heavily debated in the years since.

"The way he explained it made sense to me," said T. J. "He said afterwards he realized he couldn't beat me heads-up. He had to gamble on a hand."

"I thought there was a very small chance that I had the best hand," Chris said. "And if I had the best hand I was giving up a lot more by folding."

Whatever hopes Jesus had of seeing an inferior hand ended when T. J. revealed A♦Q♣.

The flop came 2♥K♣4♥. The K♥ fell on the turn.

"Not again," said Mike Paulle, alluding to the possibility of a third chopped pot.

"The funny part about it was I felt the nine coming," T. J. said. "In fact I even knew what suit it was going to be. It was as though I was looking right through the deck. I said, 'Don't let it be the nine of hearts,' and *bingo,* there it was."

When the 9♥ appeared on the river, Chris jumped out of his chair.

"Way to go, Jesus!" someone yelled from the gallery.

His eyes filling with tears, the new world champion embraced T. J. in an emotional hug. "Are we still friends?" he asked.

"Of course," replied T. J., as always treating difficult defeats in the same relaxed manner he does lopsided victories. "Don't feel bad. You played great." They broke their embrace. "You didn't think it would be that tough to beat me, did you?"

"Yes I did," Jesus replied.

It was the closest T. J. has ever come to winning the title and his most painful defeat. It was a loss, however, that only further demonstrated his greatness. He shook off numerous bad beats late in the tournament, arrived at the final table desperately low on chips, managed to claw his way back into contention, and got all his money in with the best hand. Those in need of more tangible evidence can point to the fact that the $900,000 he won for coming in second made him the all-time leading money winner in the history of the World Series of Poker.

"I want two things," T. J. had announced as the prize money was being dumped onto the table, "[a place in the Poker] Hall of Fame and this tournament."

While he may never luck into the elusive title, his status as one of the greatest poker players to ever play the game is assured.

· · ·

As the most successful World Series in history came to a close, Becky Binion-Behnen was rewarded with further good news. On May 19, 2000, the jury in Ted Binion's murder case returned from sixty-nine hours of deliberation with two guilty verdicts. Sandy Murphy and Rick Tabish were sentenced to twenty years' to life imprisonment.

The verdict had the unintended effect of putting the feuding Binions in the same room.

Jack remained stoic as he exited the courtroom. "There's really nothing to say. I don't have anything to say."

Becky, however, wept openly. As she left the courtroom, some fifty onlookers applauded her for her efforts to bring her brother's accused killers to justice. Outside, she was quick to congratulate the prosecutors for the work they had done.

"I feel fine with the sentence," she said. "I think these people gave their all. Nothing will bring Ted back. Inflicting more pain on their families doesn't make me feel better. So I'm satisfied with the sentence. Twenty years is a long time."

Having done her part to bring this chapter to its apparent end, Becky returned to the Horseshoe.

15

FIVE DAYS IS A LONG TIME

Before the 2001 World Series could even begin, it was already embroiled in controversy.

Most poker tournaments require players to pay two separate fees: a buy-in—the money that goes to the prize pool—and the entry fee—the money that the casino uses to pay its employees and other hosting costs. For example, entering the $5,000 Limit Hold'em event actually required $5,100, the extra Franklin getting skimmed by the house. The notable exception at the World Series was the $10,000 championship event, which had always been treated as a loss leader. Whatever it cost to host the event was more than covered by the entry fees from the smaller tournaments, the rake from the side games, the traffic that it generated for other areas of the casino, and the intangibles associated with the prestige of hosting the world's biggest game. The rise of satellites and supersatellites—which also charge entry fees—had become yet another source of profit.

Just before the 2001 World Series was about to begin, Becky announced that the Horseshoe planned to withhold 3 percent of the prize pool from *all* of the tournaments, including the main event. The money—over a half-million dollars, thanks to the $18 million-plus set to change hands over the course of the month—would ostensibly be used to supplement the pay of long-suffering dealers and floor managers, whose relatively meager salaries forced them to rely on the ever-volatile "toke pool," the tips collected from the winners, to get by. It seemed fair, and no one raised much of a fuss, until the list of "tournament personnel" slated to share in the extra pay was made public. Among the dealers and floor managers were cashiers, payroll clerks, and computer operators. Some poker players bristled at the change.

"When people hear that three percent of the prize pool has been withheld, they expect it to go to the dealers and tournament floor personnel," said professional player Paul Phillips, one of the most vocal critics of the change in policy. "If Binion's wants to supplement the salaries of its employees, they should raise the entry fees, rather than subtract from the prize pool."

Becky thought that Phillips's criticism, printed in a local newspaper, was misguided. "I'm not taking a penny of the money, and my family's not taking a penny. It's going to the employees who have to deal with the incredible month-long tournament." His comments stung enough for Becky to have Phillips 86ed from the Horseshoe. He was forcibly ejected by security guards from a late-night game in the cardroom and barred from returning. That included the World Series of Poker.

"The Horseshoe is playing with fire," observed Anthony Curtis, publisher of the *Las Vegas Advisor.* "There are rumblings that players are upset, and there are a number of casinos around the country that might think of hosting a competing world championship."

For now, however, the fire belonged to the Horseshoe, and it showed no signs of flickering out. Two new tournaments were added to the lineup, an event for seniors and a new hybrid called "S.H.O.E." that tested a player's all-around skills at alternating hands of seven-card stud, hold'em, Omaha hi-lo, and seven-card stud hi-lo.* Paul Phillips,

---

*The "E" in S.H.O.E. comes from the "eight or better" caveat to the stud hi-lo game—for a hand to qualify as a "low," none of the player's cards can be higher than 8.

having apparently made amends with Becky in time to enter, finished tenth.

But, as always, the most excitement was reserved for the championship event. The Horseshoe had been running satellites since January, and this year's championship promised to be the biggest ever. ESPN, which had temporarily abandoned its coverage of the Series during the last couple of years—only to see the rival Discovery Channel step in and achieve record ratings—would once again broadcast the finals.

Sure enough, 613 players arrived for the event. New computer software, Tex Morgan's Tournament Evaluation And Rating System, or TEARS, was introduced to better streamline the blind and ante structure. A good measure of a poker tournament is how many chips each player receives in relation to the speed of the rounds. Having enough chips to work with allows the players to better use their skill as opposed to having to push all in every other hand. Even with the help of this technology, the tournament would still last a record five days.

A lot can happen in five days. Both Annie Duke—pocket jacks—and T. J. Cloutier—pocket kings—were busted out early by Diego Cordovez, who was dealt pocket aces two times in three hands. Erik Seidel couldn't get his chip stack over $18,000 and joined Huck Seed and returning champ Chris Ferguson as first-day casualties. By the end of the second day, only Phil Hellmuth, Jr. and Jim Bechtel had any hope of becoming two-time champions. The third day saw Paul Phillips, the lightning rod for controversy, become a lightning rod for pocket aces. Unfortunately, he lost both times he was dealt them, both times to an inferior pocket pair when his opponent made a set, and exited the tournament to a round of applause. Day turned to night turned to morning until, closing in on one o'clock, the very same Diego Cordovez was eliminated forty-sixth, making him the last player plucked off the bubble.

The fourth day looked like it would belong to Daniel Negreanu, the energetic young professional from Canada who was terrorizing his opponents with a combination of brilliant play and timely courage. In one instance he bet $70,000—about a third of his chips—after three opponents joined him to see a 7-8-9 flop with two hearts. After they all folded, one asked to see his hand. Daniel reluctantly obliged, showing them a 5 and a 3, both spades, a phenomenal bluff. Fate's pendulum, however, swings both ways. It was a real hand, A-K, that contributed to his demise when he lost a $900,000 pot to nattily attired German businessman Henry Nowakowski's pocket 6s. Daniel would never recover, eventually finishing eleventh.

At a nearby table, two of the biggest personalities in poker were going at it—Phil Hellmuth, Jr. and poker-dealer-turned-pro Mike "the Mouth" Matusow. Friends apart from the game, they bickered incessantly while playing it. Phil couldn't resist any opportunity to talk about how good he was, and Mike refused to miss a chance to talk about how good he thought Phil was, only it came out as a staccato monologue with an East Coast twang drenched in sarcasm.

"You're the greatest, Phil, you're the best, Phil, no one can play like you, Phil."

A third party entered the fray when an even taller Phil—six-foot-nine professional Phil Gordon had three inches on the already giant Hellmuth—sat down to the table and declared, "I'm *en fuego*." The trio soon got mixed up in a hand that could easily have crushed two of them, but wound up demonstrating why all three had what it took to make the final table.

After Matusow opened with a $20,000 raise, Gordon reraised him $100,000. Hellmuth then moved all in for $408,500 more. For Hellmuth, a player who doesn't like to risk his chips unless he's quite sure he's got the best of it, to come over the top of a raiser meant only one thing: he had pocket aces. Matusow had pocket queens, which he flashed to the crowd as he threw them in the muck. Gordon, after careful consideration, threw his hand away as well, prompting Hellmuth to show the world his aces. This was old news to Gordon, who had made a remarkable laydown.

"I had two kings," he said, retrieving his cards from the muck and turning them over for Hellmuth to see.

"Wow," said Mike, speaking for everyone who witnessed the hand, "two queens, two kings, and two aces on the same hand!" What he neglected to point out, but was obvious to those who know the game, was just how much skill and discipline he and Gordon had demonstrated in throwing their hands away.

· · ·

The fifth day finally arrived with nine players still alive, and for the first time in the tournament's history all nine would get to be on television. Whether consciously or otherwise, they decided to make the most of their time in front of the camera. In 2000, four of the six finalists were eliminated in the first forty-five minutes. At the 2001 championship table, it took well over an hour and nearly sixty hands before the first player, John Inashima, was caught bluffing with a 10♥5♥ by twenty-nine-year-old Carlos Mortensen of Madrid, Spain, and his ace-*nueve*. A second *nueve* on the river produced the first casualty of the day. This year's Cinderella story, electrician-turned-supersatellite-winner Mike Riehle, followed shortly thereafter.

The two Phils, Hellmuth and Gordon, brought the same vibrant energy they had displayed the previous day. Hellmuth was playing some of the best poker of his life, having already cashed six times in the preliminary events that year. Throughout the championship event, he employed his preferred style of play, chipping away at his opponents for small pots, keeping himself out of situations where he might lose big ones. On his way to the final table he'd been forced to jeopardize his entire stack only once.

What Gordon lacked in experience he made up for with a combination of brains and the confidence of a man who didn't have to quit his day job. He had no day job to quit. After graduating from Georgia Tech, where he studied artificial intelligence, he moved to Northern California to work in the tech industry. A life-changing trip to a local card room nearly derailed his career—having fallen in love with poker, he mustered a $10,000 bankroll and marched into his boss's office, declaring his intention to quit his job and turn pro. The boss convinced Gordon to hang around a little while longer, as a few big changes were afoot. The biggest turned out to be the sale of their startup company to Cisco for $95 million. An instant multimillionaire, Gordon traveled around the world and, upon his return, began life as a professional poker player.

Gordon is a big believer in profiling his opponents, developing specific strategies to combat each player's tendencies before the first hand has even been dealt. Having observed Hellmuth's unwillingness to risk all of his chips, Gordon concocted an effective means of attack, unveiled when Hellmuth opened a pot with a $45,000 raise. Gordon moved all in from his blind. Hellmuth, still hesitant to risk all of his chips, mucked his hand. A cheeky Gordon showed him the cards he had come over the top with: a Q-2 offsuit. It was the beginning of a long day for the two tall Phils, who would battle like hoops players fighting for position in the paint.

"Phil Gordon was acting like there was a bounty on my head," Hellmuth said later, "and I knew that he couldn't help himself. He would continue to risk his whole stack against me time and again with weak cards."

Not one to be left out, Mike Matusow continued to play with emotion and bravado. After winning an $860,000 pot from Gordon with a full house, he turned to his friends in the gallery and yelled:

"I'm going to win this tournament!"

He suspected the road would go through Carlos Mortensen, the imaginative young Spanish star, a professional for the last four years. Carlos had entered only two major tournaments that year—the L.A. Poker Classic and Bay 101's Shooting Stars—and won them both. Like Hellmuth, he sought to increase his stack slowly by winning small pot after small pot with timely raises. Unlike Hellmuth, he was succeeding, as no one was pushing back.

Matusow sought to change that, and thought he had found his opportunity when, after Henry Nowakowski limped in from early position, Carlos raised to $80,000. Mike came over the top with a $300,000 reraise. He had forgotten about Henry, however, who pushed all of his chips into the middle. While Carlos was able to escape relatively unscathed, the pot odds demanded that Mike call the bet—it would only cost him another $65,000—with whatever two cards he happened to be holding. He happened to be holding the worst hand in hold'em, 7-2 offsuit. Henry turned over pocket kings, they held up, and Mike had lost more than half his stack. The loss did little to quiet the Mouth.

"I knew you had nothing, Carlos," he said. "We're here to play poker, boys. Back to work. Now you guys are never going to know what I have when I move in. All I have to do is get a few chips back, and we can have a little party."

The chip leader at the start of the day, Henry Nowakowski would suffer a rapid decline. After Phil Gordon opened for $65,000 with 9♠7♠, Henry's reraise to $140,000 with A♠K♥ wasn't enough to make Phil throw his hand away. Gordon was glad he didn't when 9♣5♥7♦

appeared on the board. After checking the flop, he let Henry bluff $100,000 at the pot, then came over the top of him with all of his chips. Henry called, but didn't improve his hand, and Gordon won what was almost a million-dollar pot.

Just two hands later Henry opened for $90,000, Hellmuth moved all in, and Henry called with his last $210,000.

"Just jacks, Henry," said Hellmuth, showing his hand.

Henry was in worse shape, holding "just sevens."

Shortly after Henry's exit, the ongoing battle between the two Phils resumed. Hellmuth opened with a $70,000 raise, and Gordon, as had become his habit, reraised all in.

"I called his $450,000 raise so quickly that I freaked out everyone at the table," Hellmuth later said. "I just knew that he was going to move all in with a weak hand, and I was ready for him."

Hellmuth had read his man correctly. Gordon only had a pair of 6s, a huge underdog to Hellmuth's two 9s, the same hand that had won him the 1989 championship. If the 9s held up, Gordon would be eliminated and Hellmuth would be in great shape to win his second title.

That's not how it worked out. A 6 on the flop gave Gordon a set and a $1.2-million pot, while knocking Hellmuth back to near oblivion.

"I was a five-to-one underdog to a world champion and I got lucky," Gordon said to him, not unsympathetically. It seemed logical to expect a tantrum out of Hellmuth—he was, after all, the Poker Brat—but he just sat there, perfectly still, speechless, and numb. He would later call it "the worst beat of my life," but refrained from exploding.

"I couldn't afford to bring any negative energy to that moment in time," he explained afterwards. Inside, however, he stewed.

Gordon had frustrations of his own, namely Carlos Mortensen, whose stacks of chips now rose from the table like a mountain range. Seated directly to Phil's left, Carlos seemed to perk up with a raise whenever Gordon tried to make a play.

"Anyone want a seat change?" joked Gordon.

Finally snapping out of his pained stupor, Hellmuth barked, "Oh, you're not happy with that seat where you sucked out for a million-two?"

. . .

While the others were sniping at each other, Carlos Mortensen, looking relaxed in a blue T-shirt and ratty fisherman's cap, had plowed his way into the chip lead with nearly $2 million. Big stacks allow bold play, and the Spaniard was dominating the action at the table. When Mike Matusow opened for $60,000, Carlos raised him $150,000 from the big blind with Q-8 offsuit. Mike, who had A-Q, correctly decided that Mortensen was making a move with a weaker hand, and he reraised another $350,000. Carlos moved all in, leaving Mike to make the difficult decision. Having already invested $560,000 of his chips into this pot, Mike wanted to call, but the authority with which Carlos had come over the top convinced him that he had to throw his hand away. As soon as he did Carlos showed him his inferior hand, prompting Mike to suffer what appeared to be an epileptic fit. The crowd roared its appreciation as Carlos stood and pumped his arms in triumph.

"The seven-deuce hand was in my mind," Carlos said later, referring to the play Mike had earlier attempted to make against him. "I knew he was capable of making a big raise based on position, instead of a strong hand, and I had enough chips to play at him."

Mike never recovered. Twenty minutes later Dewey Tomko—the same Dewey Tomko who finished second to Jack Straus in 1982—opened for $70,000, and Mike moved in on him. Dewey called and turned over pocket kings, which had Mike's 10s beat from start to finish. Losing $413,000 on the hand, Mike was left with only $240,000, which he shoved into the pot two hands later with pocket 8s. Hellmuth called from the small blind with pocket kings, and Mike was out in sixth place.

"You can be the best player in the world and never get here," said Mike with tears in his eyes. "I wanted this so bad. It's not about the money. I can play great poker for the next twenty years, and I still might never get back to the final table of this tournament. It's that hard to get here."

Matusow has yet to return to the final table of the championship event.

Five players remained. When a final table gets shorthanded, most pots lead to showdowns between two players. Occasionally three players will get involved. Four-way pots, like the one that came on the 149th hand of the day, are highly unusual.

Hellmuth and Gordon limped in, Mortensen and Stan Schrier, a middle-limit player who had moved to Las Vegas from Omaha, Nebraska, completed their blinds. The flop came Q♠9♦4♠, and after Carlos and Stan checked, Hellmuth bet $60,000. As quickly as Gordon folded, Carlos completed a check-raise, pushing another $200,000 into the pot.

Stan Schrier leaned back in his chair, appearing utterly absorbed, as the others waited for him to act. A minute passed. Then another. His cards sat in front of him, partially obscured by the lucky stone frog he used as a "card capper" to prevent his cards from ever getting inadvertently pushed into the muck by the dealer. It suddenly dawned on Stan that everyone was waiting for him to act. He snapped out of his daze and folded his hand, embarrassed and apologetic. Five days is a long time.

Meanwhile, Hellmuth was using the time to his advantage, calculating how to play the Q-10 he was holding. "While I was waiting for Stan to act, I spent all of my time studying Carlos, because I already knew that if Stan put a chip into this pot, I was going to fold my hand. Carlos looked very nervous to me, as we both thought that Stan was contemplating his next move. Suddenly, I began to think two things at once. First, I thought that Carlos had Q-J, which had me beat, but it would be hard for him to call my six hundred fifty thousand dollar reraise with Q-J, if I indeed raised all of my chips. My second thought was one that I don't ever remember having before in my life. I thought, 'Is it time to go home?' I have been waiting twelve years for the chance to win the World Series of Poker again. I have visualized it and seen it happen many times in my mind over the years. I thought to myself, 'I'm not going anywhere. I think I probably have Carlos beat, but even if he does have Q-J, he will fold it for a six hundred fifty thousand dollar raise right now.'"

"I'm all in," Hellmuth announced.

"Count," Carlos replied in his thick Spanish accent.

Hearing him wrong, the dealer said, "Call."

Phil flipped his cards faceup.

"Wait a minute," Carlos said. "I didn't say, 'Call.' I said, 'Count!'"

Phil quickly covered his cards with his hands, unsure if Carlos had seen them or not.

He hadn't. But Carlos, who was indeed holding Q-J, didn't need to.

"I thought he might have Q-10," he later said. "I didn't think he would limp in with K-Q or A-Q."

Carlos called and they turned over their cards. The jack that hit the turn gave Carlos two pair, but it also gave Hellmuth an open-ended straight draw. Needing an 8 or a king, Phil was eliminated when the A♠ fell on the river.

Brushing past his wife and parents who were sitting in the bleachers, Phil bolted from the room. He did not return.

Most players say the title means more to them than the money, but do they really mean it? In 2001 the enormous prize pool would award the second-place finisher nearly $1.1 million, only $400,000 less than the champion. After Carlos (pocket queens) dispatched Gordon (A-6) and Tomko (pocket kings) eliminated Schrier (Q-10), it was time to find out how much the title meant to the last two men standing.

With $4 million in chips, twice as many as Dewey, Carlos resumed his offensive, raising nearly every pot, usually to $100,000, whether he had the cards or not. The ex-kindergarten teacher—now, at fifty-four, a seasoned poker veteran—fired back with big raises of his own just often enough to stay within striking distance. To catch up, however, he knew he would have to win a big hand. On the fiftieth hand of heads-up play, Dewey found his spot.

Dealt pocket aces in the small blind, Dewey merely completed the bet, trying to lure in his opponent. Carlos took the bait, raising $100,000, a bet Dewey once again merely called. When the flop came 3♣10♣J♦, Carlos continued his assault, betting his usual $100,000. Finally revealing his strength, Dewey popped him another $400,000.

By limping in before the flop, Dewey was hoping Carlos would catch just enough of the flop to get him interested in the hand. The problem was that the flop hit Carlos a little harder than Dewey might have hoped. Holding K♣Q♣, Carlos had four cards to a flush and an open-ended straight draw. Even against pocket aces, he had a fifty-fifty chance of winning the hand. Like a bullfighter gesturing that it was time for the kill, Carlos indicated he was moving all in.

Dewey quickly called him. The crowd pushed closer to the table. The players rose to their feet. Carlos's wife, Cecilia Reyes, leaned over her husband's vacant chair. The 3♦ on the turn made Tomko a three-to-one favorite to win the hand, but the 9♦ on the river completed Carlos's straight.

Mortensen pounded his fists on the table in triumph. He then grabbed several bundles of the $1.5 million in cash he had just won, held them above his head, and cried, *"¡Viva España!"*

Friends, old and new, swooped in to congratulate him. His ecstatic wife kissed him just as he deserved to be kissed, long and hard. His ratty fisherman's hat was lost somewhere in the madness.

For the second year in row, a red 9 on the river had decided the championship and had slapped the loser with a dubious honor. Dewey Tomko joined T. J. Cloutier as the only other player to finish second in the championship event twice in his career. Also like T. J, he exhibited nothing but grace in defeat.

"He's a gentleman, and he played well all day," said Dewey of the new world champion. "A lot of the other players were talking a lot, and I'm not sure how they can do that and concentrate on the game at the same time, but this young man stayed out of that and stayed focused, and he earned his win."

While the tournament was soaring to new heights, the behind-the-scenes saga at the Horseshoe continued to search for a bottom. It began with the lingering issue of the prize money that had been withheld, nearly $550,000. The tournament's floor managers—the men and women who actually run the World Series, shifting players, monitoring dealers, resolving any disputes—expected to split about $178,000. They received less than one-sixth of that amount. When Horseshoe poker room manager Cathi Wood complained about the situation to Becky, she was summarily fired. Twelve angry managers filed a lawsuit against the Horseshoe. The Nevada Gaming Control Board began a probe into the dispute.

Hoping that a new face might alleviate some of the growing anger, Becky hired 1983 champion Tom McEvoy to take over as the manager of the poker room. "I want to bring the big games back to Binion's," Tom declared. "The high-stakes players will play for free. You can't beat that."

Fifty-three days later, he too was dismissed. "The owners never gave me an explanation for why I was fired," he told the press, "and I never asked for one."

Nor could the Horseshoe shake what had become persistent rumors of impending financial doom. An early January report in the *Las Vegas Tribune* claimed that the casino owed more than a million dollars in back rent to its landlords. Becky insisted that the allegations were untrue, that the casino was operating at a profit. There was no denying, however, that the Horseshoe had failed to pay its dues to the Fremont Street Experience. When it became apparent that Becky had no intention of coughing up the nearly $1.9 million in arrears, the governing body of the Experience filed a lawsuit of its own, ultimately winning a judgment for the full amount from the Nevada State Supreme Court.

While the Horseshoe suffered from its missteps, it looked as if the World Series might be victimized by its own success. Its popularity inspired competition. In early 2002, one of the most prestigious casinos on the swankier Las Vegas Strip, the Bellagio, announced the arrival of the Five Diamond Classic, a series of World Series-style tournaments leading up to a $10,000 buy-in championship. The Party Poker Million, a tournament held in March 2002 aboard a cruise ship—a far cry from the Horseshoe's makeshift card room—whose participants won entry via a series of online satellites, became the first such event other than the World Series to hand out a million-dollar first prize, generating even more publicity when that prize went to Kathy Liebert, the first woman to ever win a seven-digit payday. Later that year, Steven Lipscomb, the director of the Discovery Channel's coverage of the 1999 championship event, announced the formation of the "World Poker Tour," a yearlong series of nationally-televised tournaments culminating in a $25,000 buy-in championship event.

And just before the World Series was set to kick off, Becky received yet one more piece of bad news. One of Sandy Murphy's lawyers, citing new information obtained from a recently released FBI probe into the Binion family, petitioned the Las Vegas District Attorney to reopen Ted Binion's murder investigation.

. . .

Tournament poker was becoming so big that a "Tournament Directors Association" had been formed to help standardize the rules. Becky hired one of its founders, thirty-three-year-old Matt Savage, along with Hustler Casino card-room manager Jim Miller, to run the 2002 World Series of Poker. Deciding that bigger was better, the lineup of events was expanded from twenty-seven to thirty-five. The separate entry fee was eliminated from all the tournaments in favor of a 6 percent withholding from the overall prize pool. And despite a few last-minute bumps in the road—twelve dealers were fired for demanding an increase in pay—the $10,000 championship managed to attract a record 631 players, including Chip Reese who had skipped the event the last several years out of respect for his good friend Jack Binion. Another Jack loyalist, Doyle Brunson, also planned to attend, but had to withdraw from the contest at the last minute for health reasons. Becky, hoping to restore some of the tournament's legacy, had reached out to them both.

The hottest player entering the event was a rising poker star named Phil Ivey. The twenty-five-year-old Atlantic City native was being hailed as "the Tiger Woods of Poker" due to a combination of his youth, African-American heritage, and dominating play. He finished in the money in five out of the six World Series events he entered that year, and, amazingly, he went on to win three of them.

Ivey managed to survive the bloodbath that was the first day—the 283 early departures included returning champions Mortensen, Furlong, Seed, Matloubi, Bechtel, Hamilton, Preston, and Daugherty, as well as notables T. J. Cloutier, Kathy Liebert and Mike Matusow. Johnny Chan would exit on the second day, leaving Phil Hellmuth, Jr. as the only former champion still in the hunt.

With 60 of the 613 players who entered the 2002 tournament remaining, Robert Varkonyi, an amateur from Brooklyn, New York, arrived at Hellmuth's table. After winning his seat in a one-table satellite, Robert had managed to stay alive in the tournament, thanks largely to a single hand. At the very end of the second day of play Robert, holding A-K, tripled his stack by knocking out two players at the very same time, both of whom had pocket queens.

Varkonyi's demeanor is, in a word, unimposing—he's short and bald and a bit of a nebbish—but *no one* flies too low for Hellmuth's radar. "Immediately, I had a good read on him," Phil said, "and I knew whether he was weak or strong."

After Robert opened for an $8,000 raise, Hellmuth reraised to $25,000 from the small blind. Robert immediately pushed his remaining $84,500 all in, leading Phil to leap out of his chair. "They keep coming over the top of me!" he wailed.

The "they" he was referring to was mostly an aggressive player named Meng La, who had been raising Phil all day long, forcing him to muck many of his hands. This time, however, he held a strong hand, A♥K♥, and had Varkonyi slightly outchipped. Phil asked Robert to count his chips, then interrupted him before he could finish, having discovered the information he was looking for: Robert was weak.

"Never mind, I call."

Phil, as usual, had made a good read—all Robert Varkonyi could show was Q♣10♣. The flop even paired Phil's ace. Unfortunately, the other two cards were a queen and a 10, giving Robert two pair. Neither the turn nor the river helped Phil.

"Sometimes," announced Varkonyi, paraphrasing Edward G. Robinson in *The Cincinnati Kid*, "you have to do the wrong thing at the right time."

What little money Hellmuth had left Ross Boatman, one of a group of British professionals who call themselves "the Hendon Mob," took a few hands later, beating Phil's A-2 with pocket 4s. For the third year in a row Phil Hellmuth was the last former world champion to get knocked out of the World Series, and, as had become customary, he wanted everyone to know about it. In 1999 he actually challenged the player who knocked him out to play heads-up for a million dollars. This year he focused his bitterness on Varkonyi.

"If Robert Varkonyi wins the World Series of Poker," Phil declared while doing commentary with Gabe Kaplan for ESPN, "I'll shave my head."

Phil Ivey, who along with Hellmuth had hovered atop the leader board for much of the tournament, found himself crippled by an even worse beat. After flopping a set of 3s, Ivey bet enough to force his opponent, John Shipley of Birmingham, England, all in. Having flopped top pair with A-K, Shipley called. Ivey was nearly a fifty-to-one favorite to win the hand, but an ace on the turn *and* the river gave Shipley a miraculous four of a kind. As cool as they come, Phil never panicked and actually managed to survive into the following day, when, holding A-Q, he'd lose the rest of his chips to a hand he had dead to rights, A-3. In addition to winning three preliminary events that year, Ivey finished twenty-third in the main event, capping what might have been the most dominating performance in modern World Series history.

None of the players who remained had ever won a World Series event, and as these relative amateurs jockeyed for inclusion at the final table—and the chance for a $2 million payday—the attendant pressure was fully in evidence. With only ten players remaining, Russell Rosenblum, a lawyer from Bethesda, Maryland, raised before the flop with pocket jacks. Yet another Brit, twenty-three-year-old wunderkind Julian Gardner, dubbed "the Harry Potter of Poker" for his youthful appearance, called with pocket 6s. When the flop came 10-10-5, Russell led out for $100,000. Hoping his opponent was bluffing at the pot with two overcards, Gardner declared that he was moving all in. Rosenblum rose from the table and walked away, in obvious distress, mumbling about his rotten luck. He told the dealer to fold his hand.

What Russell, who had nearly a million dollars, failed to notice is that Julian only had $130,000, and that it would have cost only another $30,000 to call the all-in bet. Tournament director Matt Savage gave Russell an out, asking him again what he wanted to do.

"I fold, I fold," said Russell, a millisecond before he came to his senses. Running back to the table, he grabbed the cards he'd mucked. "How much more is it to me?"

"Russell," Savage said, "your hand is dead."

"What do you mean? It's only thirty-something-thousand more to me."

"Your hand is dead," Savage repeated before explaining that verbal declarations are binding.

Russell had been a 92 percent favorite to win the hand, which would have knocked Julian Gardner out of the tournament. Allowing Julian to survive was a mistake Russell would come to regret.

John Shipley, having single-handedly closed out the fourth day by knocking the last three players out, began the final day with just over $2 million. It was a commanding lead, given that his nearest opponent, Russell Rosenblum, was shy of a million. By the first break, however, the gap had narrowed considerably, thanks in part to a pair of very questionable plays. On the first, Shipley opened with a $42,000 raise and was called by Robert Varkonyi, who had confounded all the so-called "experts," most notably Phil Hellmuth, by making the final table.

Shipley had A-K, and when the flop came Q-8-4, bet $120,000 at the pot. Robert, who held pocket jacks, went all in with his remaining $240,000, a relatively strange decision, given the overcard on the board. Shipley made an even stranger move when he called him, earning the derision of Amarillo Slim, who watched from the sidelines.

"The only way I'da called him would have been on the phone."*

Varkonyi doubled up, while Shipley entered a tailspin from which he could not seem to escape. The two locked horns again on the eightieth hand of the day, when Shipley countered Varkonyi's $60,000 opening bet with a $150,000 reraise from the small blind. When Varkonyi moved all in with his remaining $759,000, Shipley, after a minute or so of thought, called. He shouldn't have—Varkonyi, once again blessed with pocket jacks, was a big favorite over Shipley's A-J offsuit. While the 3-3-7-J-A board gave Shipley two pair, it also gave Robert a full house. Down to his last $370,000, Shipley, brow furrowed with displeasure, jammed his hands into the pockets of what appeared to be a varsity letter jacket, looking for all the world like a guy who couldn't find a date to the prom. What had happened to his large stack? He'd handed most of it to Robert Varkonyi, along with the chip lead.

It was the first year tournament officials used pink $25,000 chips, and Robert now had a ton of them. Still enjoying his rush a half an hour later, he opened for $100,000 with A-10. Shipley moved all in, for another $250,000 more, with pocket 7s. Robert called and caught the ace he needed on the turn.

When Shipley was given the $120,000 he had earned for coming

---

*As long as it wasn't a cell phone, which had been banned—along with cigarettes and CD players—from the tournament in 2002.

in seventh, he still looked stunned. With the former table captain's departure, the championship was up for grabs.

As resilient as vampires, poker players need to have a stake driven into their hearts to convince them their tournament life is over. When given the opportunity to knock out Julian Gardner the previous day, Russell Rosenblum had failed. Now it was time for him to pay for his negligence.

Holding an ugly-looking J♦6♦ on the button, Russell tried to steal the blinds with a large raise. Julian reraised him enough to force him all in. Committed to the pot, Russell called and grimaced when he saw what he was up against: pocket aces. A five-to-one underdog, Russell reached across the table to shake Julian's hand, all but conceding the hand, until the flop came J♠8♦4♦. Suddenly blessed with fifteen outs, Russell celebrated as if he had already caught one of them, but none of them arrived. Julian pumped his fist in the air and screamed, acting his age for about two seconds before returning to the task at hand.

The hand had the opposite effect on Russell. Down to his last $95,000 he went all in on the very next hand with A-8. Ireland's Scott Gray called with A-K, and when Scott made a full house on the turn, Russell was out in sixth place.

Julian continued to ride his rush. When Californian Harley Hall, a crowd favorite who had gone all in five times on the day, made it six with A-2 in the small blind, Gardner called him from the big blind with K♣7♠. Julian caught running 7s to knock Hall out in fifth.

The chip leader, much to Phil Hellmuth's chagrin, remained Robert Varkonyi, whose towers of pink checks comprised more than half the chips on the table. When Scott Gray pushed all in after he had opened with a $100,000 raise, Robert smiled.

"I usually wouldn't," he said, "but since this is Phil's favorite hand, I guess I should play it. I call."

He flipped over the same hand he had used to eliminate Hellmuth two days earlier, Q-10. Robert's favorite hand worked its magic once again as he caught two queens on the flop to defeat Gray's A-9.

With Gray's departure, Robert enjoyed a 3–1 chip lead over his two remaining opponents, Julian Gardner and thirty-six-year-old Las

Vegas professional Ralph Perry. He suggested they cut a deal and play came to a halt as they attempted to negotiate the terms, but they failed to come to any sort of agreement. On the very next hand, Julian opened for $100,000 from the button, Ralph made it $300,000 to go from the small blind, and Robert pushed his entire $4 million stack into the pot from the big. Shaking his head, Julian folded his hand, but Ralph, who had pocket jacks, called. Robert dramatically turned over his cards one at a time: first one ace, then another. Reminiscent of Hellmuth's display in 1989, Julian jumped for joy and proudly showed everyone the pocket 10s he'd folded. Robert's aces held up, and the 631 who started the tournament were down to just two.

The matchup between Julian Gardner and Robert Varkonyi presented Phil Hellmuth with an excruciating dilemma. If Julian won, Phil would lose his title as the youngest player ever to win the World Series of Poker. The alternative was no more appealing. Gabe Kaplan thoughtfully reminded everyone of Hellmuth's promise.

"I can't believe a man like Phil would have made a statement like this," he said, "but if Robert wins the tournament, Phil has told Robert that he can shave Phil's head."

Kaplan motioned Hellmuth over to the microphone.

"I brought this on myself," Phil said, looking a little concerned. "I haven't put my foot this far into my mouth in a long time. This is tough. I lose no matter what happens."

"Just like Phil Hellmuth," Kaplan said with perfect deadpan timing, "never thinking of himself."

Phil tried to pretend he really didn't care who won, but it quickly became obvious where his heart was. While he wasn't getting any younger, his hair would surely grow back. He was quietly rooting for Robert, and Robert obliged by refusing to relinquish any of his enormous chip lead, $5.1 million to Julian's $1.2 million.

On the fifteenth hand between the two, Robert made it $80,000 to go from the button with the hand that from this tournament forward would be known as a "Varkonyi": Q-10. Julian called with J-8, both clubs. The flop came Q♣4♣4♠. Julian checked, waiting for Robert to bet a relatively paltry $50,000, and moved all in.

"I call," declared Varkonyi. The crowd began to buzz. The turn card was the 10♦, making two pair for Robert, but adding a gutshot straight draw to Julian's potential flush.

"Julian needs a club or a 9," announced Matt Savage, neglecting to mention that one of the clubs—the 10♣—would make Robert a full house. Which, as the poker gods would have it, was the very card that fell on the river.

The gallery erupted into applause, first for Varkonyi, then for the implications associated with his unlikely victory. They began to chant.

"Shave Phil's head! Shave Phil's head!"

Becky Binion-Behnen produced an electric razor, and the ecstatic Varkonyi shaved about an inch off Phil's mop before retiring to ponder what he would do with the $2 million he had just won. Becky took over the job on the surprisingly gracious Poker Brat.

"I tip my hat to him," said Phil. "I tip my hair to him."

The shears were handed to Andy Glazer, then to Devilfish Ulliott. Phil's dark locks drifted to the floor. For one glorious moment, all the strife surrounding the Horseshoe seemed to be forgotten, and the World Series was transformed into what it once had been, a fraternity party, a collegial gathering of like-minded peers.

16

PRIME TIME

Be gentle with her. She's not used to this sort of thing."

Or so went the advice a Binion family advisor offered to a reporter who was preparing to interview Becky Binion-Behnen, just after she took the reins of the Horseshoe.

The spotlight had always made Becky uncomfortable. Unfortunately, as the host of the world's biggest poker tournament and a key participant in the highest-profile murder trial Las Vegas had ever seen, the spotlight was exactly where Becky lived. And now that rumors of the casino's decline had the media smelling disaster, the scrutiny only got worse. In October 2002, after the Nevada Gaming Control Board shut down about 40 percent of the Horseshoe's slots and several table games, citing a lack of sufficient cash reserves, Becky's stress levels shot through the roof, and she checked herself into the hospital for a weekend.

The games were reopened shortly thereafter—Becky called it a "misunderstanding"—but the casino's troubles seemed to multiply. The National Labor Board filed two complaints against the Horseshoe, one on behalf of the dealers fired during the 2002 World Series, the other for the continually unhappy Bartenders and Culinary

Unions, which had been waiting six months for management to sign a collective bargaining agreement. Many employees discovered that, if they wanted medical attention, they were going to have to pay for it themselves, as several clinics stopped accepting their insurance—the Horseshoe had apparently failed to appropriately fund their health care plan. The Gaming Control Board began an investigation into the matter, as well as "several other issues" they refused to specify.

Some blamed 9/11. The 2001 tragedy was followed by a dramatic dip in tourism, compelling the upscale casinos along the Las Vegas Strip to lower their rates, siphoning traffic away from downtown establishments like the Horseshoe.

Others blamed Nick Behnen. Becky's husband was supposed to have nothing to do with the operation of the casino, but there were persistent rumors that, while she held the license, he called the shots from behind the scenes.

"Nick was in there all the time," a former blackjack dealer would later declare. "If you told me he wasn't in there every day, I wouldn't believe it. He'd fire people on the spot." Others called him a "boorish Svengali" who verbally abused the Horseshoe staff. In one instance, claimed another former employee, he threw a half-eaten hot dog at a snack bar attendant.

In January 2003, Nick quietly received a work card from the Las Vegas Police Department allowing him to call himself the Horseshoe's vice president of marketing. He also initiated proceedings to once again apply for a gaming license.

In one of his first public statements as an official Horseshoe executive, Nick announced that a live video broadcast of the 2003 World Series of Poker would be available on the World Wide Web. For the first time, a dedicated fan—yes, the World Series now had dedicated fans—didn't have to wait for the packaged highlight reel that would be broadcast months later on television, but could watch the entire tournament, from start to finish, in real time.

But the most significant advantage the Internet had over television wouldn't make itself clear until the day the championship event was set to begin. Television is a passive medium, good for delivering content to ready viewers. The Internet is a two-way medium equally capable of delivering the viewers to the content.

Online poker was growing in popularity at an exponential rate, its players harboring the same dream as every other poker player: a gold bracelet at the World Series. It was only natural that some of these new online cardrooms, virtual casinos with names like PokerStars, Paradise Poker, and UltimateBet, would start hosting their own satellites and supersatellites. What was surprising is just how successful these Web sites were at turning out players. Over fifty entrants to the 2003 championship event won their way in via online tournaments. PokerStars alone sent thirty-seven.

The virtual card rooms weren't the only destination for those gripped by poker fever. Many took advantage of the recent proliferation of brick-and-mortar casinos on Indian reservations, which responded by offering their own recruiting drives for the big event—Connecticut's Mohegan Sun supplied fourteen aspirants to the championship event. Others made the pilgrimage to the Horseshoe, where one-table satellites, two-tier satellites, supersatellites, and supersupersatellites were being run around the clock.

The end result was a record-shattering 839 entrants, a whopping 33 percent increase over the previous year. Tournament codirectors Matt Savage and Jim Miller, who had optimistically hoped for 700, found themselves mimicking the frenzied behavior of their predecessors. In a last-minute scramble to provide enough seats, they were forced to borrow tables from neighboring casinos. The lucrative side games that had once played such a key role in attracting big money players to the World Series were all but extinguished, as nearly every card table in the casino was dedicated to the primetime event. High rollers would have to content themselves with taking a shot at the $2.5 million first prize. Or even sixty-third place, which paid $15,000.

Perhaps the most amazing fact about the composition of the field was that only 63 players actually shelled out the $10,000 entry fee—everyone else had won their seat by winning some smaller buy-in affair. It was obvious that the thirty-fourth annual championship was a radically different beast from the ones that had preceded it. Less clear was the impact the transformation would have on the ensuing drama. This was no longer an exhibition for the world's finest players to strut their stuff, but a lottery to see which lucky ticket holder would win the immense prize. How interesting could that be?

The answer turned out to be an unqualified "very." The 2003 World Series produced the singular story of a man who embodied both the old and new worlds. On the one hand, he was an infidel at the gates, a professed amateur who never had to play poker in a backroom, or an Elks Lodge, or even in a live venue. In other ways, however, he was a throwback to the Texas road gamblers, willing to risk everything he had, even some things he didn't have, on the turn of a card. And as if this fable needed any more juice, there was the matter of his impossible but true name: Chris Moneymaker.

For the first twenty-seven years of his life, the name had seemed less like a portent of riches than a cruel joke. Chris Moneymaker had demonstrated a remarkable inability for holding onto money. He loved to gamble on sports, which isn't to say he was any good at it. As a student at the University of Tennessee, he once lost $60,000 in a single day. Chris's bankroll had mostly been financed by credit cards, a misstep trumpeted by the arrival of his monthly statements. His situation did not improve after he married his longtime girlfriend Kelly, as the two shared the same "spending problem," building a house and taking vacations they really couldn't afford. The man who had earned a masters degree in accounting could hardly balance his own books.

The $32,000 yearly salary he made as a comptroller for a restaurant in Nashville, Tennessee, was enough to cover the mortgage and service his massive credit card debt, but not much else. Kelly pressured him to stop betting on sports, which he did, but what to do with his inner gambler? In 2000 he discovered poker, a game that satisfied his jones while depending much less on the vagaries of luck. He began to dabble in the low-limit games at casinos in Las Vegas and nearby Tunica, Mississippi, until he discovered he could play on the Internet. PokerStars became his online casino of choice; his screen name was—and still is—Money800. He played after work. He played during his lunch hour. He played in hotel rooms. He occasionally played all weekend long. He lost, in his first year, nearly $15,000. Compared to the lightning-bolt sting of sports gambling, it didn't hurt so badly. The night he ventured into a Tunica casino and dropped $4,000 was an entirely different matter. Kelly made him sleep on the couch for a week.

His bankroll had been obliterated, cruelly leaving only the desire behind. Chris turned to online poker tournaments, which offered plenty of action for a very low entry fee. In his mind they were just something to do, a distraction from worrying about money and the anxiety of never having enough, exacerbated by the arrival of a baby daughter, Ashley. On a rainy Saturday in April of 2003, Chris entered a $40 supersatellite for the World Series championship event along with eighteen other PokerStars players. The winner would earn a "free" seat in a $600 buy-in tournament the following weekend. It was a lark, and he treated it as such, watching television and helping Kelly with mommy duties in between hands. Before he knew it he had won the thing.

He took the next tournament more seriously, as the stakes demanded it. Of the sixty-nine players entered, the top three finishers would earn a seat in the $10,000 championship event plus $1,000 in cash. In truth, Chris really didn't want to win—he was hoping to finish fourth, an $8,000 cash prize that would put a decent dent in his household debt. As the day wore to a close, he miraculously found himself in position to do so, enjoying a two-to-one lead over his closest rival with only six players left. He prepared to throw off his chips to the other players and glide into the fourth-place payday, until a friend who was watching him play begged him to reconsider, offering to buy half his entry fee for $5,000 in exchange for half of whatever he won at the World Series. Considering that in all likelihood there were going to be no winnings at the World Series, Chris thought it was a generous offer, agreed to the deal, and went on to win the tournament.

The friend's own financial difficulties led him to pull out of the deal a week later, but Chris's inner circle was abuzz with the fever. His father Mike and another friend, appropriately named David Gamble, each gave Chris $2,000 in exchange for 20 percent of his winnings, while two other friends kicked in $500 apiece.

The trip was back on. Chris Moneymaker, a lowly Internet player from Tennessee, was going to Las Vegas to play in the world championship of poker. Only one problem remained. He had never played in a live poker tournament before. He was the definition of "dead money." He didn't stand a chance.

.   .   .

Chris flew to Las Vegas a week before the start of the tournament to get a crash course in live tournament play. Using the money he had collected from his backers, he entered a series of satellites and super-satellites. He won a few, lost a few more, and threw away a lot of money making stupid bets on baseball. He also discovered that he had a "tell," looking away from his opponents when bluffing. A friend bought him a pair of Oakley sunglasses to cover his eyes.

At noon on May 20, the 839 hopefuls took their seats. Chris was initially comforted by the fact that half the players at his table were wearing shirts from online poker rooms, one of whom had won a seat simply by winning the two-millionth hand ever played at the site he favored. Only later did he discover that the man in the PokerStars shirt was Jim Worth, a.k.a. "Krazy Kanuck," a guy who had built a reputation as being one of the best online players in the world—and that the older gentleman in the green 888.com shirt and hat was 1995 champion Dan Harrington.

Chris managed to build his stack to about $20,000 by the time his table was reshuffled at ten that evening. He caught a couple of big hands at his new table, eliminating two players from the tournament. By the time the first day came to a close, just after one A.M., he had accumulated over $60,000 in chips, good for eleventh place among the 385 players who remained. Utterly exhausted, he went to sleep that night with a sweet dream filling his head: maybe, just maybe, he could finish in the money.

The beginning of the second day fueled his optimism. He knocked several more players out of the tournament, building his stack to $180,000. He became his table's captain, bullying the shorter stacks with aggressive play, until a new arrival put a serious crimp in his plan.

Johnny Chan. While Chris might not have recognized Dan Harrington, he certainly knew Chan, having watched *Rounders* too many times to count. The two-time champion took a seat at Chris's table and immediately began flinging chips with seemingly reckless abandon, at one point pushing all in six hands in a row.

Bad went to worse when they were joined by Phil Ivey. The two professionals proceeded to stage a hold'em clinic, taking turns, in

Moneymaker's words, "slapping me around." When the day finally ended just past midnight, Chris's stack had been chopped down to $100,000. He slumped down in his chair, looking like a beaten man.

He took the edge off with a couple of beers and staggered back to his hotel room where he evaluated what had happened. "I kept on thinking, how often do these guys have aces or flop sets?" He realized the two professionals had thrown him off his game. He had been playing scared, and he vowed to play more aggressively the next day.

"I went to bed that night and I made a decision," he said, echoing the spirit of Bobby Baldwin in 1978. "I said I'm not going to be afraid anymore. If I get beat, I get beat. I'm going to play my game."

The next day Chris had trouble finding his table, number seventy-one, until someone pointed out that it was the "TV table" that ESPN would feature on its upcoming broadcast. It was rigged with microphones and "lipstick" cameras, which allowed viewers at home to see the players' hole cards. Prior to this technological advance, viewing poker tournaments on television was about as exciting as watching paint dry. These lipstick cameras changed everything. Now every successful bluff and every carefully laid trap was like an inside joke shared between the winner and the television audience. A miraculous river card let the viewer experience, at the same time, the thrill of making a long shot draw and the agony of suffering a bad beat.

When Chris sat down at the table, it wasn't the bells and whistles that frightened him as much as the intimidating lineup of players, which included Howard Lederer, professionals Phil Darden and Brian Haveson, and, once again, Johnny Chan.

Was Chris nervous? On one hand, he watched Chan open for a raise, only to be reraised by Lederer. Moneymaker stared at the pros, wondering what would happen next. A couple of minutes passed before Chan looked directly at Chris.

"You know it's up to you, right?"

Chris's cheeks turned red as a fire truck—he hadn't even realized he was in the big blind. He quickly mucked his hand.

On the very last hand before the six-thirty dinner break he was dealt A♥8♥ on the button and raised $8,000. Everyone else departed the table except for Chan, who called him from the big blind. The two were left to battle it out with only the television cameras for witnesses.

The flop came A♦3♥4♥, giving Chris top pair and the nut flush draw. Playing the part of a weak amateur, he made a timid bet, only $4,500. Johnny did what he usually did, raising another $15,000.

Chris took off his glasses and thought about it, suddenly plagued by doubts. Maybe Johnny had a bigger ace. But, with a four-to-one chip lead, Chris could afford to be wrong.

"If I lost the hand, I lost the hand," he said, "but I didn't want to get outplayed by the great Johnny Chan."

Chris pushed all in. Word spread like a virus that some Internet player had made a move on Johnny Chan, and a crowd gathered around the table to watch.

Johnny gnawed on his swizzle stick and fondled his ever-present orange. He needed some luck. It had been a frustrating day for him, one where the cards never seemed to cooperate. His hole cards, K♥5♥, gave him draws at a gutshot straight and a flush. He was ready to double up or go home. It was time to gamble.

"All right," he said, pushing his chips into the middle.

It was all over on the next card: the 9♥ completed flushes for both men; however, Moneymaker's went to the ace. He had knocked out the former world champion.

"At that moment," he said, "I thought I was good enough to at least be at the same table with these guys."

A couple of hours later, John Strzemp, the runner-up to Stuey Ungar in 1997, was eliminated on the bubble in sixty-fourth place. Whatever happened next, Chris would live up to his surname and return to Tennessee having finished in the money.

Even Chris's mistakes seemed to be going his way. On the fourth day of the tournament, he got all in with pocket 8s against Humberto Brenes's pocket aces, then sent Humberto back to Costa Rica when he spiked a third 8 on the turn.

He wasn't just getting lucky—he was playing with an incredible new sense of confidence. In a confrontation with young professional Russ "Dutch" Boyd, he bet $100,000 into a 9♥2♣5♦ flop. Chris only had pocket 3s, but he was convinced Dutch had failed to connect with the board. When Dutch removed his sunglasses, smiled, and announced that he was all in, Chris called and slammed his hand faceup on the table.

"Low cards!" he implored the dealer. Sure enough, all Dutch could show was K♦Q♣.

"What a call!" a spectator yelled from the gallery. The Internet player hadn't just won a new fan. After the dealer complied with Chris request, he raked in a $1,275,000 pot, making him the new chip leader.

With the hour nearing 3 A.M. and just ten players left—only nine would go on to the next day's final table—all eyes were on Phil Ivey. The young pro, wearing a Steve Francis basketball jersey, was playing some of the best poker of his life.

"He is absolutely fearless," observed Howard Lederer, who was dispatched by Ivey in nineteenth place. "He can have any two cards at any time and he will play them like they were aces. That puts people under a tremendous amount of pressure. It's very hard to play against Phil."

Upon discovering A♥Q♦, Chris Moneymaker opened with a $60,000 raise. Phil opted to just call with his pocket 9s, while tournament veteran Jason Lester, the former backgammon pro and options trader from New York City, called with pocket 10s. The flop must have looked like a dream for Chris: not one, but two queens fell, accompanied by a harmless 6. After Lester checked, Chris bet $70,000, a surprisingly small bet for such a large pot. Having made trips, he didn't want to scare anyone away. He was looking for action, and he got it. Phil called.

Chris appeared to have tricked himself when the 9♣ appeared on the turn. When he fired $200,000 at the pot, Ivey quickly pushed all in. Chris wasn't about to lay down his three queens with an ace kicker. He called the bet, grimacing in pain when Phil turned over his cards—the turn had given Ivey a full house.

But once again, Phil Ivey would be viciously denied his chance at the title. The A♠ on the river made Moneymaker an even bigger full house. He pumped his fist in the air and screamed. With one card he won an enormous pot, knocked out the most dangerous player left in the tournament, and ensured himself a spot at the next day's final table.

.   .   .

Chris arrived at the final table with over $2.3 million in chips, about a million more than his closest competitor, Amir Vahedi. While the final nine lacked star power, it was loaded with talent. Vahedi, a goateed, bespectacled poker pro from California who almost always has a cigar in his mouth, won his first World Series event two weeks earlier in the $1,500 No-Limit Hold'em tournament, one of four money finishes he'd enjoy that year. Dan Harrington, the 1995 champion, was in good shape with more than a half-million in chips. Moneymaker was flanked by two renowned high-stakes money players named David, Grey and Singer. And seated across the table was one of the more unpredictable players in that game or any other, Ihsan "Houston Sammy" Farha.

If Sammy Farha didn't exist, you'd have to invent him. From Lebanon by way of Texas, he looks like central casting's idea of a poker shark: sports jacket and a shirt open at the neck revealing the requisite gold chain; an ever-present cigarette, which, thanks to the new antismoking policy, remained unlit; probing eyes that seem to miss nothing; and a certain quality of implied menace that belies his smallish frame.

Farha, considered one of the best pot-limit Omaha players in the world, also possesses a sort of devil-may-care attitude that, at times, borders on recklessness. During the fourth day of the tournament, Phil Hellmuth threw a temper tantrum after Sammy called his preflop raise with a relatively weak Q♦J♦. The fit came, of course, shortly after Sammy won the hand, and a large chunk of Hellmuth's stack was relocated into Farha's growing pile of chips. It was all in a day's work for Sam, whose wildly up-and-down progress through the tournament resembled a seismograph in the midst of an earthquake. He came to the table with just under a million in chips, more than enough to create a few tremors of his own.

It was only a matter of time before he got into a showdown with Amir Vahedi. As the only full-time tournament pro at the final table, Amir seemed poised to become its table captain; but, after knocking David Singer out in ninth place, he quickly fell apart. Vahedi lost a large chunk of his chip stack to Jason Lester after flopping two pair with K♦J♦, only to see Lester make a better two pair with A♦K♠.

"That's the beauty of this game," Amir said, seemingly unfazed. "In order to live, you have to be willing to die."

Just how willing he was became apparent fourteen hands later when, holding a junk hand, 10♦8♣, he joined Chris Moneymaker in calling Sammy Farha's $60,000 preflop raise. Sammy, who held pocket 9s, flopped top set when the first three cards off the deck were 9♠6♠4♥. He bet $80,000, which both Chris and Amir called.

The 6♥ fell on the turn. Vahedi—taking a shot, trying to make a play—led out for $300,000. Having made a full house, Sam was delighted to call and hoped Moneymaker would come along for the ride. Chris prudently folded, saying, "You gentlemen have fun."

Amir finally came to his senses after the 3♣ hit the river and checked. When Farha bet $300,000, Amir pretended to be wrestling with an agonizing decision, but it wasn't the decision that was causing him such agony. It was the fact that he had nothing but 10-high and no choice but to fold. In just two hands—the one with Lester, the other with Farha—Vahedi lost $1 million.

Playing even faster than usual, it didn't take too much longer for him to throw away the last of his chips. After the dinner break he called Farha's $80,000 raise before the flop with a hand as doomed as his 10♦8♣ had been: 6♥4♥. When the flop came A♠Q♥9♣, Amir pushed all in for his last $535,000. Sammy had made top pair with A♥5♠, but his weak kicker concerned him. He seemed undecided as to what to do until Amir demanded, "You go against them. You've got to go against me too."

The most common tell in poker has nothing to do with twitching eyes or nervous hands, but with a player's attitude. Strong usually means weak, while weak almost always means strong. Sammy read Amir's apparent bluster for what it was, a bluff. He called, Amir was out in sixth place, and Sammy Farha became the new top dog with $3.76 million, nearly half of the chips in play.

Despite entering the day as the chip leader, Chris Moneymaker remained relatively quiet early on as the more experienced players took turns beating up on one another. During the dinner break he decided that it was time to change gears.

"I was tired of getting run over," he'd later say.

His plan worked to perfection when, thanks to a little assistance from Lady Luck, he transformed several average hands into very big winners. Many players, respecting Dan Harrington's tight image, would have folded their A♣2♠ after the former champion opened for $90,000, and yet Chris called. Sensing a good opportunity to steal some much needed chips, Tomer Benvenisti, an expedition tour guide who had won his seat for $125 in a two-tier satellite, moved in for another $490,000 with J♥10♦. Dan mucked his pocket 4s, but Chris made a gutsy, some might say foolish, call. When Chris caught an ace on the flop to end Tomer's day, ESPN commentator Norman Chad hit the nail on the head when he said, "Moneymaker continues to sleep with angels."

He wasn't ready to wake up. Thirteen hands later, he raised $100,000 from the button with Q♠J♦, only to be reraised $450,000 by Jason Lester, who had A♥Q♥. Lester's dominant hand was snapped like a twig when the 10-9-8 flop gave Chris the nut straight. Making the right move at the wrong time, Lester moved all in. Chris called and knocked out his second consecutive player, pulling into a virtual tie for first place with Farha. Dan Harrington remained a distant third.

Sammy didn't have a lot of respect for Moneymaker's game and he had a difficult time hiding it. As midnight approached, Farha jokingly suggested that all three of them risk their entire stacks on the next hand.

"You'll have a better shot this way," he told Chris before quickly correcting himself. "I mean *I'll* have a better shot this way."

A half hour later, Chris eliminated the short-stacked Dan Harrington. Despite a nearly two-to-one chip advantage over Farha, Moneymaker offered to split the remaining first and second place prize money—$3.8 million dollars—right down the middle. Sammy dismissed the proposal, confident his superior talents would carry the day. He was, after all, a professional—while Chris Moneymaker was just a lowly amateur.

Back in Spring Hill, Tennessee—where the hour was nearing 5 A.M.— Chris's wife Kelly and a group of friends and family took advantage of the live Internet coverage to track the progress of their beloved hometown hero. Moneymaker, meanwhile, prepared to take advantage of Farha's hubris.

After twenty uneventful hands, Chris received K♠7♥ and contemplated a preflop raise. Farha, sensing his indecision, lowered his unlit cigarette and said, "Don't do it."

Chris ignored the warning, making it $100,000 to go, a bet Sam called with Q♠9♥. When the flop came 9♠6♠2♦, Sam checked his top pair, perhaps looking to check-raise, but the opportunity vanished when Chris checked behind him. When the 8♠ fell on the turn, Sam fired $300,000 at the pot.

Chris only had draws to open-ended straight and a king-high flush, but that was enough to convince him it was time to make a move. He raised to $800,000. Sammy smiled tightly as he called, unsure what to make of the play. He was further confounded when, after a 3♥ fell on the river, Moneymaker confidently pushed his remaining chips into the middle.

"I'm all in."

To Farha's credit, he smelled a rat. "You must have missed your flush, huh?" he asked, fishing for information. Moneymaker remained impassive, the Oakleys covering his eyes, his hand across his mouth, betraying nothing. "I could make a crazy call on you," Sammy continued, while contemplating the relative strength of the top pair he had made. "Could be the best hand." He continued to agonize for several minutes.

Moneymaker's all-in bluff, pitted against Farha's gnawing suspicion that he was being bluffed, represented a true test of heart. Perhaps allowing his ego to get the better of his instincts, Farha decided that the amateur simply couldn't have the courage to make such a play against him. He folded his hand with a growl.

"The price of poker is going to go high now."

"I figured it would," Chris replied as soon as he was able to breathe again. The announcers on ESPN were quick to call it "the bluff of the century." Considering the circumstances, and the fact that the century was barely three years old, it very well might have been.

Moneymaker now had $6.6 million to Farha's $1.8 million. The end was near. With such a massive chip lead, Chris could afford to call a raise with a hand like 5♦4♠, which he proceeded to do after Sammy made it $100,000 to go with J♥10♦. The J♠5♠4♣ flop looked pretty good to Sam, but it looked even better to Chris, as it gave him a sneaky two pair. Chris checked, and Sam bet $175,000.

Rubbing his chin, Chris said, "I'm gonna raise $100,000."

"Let's go," Sam said, indicating he was all in.

Chris quickly called.

The 5♥ on the river gave Chris a full house, 5s full of 4s, the championship, and enough cash to pay off his credit card debt and then some—$2.5 million. He bounded towards his father Mike, who had flown in to watch his son play, and the two large men hugged like dancing bears. A good Southern boy, Chris quickly remembered his manners, removed his hat, and shook Sammy's hand. He even tried to make the man feel better by coming clean about his bluff.

"I missed the flush and I missed the straight draw on that one, that king high," he confessed.

"I made one bad mistake," Sam said, shrugging it off.* "Good job."

They were *still* talking about that hand, and rightfully so. It was the bluff of the century.

If he had been named Chris Smith, it probably would have been a completely different story. Chris Moneymaker, however, became an instant celebrity. He appeared on *Late Show with David Letterman* and *Jimmy Kimmel Live*. Hundreds of newspapers and magazine articles were written about him. Despite his being two years shy of thirty and having but one major tournament win to his credit, plans were made to publish his memoirs. Moneymaker not only became a household name, but a folk hero to any would-be rounder with dreams of sitting down with the professionals. There was no doubt that next year's World Series would be bigger than ever.

Assuming there was a next year.

That summer the Binion family received two pieces of jolting news.

The first came from the Nevada State Supreme Court, who in a four-to-three decision overturned the murder convictions against Sandy Murphy and Rick Tabish. "It's going to be disturbing for Ted's

---

*Actually, Farha made *two* mistakes: his refusal to make a deal with Chris cost him a half-million dollars.

family to have to relive this ordeal," observed a family spokesman in what was surely an understatement.

The second came from halfway across the country, where Jack Binion sold his riverboat casinos to the Harrah's corporation. The deal netted him nearly a billion dollars. For Harrah's, the biggest asset they received in the acquisition might have been a debt: the IOU Becky had written Jack for his share of the Las Vegas Horseshoe was now worth, with interest, nearly $20 million. The corporation intended to use the marker as leverage, hoping to get Becky to sell them what they saw to be the crown jewel of this or any deal, the World Series of Poker.

As the financial climate at the casino went from bad to worse, Becky was running out of options. Nick withdrew his application for a gaming license, a sign that many took to reflect the imminent demise of the Horseshoe. Speculation soon turned to fact. In January 2004, on an otherwise normal Friday evening, the casino's staff and patrons were jolted from their workday routines by an old-fashioned raid. U.S. Marshals and IRS agents stormed the joint, armed with a court order for nonpayment of union benefits. Tables were closed, slot machines silenced. Customers were told to cash in their chips. Whatever money remained in the casino cages was seized.

After more than fifty years, the relationship between the Binion family and the Horseshoe was over. So, it appeared, was the World Series of Poker.

17

REFORMATION

ocal media pundits took turns dissecting the Horseshoe's demise—BLAME BECKY, read one headline. Another article accused Nick of frittering away the family's assets. For the growing legion of poker players around the world, the question was far simpler: Would there be a World Series in 2004?

They didn't have to wait long for an answer. Two days after the shutdown, Harrah's announced they were buying the Horseshoe. Actually, they had little interest in the casino itself, having already sold the physical premises to another corporation that would manage the property. Just exactly what attracted them to the deal could be easily ascertained from the asset they kept—and the nearly $40 million they had paid for it—the World Series of Poker. And yes, the tournament would go on as usual this spring.

Well, maybe not "as usual." Just how hot had the Series become? On the other side of the country, a superior court judge in New Jersey, expecting to deliver sentencing in an investment fraud case, instead received a fax from the defendant—he was in Las Vegas, at the World Series of Poker, where he hoped to win restitution for the investors he had victimized. He happily reported that he was well on his way, thanks to a money finish in the $5,000 Seven-Card Stud event. The judge was less amused, issuing a bench warrant for the absent defendant, who he called "a degenerate gambler."

Everyone knew that Chris Moneymaker's highly publicized win would inspire gamblers everywhere, degenerate or otherwise. The new game within the game was predicting just how many people would show up for the championship event.

Detractors pointed to the increased competition from other poker tournaments. A week before the 2004 Series began, the rival World Poker Tour staged a $25,000 buy-in event at the Bellagio and awarded its champion, Martin DeKnijff, a record $2.7 million first prize. The World Series was no longer the biggest game in town.

The new management at the Horseshoe, however, predicted that this record would be short-lived, as they expected a thousand players for the main event, creating a $10 million prize pool. Amarillo Slim, undoubtedly amused at just how popular this reunion for old Texas gamblers had become, bet $50,000 at six-to-five odds that the field would break a thousand, then the same sum at seven-to-five that there would be more than twelve hundred players. The day before the tournament began, organizers were bandying about the number two thousand.

They weren't even close. The 2,576 entrants who ultimately arrived shattered every poker tournament attendance record in existence. There were so many players that they had to be split into two separate groups, each starting the tournament on a different day. PokerStars, the online poker room that had catapulted Moneymaker into stardom, was alone responsible for 315 entries. The better-than-$24 million prize pool meant that the top 225 players would get paid and that the *second* place finisher would receive the biggest payout in tournament poker history—$3.5 million—next to, of course, the winner, who would earn a ridiculous $5 million for what was now a full seven days of work.

The atmosphere was pure circus. The list of celebrity players included Tobey Maguire, James Woods, and about half the cast of *That '70s Show*. A conga line of twenty-six topless women in body paint paraded through the casino just as the action got underway, a promotion for an online poker site that would have been a lot more successful if anyone had actually noticed. Far more attention was directed towards the man who represented the spiritual essence of what the tournament had become—Chris Moneymaker—who had chosen to handle any pressures associated with repeating as champion in typical Las Vegas style.

"I should have slept last night," he said. "I got drunk til six o'clock this morning."

As the old poker saying goes, "Nobody wins a tournament on the first day, but a lot of people lose it." Three hours after the tournament began, Moneymaker's stack was decimated by an amateur who had pushed all in against him, then caught a two-outer on the river to beat his three aces with a full house. A few hands later, the 2003 champion was gone.

Nearly two-thirds of the entrants were playing in their first ever World Series event. They may have lacked experience, but they had certainly watched a lot of poker on television. That is to say, they had seen a lot of *highlights,* as televised poker generally edits out the meat of any game—hours and hours of folding hand after hand—in favor of the critical confrontations where all of a player's chips are on the line. Devoid of context, these new Internet and television babies knew only one speed, summed up by what quickly became their familiar battle cry:

"All in!"

"I tell you Phil, it's gettin' rough," Doyle Brunson complained to fellow champion Phil Hellmuth, Jr., now more eminence grise than Poker Brat. "I had one of these Internet players on my left almost all day, and just about any time I made a bet, it was 'all in, all in.' It was the first time he had ever played live poker, ever, in his life, and unless a man feels like gamblin' his entire stack, these young 'uns can be a hatful o' trouble."

Hellmuth readily agreed as he navigated through what he called a "minefield" of bad plays and bad beats. He lasted until the third day, when he joined fellow bracelet winners Slim, Chan, McEvoy, and Bechtel on the sidelines.

Texas Dolly enjoyed slightly better luck. The new Grand Old Man of Poker had sat out the Series through most of the tumultuous Becky years, but had returned to play the previous year, winning his ninth World Series tournament, the $2,000 "H.O.R.S.E." event, which alternated among hold'em, Omaha, razz, seven-card stud, and Omaha hi-lo.

This year, seated at ESPN's featured television table on the second day, Doyle went on a tear that brought to mind Jack Nicklaus's 1986 victory at the Masters at forty-six years old. Seventy years young, Doyle was playing as well as he ever had, knocking player after player from the tournament. He took out this year's H.O.R.S.E. winner—rising star Scott Fischman—along with experienced pro David Plastik, on the same hand. That evening, he dispatched Howard Lederer, rivering a flush to overcome a set.

On the fifth day of the tournament, his magnificent run seemed like it might never end when he was dealt pocket 10s and announced before the flop that he was all in. The perpetual crowd that buzzed around him like bees at a bad picnic, however, created so much noise that the player in the small blind, Bradley Berman, son of the World Poker Tour financier Lyle, failed to hear what he'd said. Believing that he was alone against the big blind, Berman announced his intention to raise. Because verbal declarations are binding, Berman was forced to call Doyle's bet with A-7, a hand he surely would have folded had he known his opponent had raised all in. A 2½–1 underdog, Berman defied the odds and won the pot when an ace appeared on the flop. Texas Dolly lumbered out of the room, collecting $45,000 for his fifty-third-place finish and a thunderous round of applause from his appreciative fans, which included nearly every player in the room.

As champions continued to fall, several players began to distinguish themselves from the increasingly obscure field. Josh Arieh, a twenty-nine-year-old professional from Atlanta, was playing like he'd been here before because, in fact, he had. In 1999 he won the $3,000 Limit Hold'em event; the following year he came in second to Johnny Chan in the $1,500 Pot-Limit Omaha event. On the third day of the 2004 tournament he went on a Farha-like roller-coaster ride, starting the day with $60,500 before dropping to $20,000, which he used to go all in with A-Q against another player's A-K. He was halfway out the door when he caught a queen to win the hand. Taking full advantage of his new lease on life, Josh went on a torrid run to end the day with

$754,000, good for second place among the 276 players who remained.

"Josh plays a very aggressive, wide open, pedal-to-the-metal kind of poker," commented Andy Glazer. "He likes to put a lot of pressure on his opponents and really put them to the decision."

The other player making noise was Greg Raymer, a thirty-nine year-old patent attorney from Connecticut who, like Moneymaker before him, won his seat in a satellite on PokerStars. The man better known as "Fossilman," a nickname derived from his passion for collecting and occasionally peddling fossils, had a few advantages over last year's champion. One was his discipline—he had promised his wife at the start of his poker career that he'd quit were he ever to lose his initial thousand-dollar bankroll, a vow he had never been forced to carry out. The other was his experience. As he lived a stone's throw from Foxwoods Casino, he had accrued plenty of live tournament experience, including a third-place finish in the 2000 World Poker Finals.

Raymer also came from the school of thought that espoused aggressive play from the very start of the tournament. For years, the strategy for most of the top players was to play conservatively in the early going of the major tournaments. That started to change once so many online players began to enter them.

"Many old-school thinkers believe that day one is a day of survival," said Daniel Negreanu. "While I respect them, they are just wrong. Poker's changed so much in the last five years that surviving on day one should take a backseat to scooping up some dead money."

Like Negreanu, Raymer saw the advantages of attacking the weaker players on the first day, believing that in an event with such a large field it made more sense to gamble early and often.

"My style either accumulates a lot of chips or has me on the sidelines early," he admitted.

The strategy produced mixed results for its two proponents. Negreanu was knocked out on the first day. Raymer, however, managed to stockpile a small mountain of chips early on, which he used to acquire even more.

By the end of the fourth day, Fossilman sat behind the biggest stack in the tournament, some $1.8 million. He had acquired a substantial portion of those checks from Mike Matusow in a series of highly entertaining altercations. In their first major battle, Raymer made a $20,000 raise, only to throw his hand away when Matusow raised $40,000. The Mouth started yakking.

"You got to stop fucking with me, buddy," Mike said. "I'm going to bust you. You ain't playing with kids, buddy. I got big *cojones*." Perhaps hearing himself for the first time, he suddenly stopped, smiled, and extended his hand to Greg. "I'm just joking. I'm sorry, bro'. I'm just messing with you."

Raymer refused to shake Mike's hand, and, like an elephant, he would not forget the incident. Instead, he would wait for Matusow to do what he had done so often before: implode.

For those who had never witnessed the infamous Mike Matusow blowup, ESPN analyst Norman Chad drew a vivid picture:

"That's where he shoots himself in the foot, then takes off his other shoe, then shoots himself in that foot, then takes both injured feet and sticks them in his mouth."

No one was more aware of Mike's predilection for disaster than he himself. "Three and a half days in, the Mike Matusow blowup hasn't happened yet," he announced to the table without any prompting. "They should have like a lottery out there like on the betting board. When will Mike Matusow blow up today in the tournament?"

Talk about self-fulfilling prophecies. On a hand he undoubtedly wishes he had never gotten involved in, Matusow raised the pot with 9♠7♠, then called a reraise from Raymer, who held A♦J♦. The 9♦3♦10♥ hadn't made Raymer's hand, but with two overcards and a nut flush draw, he decided to push all in for $241,000. Matusow stared at Greg, who was hiding behind the goofy funhouse glasses he had bought at the Tower of Terror gift shop at Disney World while vacationing with his family. Glazed with a holographic swirl, they were incredibly annoying to look at for any length of time and turned most staredowns into comic routines.

"I told you I was going to bust you when you came after me, didn't I?" Mike taunted Greg as he called the bet. Matusow was initially pleased with himself, as his pair of 9s was currently the best hand. He had completely ignored the fact that Raymer had a better than 50 percent chance of drawing to an even better hand, which is exactly what happened when the 2♦ appeared on the turn, completing his flush.

Fossilman raised his hands in a gesture that said "Who's got the *cojones* now?" The Mouth was momentarily silenced.

A few hands later, a crippled Matusow pushed all in with A♦K♠, got called by A♣Q♠, and lost when the river paired his opponent's queen. Knocked out of the tournament before he was ready to go, Mike staggered off to do what every single player but the champion feels like doing each and every year—he got as far away from the table as he could and cried.

When there were only ten players left fighting for the coveted nine seats at the final table, every player tightened up except for one, Josh Arieh. Like a true professional, he was playing to win the championship, instead of watching and waiting for others to eliminate themselves. He had already knocked out the eleventh- and twelfth-place finishers, and with pocket 10s in the big blind he was looking to bust one more. David Williams, a twenty-three-year-old student at Southern Methodist University, had already raised $400,000 with A♠Q♦. Arieh popped him back for $600,000 more.

"If I had folded," Williams said afterwards, "I might have been able to make the final table, but even though you never know for sure what can happen, I would have been getting there with such a small stack that I probably would have gone out ninth or eighth." Already guaranteed at least $373,000—a massive windfall for any college student—Williams moved all in. It wasn't much more for Josh to call, and so he did without hesitation.

The flop was no help to David, who looked to the man sitting next to him for reassurance. Marcel Luske, a professional from Holland, is not only one of the finest players in the world, but one of the most entertaining. Throughout the tournament he had worn his sunglasses upside down, donned a different suit each day, and frequently broke into song. He and Williams had improbably found themselves at the same table on four separate occasions during the first six days and had developed a bond. Now Marcel winked at David and said, "The ace is coming."

And so it did on the very next card, earning Williams a $2 million pot and almost guaranteeing him a spot at the final table. Ironically, it was Luske who assured him of that honor a few hands later, when he decided that a Q♣8♣6♣ flop had missed Dan Harrington and moved all in with his pocket 4s. He was right, but Dan called with his A♣J♦ and caught a jack on the turn to knock the charismatic Dutchman out in tenth place.

Despite the overwhelming number of amateurs who had started the event, the final table wasn't completely devoid of star power. Former champion Dan Harrington was there for the second year in a row, which—given the tremendous size of the fields—represented one of the more amazing accomplishments in modern poker history. Fellow Mayfair Club alum Al Krux had earned his third trip to the championship table. But the big stack and the momentum belonged to the Fossilman: Greg Raymer's more than $8 million was almost twice as many as the man in second, Matt Dean, a twenty-five-year-old Texan studying to be a math teacher.

More importantly, Raymer knew how to wield a large stack of chips. He began the seventh and final day of the tournament by knocking out four of the first five players himself, thanks in large part to his chip lead, which allowed him to call his opponents' all-in bets with inferior hands. Raymer's pocket 10s beat poker pro Mike Mc-Clain's pocket aces when a 10 showed up on the flop. Next to go was Mattias Andersson, a twenty-four-year-old Swede who ran around the table screaming "Daaaaaa!" every time he won a big hand. Andersson had Raymer dominated, A♦K♣ against A♠10♦, but the 8♠ on the river completed an unlikely straight for the Fossilman. Like Chris Money-maker the year before, Greg Raymer was sleeping with angels.

So too was David Williams. Shortly after the game was interrupted by Matt Savage, who used his bully pulpit as tournament codirector to propose to his girlfriend seated in the VIP row, Williams opened for $120,000 with pocket 5s. After Josh Arieh reraised to $500,000 with A♥K♥, Williams decided to simply call, then, stealing a page from Marcel Luske's book of tricks, announced he would "check in the dark" when the flop arrived. This bit of eccentricity worked to perfection when the dealer laid down both an ace and a 5. Arieh quickly moved all in, a bet Williams was even faster to call, having flopped a set. Williams's hand held up, leading Arieh to take a page out of Phil Hellmuth's book.

"What a joke," he said of Williams. "He's got a million and a half dollars and he calls five hundred thousand with two 5s."

"I felt it," was all Williams needed to say about the play. He now had $3,610,000 and was suddenly a serious threat, so much so that Arieh was forced to start picking on someone else. Josh selected Matt Dean, coming over the top of him with a big raise whenever he entered a pot, forcing him to fold. When Dean finally made a stand, it was with the wrong hand against the wrong player, pocket 9s against the red-hot Williams's pocket aces. The would-be math teacher was out in seventh, but won the right to brag to future classes that he could count all the way up to $675,000.

Al Krux followed soon afterward, when Raymer's A♥Q♦ beat his A♠9♥. His old friend Dan Harrington rushed over to shake his hand.

"Al, you did it. I mean, do you understand coming in this position was tougher than winning the tournament ten years ago?" It was also far more lucrative, as the $800,000, sixth-place prize dwarfed the $58,450 he earned for the identical accomplishment in 1990.

Shortly after Arizonan Glenn Hughes was eliminated in fifth—yet another scalp for the Fossilman—Harrington found himself on the ropes. At age fifty-eight, the oldest man at the table, Dan showed few signs of slowing down after six consecutive days of play.

"The only reason he doesn't dominate the tour," said Mike Matusow of the remarkable Harrington, "is that he doesn't have that fifth gear, but he does damn well with the other four."

He finally ran out of gas when, with only a gutshot straight draw, he moved in on David Williams, who called instantly with his two pair. The river gave David a full house, his third of the day, and Dan was out. Asked who he thought would win it all, Dan nodded towards the Fossilman.

"Raymer is going to be very hard to stop," he said. "Only David has enough chips, but he doesn't have the experience. He has the heart, though. Josh has the experience, but not the chips."

Knowing he needed to make a move while he still had any chips, Josh pushed all in with his last $2.1 million just after the dinner break with pocket 9s. Raymer called with A♣Q♠, and the flop nailed him: Q♦Q♣J♣. Arieh needed a miracle 9. When it didn't come, he was out in third place, disgruntled, yet $2.5 million richer.

. . .

Lost in all the praise for Josh's game and awe over the size of Greg's chip stack was the fact that David Williams was playing some very solid poker. Like Raymer, he had won his seat via a "double shootout" satellite at PokerStars and, although the vast majority of his experience was gained online, he had adapted well to the pressure of playing for the world championship. Andy Glazer—the great chronicler of the game who would tragically pass away a few months later—had recognized this early on, making Williams his "number-one intuition pick" to make the final table.

As heads-up play began, David Williams wasn't thinking about anything beyond winning the tournament. Only later would he discover the magnitude of the opportunity that had been presented to him. If he won, he would become, in no particular order, the first African American to win the championship, the first Texan since 1985, and, at the age of twenty-three, the youngest world champion, eclipsing the record Phil Hellmuth set in 1989.

To achieve these honors, he had a long way to go, as Raymer, with over $17 million, had nearly twice as many chips as him. With so much money on the table, it appeared the contest might drag into the early morning.

On the seventh hand Williams bet $300,000 with A♥4♠, and Raymer called with pocket 8s. The flop came low: 4♦2♦5♠.

"I had been looking at Greg when he looked at his cards," David said, "and I got the feeling he had a good hand, but not something great. I put him on two big cards. It honestly never occurred to me that he might have a decent pocket pair. Once that flop came, I figured I had the best hand, and if not, I had nine outs."

Greg checked, David bet $500,000, and Greg raised him $1.1 million. David called with his usual alacrity.

When the 2♥ hit the turn, Greg upped the stakes considerably, betting $2.5 million. Williams called, again with surprising speed.

"That's when I really thought he was trying to pressure me," he explained. "I thought he had a weak hand and had to bet."

A third deuce, the 2♣, arrived on fifth street.

Raymer moved in. "In hindsight I shouldn't have bet the river," he said afterward. "I was moving pretty quickly—I had all week—and I think if I had taken more time, I would have thought, 'What would he call me with that I can beat?' But there was so much energy in the air, I think I reverted to Level One thinking, 'I have a strong hand, I should bet,' and I got lucky that he did call."

Raymer is alluding to a concept presented by David Sklansky and Mason Malmuth in their *Hold'em Poker for Advanced Players,* a book many argue is the best ever written on the game. "Level One" thinking looks only at the strength of one's own cards. A "Level Two" thinker considers what his opponent might have. At "Level Three," a player is contemplating what his opponent might think that he is holding. And so it goes into Levels Four, Five, and beyond. When two experienced pros collide, their thought processes can become so labyrinthine that the best play is often to get off the merry-go-round altogether and do something completely at random.

By that point in the hand, however, it was too late for David to do a lot of thinking. He had done the math in his head, and he understood what a huge deficit—roughly seven to one—he would be facing if he folded, and decided that he was too committed to the pot to lay his hand down. Williams called and showed his full house, deuces full of 4s.

It took a second for Greg to realize that his bigger full house— deuces full of 8s—had earned him the championship. He raised his arms in triumph, but accepted his victory with appropriate humility, acknowledging just how much the meaning of this "championship" had changed in its thirty-five-year history.

"I played well, but I was the luckiest," he told the press while posing for pictures with those goofy glasses of his. "I don't think I'm one of the world's best poker players. There were probably fifteen hundred players in this field better than me."

AFTERWORD:
TO INFINITY AND BEYOND

The retrial of Sandy Murphy and Rick Tabish lasted six weeks during the fall of 2004 and featured one hundred and fifty witnesses and more than eight-hundred pieces of evidence. Attorney Tony Serra, the quirky iconoclast who was the inspiration for James Woods's character in the movie *True Believer*, provided Tabish with a spirited defense, using his closing statement to compare the Binion family to emperors of old.

"Mr. Ted Binion was a demigod—Hail Caesar!" he addressed the jury, as Sandy Murphy wept into a tissue. "We will find an assailant. The head must be brought forth and placed on a stick by dusk! We will not allow a mistress to live in the hallowed ground of our royalty! The offense is that royalty has been insulted."

The eccentric argument—along with a sustained attack on the medical expert who had developed the "burking" theory—was enough to convince the jury to acquit Murphy and Tabish of murder. Tabish remains in jail on a separate charge, but Murphy, still guilty of conspiring to steal Ted Binion's silver collection, was released for time served. She has—thanks to the largesse of octogenarian businessman William Fuller, who footed the bill for her bail as well as much of her defense—resumed her life in Las Vegas. She has become a professional gold miner, that is to say, she manages several of Fuller's investments, which include real estate developments and several active gold mines.

Both Becky and Jack were on hand to hear the acquittals. Both seemed prepared to move on with their lives.

"I was hoping for better, but it is what it is," said Jack. "I felt like it would be a guilty verdict."

Becky actually hugged Tabish's mother outside the courthouse, her empathy towards maternal suffering outweighing any feelings of animosity. "I am a little disappointed, but justice has been served and so be it," she said. "They've served time, and what can I say?" With that, she stepped away from the trial and, finally, from the spotlight.

Jack, still feeling great at sixty-eight, is revved up for his next adventure. While his sister rightly or wrongly took the brunt for everything that went wrong with the Horseshoe, Jack's image only got better as his riverboat casinos enjoyed a wealth of success.

"One reason Harrah's bought [Jack's riverboat] properties is that they were so well run," observed Eric Hausler, a financial analyst with Susquehanna Financial Group. "They were Class-A assets in every market in which they operated."

Armed with almost a billion dollars from their sale, Jack is actively looking for a new casino to run. As a noncompete clause with Harrah's forbids him from operating one anywhere in the continental United States other than Las Vegas, there are rumors that his next project will be a resort along the Strip. He also continues to make promotional appearances at Harrah's poker tournaments, including this year's World Series.

The Horseshoe, at least in its original incarnation, is over. In March 2005, the "Horseshoe" name was officially stripped from the premises. The signage, the napkins, even the carpets on the floor—the patterns consisting of gold horseshoes—were all discarded. The casino is now called Binion's Hotel and Casino, although no actual Binions are currently involved in the property.

Both the staff and the regulars are hopeful that the new management, a company called MTR, will improve the working and playing conditions. Becky Binion-Behnen's skills as a manager have to an extent been vindicated by the style that Harrah's employed during its interim stewardship. In order to keep down costs at a casino it never intended to run, Harrah's reduced the Horseshoe's staff to nearly skeleton crews, began charging employees to park their cars, and did little if anything to maintain the physical premises.

The actual building will for the last time play host to the final two tables of the 2005 World Series championship event, part of an arrangement with the city of Las Vegas to celebrate its centennial anniversary. The rest of the tournament, as well as all future tournaments, will take place on the Las Vegas Strip at the Rio Hotel and Casino, where Harrah's has shown far less reticence in spending their money, having constructed a brand-new poker room with a capacity for two-hundred tables. The entire affair has been moved from the beginning of spring to the middle of summer, perhaps in the hopes of attracting more vacationing amateurs.

Gone are the days of anything resembling intimacy. "Everybody wants to play in the World Series of Poker," says Howard Greenbaum, a vice president of Harrah's. "It's dying and going to heaven for the poker player." They expect to far surpass last year's record field, attracting as many as 6,600 entrants and a first prize that may reach eight digits. Harrah's, in an effort to both maximize their investment in the brand and duplicate the runaway success of the World Poker Tour, has also announced the start of a World Series of Poker Circuit, seven televised tournaments held in various spots around the country, that will culminate in the championship event, which has been moved from May to July.

Only time will tell whether or not the stratagem further builds upon the tournament's mystique, dilutes it with oversaturation, or kills it altogether by competing head-on with the already established World Poker Tour. What is clear is that poker has become big business. ESPN paid only $55,000 for the rights to broadcast the 2004 Series, a huge win for the network, as more than 2.5 million households tuned in to see Greg Raymer take the crown, creating the highest-rated poker broadcast in history. There will be no such bargain this year, as Harrah's has retained Pilson Communications—the group that helped to negotiate NASCAR's $2.4 billion television deal—to handle the negotiations. "We need to see what the . . . market will bear," says Ginny Shanks, a senior vice president of Harrah's.

ESPN, for its part, seems resigned to its fate. "The World Series of Poker is it," said Bob Chesterman, coordinating producer for ESPN Original Entertainment. "It's the pinnacle of poker. The players know that and the viewers know it."

As for the players whose faces compose the Gallery of Champions and those who have endeavored to join them, their destinies have proven as varied as their personalities. Many have parlayed their celebrity into other successes. Phil Hellmuth, Jr. still plays the big tournaments, but he dedicates much of his time to the business of being Phil Hellmuth. And business is good, including videos, pay-per-view tutorials, and several well-performing books.

It seems nowadays if the professionals aren't playing poker they're writing books—or at least encouraging their ghost writers to hurry up and finish before poker's current explosion begins to wane. The collected works of Dan Harrington, Chris Moneymaker, and Tom McEvoy can all be found at your local bookstore. While writing about poker has become a fairly lucrative sideline activity for some, others have discovered where the real money lays, the Internet. Erik Seidel and Jesus Ferguson have teamed up with a collection of all-star players—including Phil Gordon, Howard Lederer, and Phil Ivey—to start their own online poker room, Full Tilt Poker.

Other players have moved into completely different lines of work, relegating poker to a recreational passion. Bobby Baldwin remains one of the most powerful executives in Las Vegas—as CEO of the Mirage Resort group, he oversees some of the most prosperous casinos in the world, including the Bellagio, the Mirage, and Treasure Island. Tuna Lund, still residing in Reno, took some time off from the tournament circuit in the late 1990s to concentrate on raising his children.

Doyle Brunson can still be found, nearly every afternoon, playing high stakes cash games at the Bellagio. Johnny Chan and Chip Reese are likely to be sitting at the same table. Dolly recently released *Super/System 2* with help from a couple of old friends, including Crandell Addington.

Amarillo Slim still haunts the tournaments like a ghost—he has been in intensive care three times in the past year and recently had a "peacemaker" installed in his chest. His hair is currently quite long, and when he dons his Stetson he earns comparisons to General Custer. It's because of a wager, of course—someone was dumb enough to bet him that he couldn't go without cutting his hair for some length of time that wasn't long enough to dissuade Slim. Hollywood recently discovered the work of art that is his life. A movie directed by Milos Foreman and starring Nicholas Cage is currently in the works.

Both Doyle and Slim, as well as Puggy Pearson—who will certainly be dressed in some outlandish costume—will be at the Rio this July, health permitting. So too will T. J. Cloutier, Annie Duke, Scotty Nguyen, Kathy Liebert, Huck Seed, and nearly every other person mentioned in this book who hasn't moved on to the great poker table in the sky.

The World Series of Poker, once it gets into your blood, will never let go.

ACKNOWLEDGMENTS

While we would like to be able to claim attendance at the original Texas Gamblers' Reunion, our love affair with the game of poker didn't begin until James McManus documented his extraordinary adventure at the 1999 World Series of Poker in his classic article for *Harper's Magazine*. Our lives have never been the same. Whether or not this is a good thing is open to debate.

Many of the people instrumental to the tournament's evolution and success were gracious in sharing their time and memories, but none more than the legendary T. J. Cloutier. Few players better embody the spirit of the World Series, in all of its glory and pain, and no man deserves a championship more than he does.

We were very fortunate for the attention lavished upon us by two of the men most responsible for the World Series' early evolution, longtime tournament director Eric Drache and the one and only Thomas Austin Preston, Jr., better known to the world as Amarillo Slim. Thanks also to the other tournament veterans and behind-the-scenes participants who helped us paint a better picture, especially Henri Bollinger, Doyle Brunson, Frank Cutrona, Nolan Dalla, Barbara Enright, Rafe Furst, Phil Gordon, and Howard Lederer.

Research is rarely easy, but we were greatly assisted by two of the tournament's most ardent fans who opened their personal archives to us: Howard Schwartz, owner and proprietor of the singular Gamblers Book Shop in downtown Las Vegas, and reporter Ed Koch of the *Las Vegas Sun*, who was providing excellent coverage of the World Series long before it was in vogue to do so. Thanks also to Jeff German, Galen Hardy, Jackie Lapin, Jessie May, Jane Ann Morrison, Todd Pellegrino, Al Roth, Jason Sklar, and Howard Stutz for the help they provided.

We never got the chance to talk to the late, great Andy Glazer, but we sorely wish that we had. Andy single-handedly turned the once dry business of poker reporting into an art form. He also died much earlier than he should have. Nor did we ever speak to anybody associated with the ConJelCo Archives or the Hendon Mob's vast online poker database, but we would have had a hell of a time writing this book without them. We relied, in our reporting, on far too many writers to acknowledge them all here, but we urge you to peruse the bibliography to get a better sense of the enormous extent to which we owe thanks.

Thanks as usual to our agents, Greg Dinkin and Frank Scatoni of Venture Literary. Without their unwavering enthusiasm, this book never would have happened. It has been a tremendous pleasure working with Pete Wolverton, Katie Gilligan, and all of the other brilliant and hard-toiling people at Thomas Dunne/St. Martin's Press.

Storms would be remiss if he didn't single out the individuals who helped sustain him during this undertaking as well as throughout the ongoing project that is his life. Without the support of Byron and Linda Smiley this book simply could not have been written. To Linda, in particular, who sacrificed her time and energy for the good of the team, I have accrued a debt that I will forever be trying to repay. My dream of being a writer surely arose from a childhood spent living under the same roof as Debbie O'Brien. She is not only one of the sharpest editors in the business but a damn fine mother as well. My many adventures on the high seas with Forbes Reback contributed to my wanderlust and perhaps made me the road gambler I am today. Thanks for always coming though in the clutch. And finally to all those who helped support my writerly lifestyle by providing encouragement—and, more importantly, housing—during the lean years:

Frates and Josie Seeligson (ranch house); Debbie Schlinger (log cabin); Jennifer Jill Ramberg, Erick Brownstein, Kristen Muller, and Bill Rotko (Hollywood bungalows); Trip "Pants" Johnston and Gray "Eazy-G" Harley (beach houses); Jim Stanford and Amy Brennan (mountain chalets); and Chris McShane and Rocky McMurtray (the "Dank").

Jonathan would simply like to thank everyone he thanked in his last book, only more so.

Finally, to Zephyr Reback and Sam Grotenstein, two little men who will undoubtedly be world champions in whatever they choose to do.

BIBLIOGRAPHY

"About the Fremont Street Experience." VegasExperience.com.

"Binion Firm Moving to Las Vegas." *Las Vegas Sun* (17 February 2003).

"Binion Verdict: Not Guilty." *Las Vegas Review-Journal* (24 November 2004): 8A.

"Binions Fires 12 Poker Dealers During World Series Tournament." *Las Vegas Sun* (22 May 2002).

"Binions Sued Over Tip Pool." *Las Vegas Sun* (25 January 2002).

"Board Recommends Against Reinstating Binion's License." *Las Vegas Sun* (26 April 1996).

"Brad Daugherty: A Poker Legend." EmpirePoker.com.

"Brooklyn Systems Analyst Wins World Series of Poker." *Las Vegas Sun* (24 May 2002).

"Calling the Odds with Theatrical Flair." *The Irish Times* (13 November 1999): 18.

"Casino Denies Report Alleging Financial Woes." *Las Vegas Sun* (19 January 2001).

"Control Board Loses Bid to Delay Binion Hearing." *Las Vegas Sun* (26 April 1996).

"Dealers File Suit, Complaint." *Las Vegas Sun* (24 May 2002).

"Defending Poker Champion Knocked Out of Famous Tournament." *Las Vegas Sun* (23 May 2004).

"Does He Like His Work? You Bet!" *Los Angeles Times*, July 10, 1979.

"Economists Call It Recession." *CNNMoney* (26 November 2001).

"Editorial: The Jurors Have Spoken." *Las Vegas Sun* (26 November 2004).

"Eric Drache: Poker Wizard." *The Gambling Scene* (March-April 1980).

"Experts: Mismanagement Brought Down Landmark Vegas Casino." *Las Vegas Sun* (18 January 2004).

"Family Helps Celebrate $268,000 Win." *Las Vegas Review-Journal* (14 May 1990).

" 'Fat Man' Winner of Poker Series." *Las Vegas Sun* (18 May 1976).

"Five Card Stud Tournament Off." *Las Vegas Sun* (10 May 1978).

"Former Casino Owner Sues Horseshoe Over Chip Dispute." *Las Vegas Sun* (10 November 1998).

"Gaming License Denied." *Las Vegas Sun* (8 May 1997).

"Harrah's Announces Purchase of Horseshoe Casinos." *Reno Gazette-Journal* (12 September 2003): 1D.

"Harrah's Announces 2005 World Series of Poker Schedule." PR Newswire (25 October 2004).

"Harrah's Reveals Price for Name, World Series of Poker." *Las Vegas Sun* (7 May 2004).

"The Hendon Mob Poker Database." TheHendonMob.com

"Hold'em Poker Set Next Week for World Series." *Las Vegas Sun* (11 May 1978).

"Indian Gaming Company Launches New TV Production Unit." *Las Vegas Sun* (6 June 2002).

"Larry King Live." CNN (1 December 2004).

"Las Vegas Ace Takes Lead in World Series Poker." Associated Press (21 May 1981).

"Locations for Poker Championship Set." *Las Vegas Sun* (21 May 2004).

"LV Man Wins Hold'em Championship Game." United Press International (13 May 1990).

"McEvoy Wins Irish Poker Tournament." United Press International (16 September 1983).

"MTR Gaming Discloses Details of Horseshoe Sale." *Las Vegas Sun* (11 May 2004).

"NBER Business Cycle Dating Committee Determines That Recession Ended in March 1991." National Bureau of Economic Research (22 December 1992).

"Nevada Gaming Win Again Up." *Las Vegas Sun* (9 July 2004).

"Nevada High Court Says Binion's Should Pay Fremont Street Dues." *Las Vegas Sun* (11 April 2002).

"Oklahoman Takes $210,000 Poker Pot." *Las Vegas Sun* (20 May 1978).

"Panel Says Gaming Chief Violated Ethics Law." *Las Vegas Sun* (16 August 1996).

"Poker Legend Jack Binion to Host Tournament." *Las Vegas Sun* (15 October 2004).

"Poker Players Down to Five." *Las Vegas Sun* (16 May 1975).

"Poker Series Narrows." *Las Vegas Sun* (17 May 1976).

"Poker Tournament Used Restitution in Fraud Case." *Las Vegas Sun* (17 May 2004).

"Record Field Begins Play for Poker Title." *Las Vegas Review-Journal* (14 May 1991).

"Record Poker Payout Awarded." *Las Vegas Sun* (26 April 2004).

"Resort Launching Poker Tourney." *Las Vegas Sun* (22 February 2002).

"Roberts is Poker Champ." *Las Vegas Sun* (18 May 1975).

"Ted Binion Stripped of State Licenses." *Las Vegas Sun* (23 March 1998).

"Terry Rogers Dies in Gran Canaria." *Gambling News*.

"Texans Dominate World Series." *Poker Player* (17 June 1985).

"This Week They Said." *The Irish Times* (13 November 1999): 16.

"Troubled Downtown Casino Looks Set to Reopen." *Las Vegas Business Press* (1 March 2004): 12.

"Ungar." *Las Vegas Sun* (22 December 1998).

"Vegas Dealer New Woman Poker Champ." *Las Vegas Review-Journal* (15 May 1978): 1A.

"Vegas Hotel Tip Plan Annoys World Series Poker Players." Associated Press (19 April 2001).

"Video Game to be Unveiled Based on Poker Tourney." *Las Vegas Review-Journal* (10 May 1992).

"Women to Compete for World Poker Title in LV." *Las Vegas Valley Times* (7 March 1977).

"World Series of Poker Begins." *Las Vegas Sun* (22 April 2002).

"World Series of Poker Dominated by Texans." *Las Vegas Sun* (16 May 1976).

World Series of Poker Media Guide. Binion's Horseshoe (1986–1995).

"World Series of Poker Set to Begin." *Las Vegas Sun* (5 April 2002).

"World Series of Poker Winners 1970–2004." PlayWinningPoker.com.

Addy, Steve. "Poker World Ready for New Champion." *Las Vegas Sun* (24 May 2002).

Almeida, Christina. "Player Named Moneymaker Wins $2.5 Million at Poker World Series." *Las Vegas Sun* (24 May 2003).

Alvarez, A. *The Biggest Game in Town.* San Francisco: Chronicle Books, 1983.

———. "No Limit." *The New Yorker* (8 August 1994).

———. *Poker: Bets, Bluffs, and Bad Beats.* San Francisco: Chronicle Books, 2001.

Alvarez, Al. "The World Series of Poker." *Poker Digest* (4 May 2000): 34–37.

Arnold, Patrick. "Poker Battle Begins." Associated Press (19 May 1981).

Baldwin, Bobby. *Tales out of Tulsa.* Hollywood: Gambling Times, 1984.

Bates, Warren. "Luck of the Irish." *Las Vegas Review-Journal* (14 May 1999).

Beam, Alex. "Vegas Family Values." *Forbes* (21 November 1994): 88.

Behnen, Becky. KLAS Channel 8 (7 October 2002).

Benston, Liz. "Binion Eyeing LV Casino Opportunities." *Las Vegas Sun* (4 February 2005).

———. "Binion's Plans to Launch Internet Casino." *Las Vegas Sun* (13 December 2002).

———. "Binion's Pulls Poker Contest from Website." *Las Vegas Sun* (10 April 2003).

———. "Downtown Attraction May Receive Upgrade." *Las Vegas Sun* (5 November 2002).

———. "MTR to Take Over Binion's in March." *Las Vegas Sun* (9 November 2004).

———. "Owner Behnen Denies Horseshoe Is in Trouble." *Las Vegas Sun* (14 October 2002).

———. "Poker Takes Center Stage at Revamped Binion's." *Las Vegas Sun* (23 April 2004).

———. "World Series of Poker Makes Internet Debut." *Las Vegas Sun* (18 April 2003).

Berns, Dave. "Becky Behnen Makes Her Mark at the Horseshoe." *Las Vegas Review-Journal* (14 December 1998).

———. "Downtown Venue Seeks Seizure of Debt." *Las Vegas Review-Journal* (6 January 2002): 1F.

———. "Poker Prize Pool Prompts Probe." *Las Vegas Review-Journal* (17 June 2001): 1F.

———. "Stupak to Drop Lawsuit over Unredeemed Chips." *Las Vegas Review-Journal* (22 April 1999).

Binion, Benny. *Lester Ben 'Benny' Binion: Some Recollections of a Texas and Las Vegas Gambling Operator. An Oral History Conducted by Mary Ellen Glass.* Reno: University of Nevada, Reno, 1976.

Bluethman, Angie. "Binion's Gaming License Suspended Indefinitely." *Las Vegas Sun* (22 May 1997).

Bollinger, Henri. Telephone interview (2 March 2005).

Bradshaw, Jon. *Fast Company*. London: High Stakes Publishing, 1975.

Brindley, Roy. "Harrah's Retain Pilson to Negotiate Deal with ESPN." Pokernews.com (13 January 2005).

Brunson, Doyle. *Poker Wisdom of a Champion*. New York: Cardoza Publishing, 1984.

———. *Super/System*. Las Vegas: B & G Publishing, 1978.

Burbank, Jeff. "IRS Yields: Let the Games Begin." *Las Vegas Review-Journal* (27 October 1992): 1A.

Burris, Jim. "John Moss Named Mr. Poker." *Las Vegas Sun* (20 April 1970).

Carr, David. "Poker Pros, Now in TV's Glare, Always Want 'In.'" *The New York Times* (23 September 2004).

Cartwright, Gary. "Benny and the Boys." *Texas Monthly* (October 1991).

———. "Forget the Sopranos. Meet the Binions." *Texas Monthly* (November 1999).

Cavanangh, Wade. "British Seeks Binion's Poker Chips." *Las Vegas Sun* (22 March 1978).

———. "Doyle Brunson Still Poker King." *Las Vegas Sun* (12 May 1977).

———. "First Day of Final Play in Poker Warfare." *Las Vegas Sun* (19 May 1981).

———. "Former Cop Aces Poker Queen Title." *Las Vegas Sun* (6 May 1977).

———. "Former Poker King Ousted." *Las Vegas Sun* (23 May 1979).

———. "Huber Tops Poker Pack With $55,000." *Las Vegas Sun* (18 May 1978).

———. "Kaplan a Smash, Poker Leader." *Las Vegas Sun* (21 May 1980).

———. "Mr. Kotter, Champ Lose Poker Stakes." *Las Vegas Sun* (17 May 1978).

———. "Players Dwindle Fast at Binion's." *Las Vegas Sun* (24 May 1982).

———. "Players Vie For Poker Title." *Las Vegas Sun* (8 May 1977).

———. "Southerners Sweep World Series of Poker Final." *Las Vegas Sun* (25 May 1979).

———. "Stu Ungar Wins Crown Again in Binion Poker Tournament." *Las Vegas Sun* (22 May 1981).

———. "Tap City Comes Quickly in World Series of Poker." *Las Vegas Sun* (11 May 1977).

———. "Texas Moon Tops Field in Rich Poker Play." *Las Vegas Sun* (20 May 1980).

———. "Ungar New Poker King." *Las Vegas Sun* (22 May 1980).

———. "Unger [*sic*] Up, Kaplan Out, In Poker." *Las Vegas Sun* (22 May 1980).

———. "Ungar Wins $90,000 in Poker Series." *Las Vegas Sun* (7 May 1980).

Chan, Johnny. "Poker Can Lead to Big Things." *Card Player* (15 February 2002).

———. "No Title." *Card Player* (13 April 2001).

Chun, Gary C. W. "TV Tourneys Fuel a Rage." *Honolulu Star-Bulletin* (1 August 2004).

Ciaffone, Bob. "Jack Keller." *Card Player* (27 February 2004).

———. "Q&A With a WSP Champ." *Poker Player* (23 June 1986).

———. "Remembering Iron Man." *Card Player* (25 April 2003).

———. "Stu Ungar." *Card Player* (18 July 2003).

Clarke, Norm. "Murphy Prepare to Work, Live Life." *Las Vegas Review-Journal* (10 December 2004): 3A.

Cloutier, T. J. *Championship No-Limit & Pot-Limit Hold'em*. Las Vegas: Cardsmith Publishing, 1997.

———. Personal interview (3 January 2005).

———. "The Sailor and the Owl." *Card Player* (11 May 2001).

———. "Thoughts on the Series." *Card Player* (21 May 2004).

Collins, Claudia. " 'Costly' Poker Series Pays Off for Binion's." *Las Vegas Valley Times* (9 May 1978).

———. "LV Poker Struggle Kicks Off." *Las Vegas Valley Times* (26 April 1977).

———. "No Defending Champs Left in LV Poker Game." *Las Vegas Valley Times* (18 May 1978).

Cooke, Roy. "If We Wanna Be Big Time." *Card Player* (11 February 2005).

Cordovez, Diego. "A Star is Born." *Card Player* (25 October 2002).

Curtis, Gregory. "The World's Greatest Poker Player." *Texas Monthly* (May 1989).

Cutrona, Frank. Telephone interview (2 March 2005).

D.J. "Sympathy for the Devil." PokerPages.com.

Dahlberg, Tim. "Gaming Board Rejects Binion's Licensing." *Las Vegas Sun* (15 May 1997).

———. "LV Gamblers in Showdown for $540,000 Poker Prize." Associated Press (20 May 1983).

Dalla, Nolan. "Event #17: Limit Hold'em Shootout." PokerPages.com (7 May 2004).

———. "Every Poker Player's Dream: Going for the Gold at the World Series of Poker." *Card Player* (25 April 2003).

———. "From Longworth to Las Vegas and 70 Years In Between: Poker Legend Doyle Brunson Tells His Story and Shares His Views on Life as a Gambler." PokerPages.com (May 2003).

———. "It Was 20 Years Ago Today." *Card Player* (27 April 2001).

Dearing, David. "Richest Poker Tournament Scheduled in Las Vegas." *Las Vegas Sun* (13 December 1978).

Dionne, Roger. "Youth Can Age You." *Sports Illustrated* (14 May 1979).

Drache, Eric. Telephone interview (26 February 2005).

Evensen, Jay D. "Vegan Wins $660,000 in Poker Match." *Las Vegas Review-Journal* (18 May 1984).

Fink, Jerry. "Kaplan Launches Comeback with Namesake Comedy Club." *Las Vegas Sun* (17 May 2002).

Fisher, Jan. "Interview with Jim Albrecht." PokerPages.com.

Fishman, Steve. "The End of the Game." *New York* (29 March 1999): 43–49.

Fitch, Stephanie. "Poker's New Suit." *Forbes* (1 November 2004): 62.

Gang, Bill. "Binion Co-President Claims Family Feud Hurts Business." *Las Vegas Sun* (3 June 1996).

———. "Charges Dropped Against Binion in Alleged Gas Station Altercation." *Las Vegas Sun* (2 December 1997).

———. "Horseshoe Dispute May Reach Settlement." *Las Vegas Sun* (6 August 1996).

———. "Jack Binion Defends His Management of Horseshoe." *Las Vegas Sun* (29 March 1996).

———. "Lawsuit Says Security Firm Botched Call from Brunsons." *Las Vegas Sun* (15 June 1998).

Gasson, Peggy. "10th Annual World Series of Poker."

Gatewood, Jim. *Benny Binion*. Garland, Texas: Mullaney Corporation, 2002.

Geranios, Nicholas K. "Beginner's Luck? Novice in World Series of Poker in Las Vegas." *Las Vegas Sun* (20 May 2004).

German, Jeff. "Behnen, Horseshoe Were Victims of Changing Times." *Las Vegas Sun* (14 January 2004): 1B.

———. "Binion Admits Association with Reputed Mob Figure." *Las Vegas Sun* (11 April 1996).

———. "Binion Family Still Fighting for Control of Horseshoe Club." *Las Vegas Sun* (10 September 1996).

———. "Binion, Gaming Control Board Headed for Showdown." *Las Vegas Sun* (26 February 1998).

———. "Binion Suspended for Another Year." *Las Vegas Sun* (1 May 1996).

———. "Binion Suspension Upheld by Gamers." *Las Vegas Sun* (23 May 1997).

———. "Binion's Sister Asked for Stand-In." *Las Vegas Sun* (24 April 1998).

———. "Chief Witness Against Ted Binion in Jail on Outstanding Warrants." *Las Vegas Sun* (15 August 1997).

———. "Control Board: Binion Not Fit for New License." *Las Vegas Sun* (16 May 1997).

———. "Control Board Extends Probe of Ted Binion." *Las Vegas Sun* (20 March 1996).

———. "Control Board Investigates Binion." *Las Vegas Sun* (5 March 1996).

———. "D.A. Still Seeking Solution to Binion 'Jigsaw Puzzle.'" *Las Vegas Sun* (27 May 1999).

———. "Despite Objections, Binion's Deposition Begins." *Las Vegas Sun* (10 April 1996.)

———. "Detectives Conclude Binion Drug Overdose Was Staged." *Las Vegas Sun* (25 June 1999).

———. "Frontier Deal Raises Wilhelm's Image." *Las Vegas Sun* (1 November 1997).

———. "Gamers Probing Binion's Arrest." *Las Vegas Sun* (14 August 1997).

———. "Gamers to Grill Ted Binion in Public." *Las Vegas Sun* (25 March 1996).

———. "Gaming Chairman Steps Away from Binion Decision." *Las Vegas Sun* (17 April 1996).

———. "Horseshoe Club Layoffs in Works Amid Binion Battle." *Las Vegas Sun* (9 September 1997).

———. "Horseshoe's Big Cash-In of Chips Comes to Quiet End." *Las Vegas Sun* (14 January 1999).

———. "Horseshoe's Records Don't Show Stupak Won Chips." *Las Vegas Sun* (20 November 1998).

———. "Hotel Executive Binion Told His Life May Be in Danger." *Las Vegas Sun* (6 February 1997).

———. "Lawyer: FBI Leads May Justify New Binion Probe." *Las Vegas Sun* (25 April 2002).

———. "Mob Adds Another Twist to Binion Tale." *Las Vegas Sun* (30 July 2000).

———. "More Trouble for Embattled Taxicab Industry and its Regulators." *Las Vegas Sun* (7 April 1998).

———. *Murder in Sin City*. New York: Avon Books, 2001.

———. "Poker Player Brunson Robbed by Armed Men." *Las Vegas Sun* (29 April 1998).

———. "Reputed Mobster Mum on Binion." *Las Vegas Sun* (18 March 1996).

———. "'Royalty' Missing in Binion Family." *Las Vegas Sun* (19 November 2004).

———. "Sawyer Remembered as a Pillar of Strength and Integrity." *Las Vegas Sun* (22 February 1996).

———. "Strip High-Roller Battle Brewing." *Las Vegas Sun* (19 February 1996).

———. "Stupak, Behnen Animosity Heats Up." *Las Vegas Sun* (29 August 2000).

———. "Subpoenas Served in Hearing Targeting Casino Executive Ted Binion." *Las Vegas Sun* (12 March 1996).

———. "Subpoenas Target 15 for Binion Hearing." *Las Vegas Sun* (13 March 1996).

———. "Suspended Horseshoe Exec Fails to Appear Before Board." *Las Vegas Sun* (28 March 1996).

———. "Ted Binion's Home Sprayed With Bullets." *Las Vegas Sun* (5 June 1997).

———. "Trying to Blame the Behnens." *Las Vegas Sun* (4 May 2004).

German, Jeff, and Jace Radke. "Arrests Provide Sense of Relief to Family, Friends of Binion." *Las Vegas Sun* (25 June 1999).

———. "Cause Debated in Death of Ted Binion." *Las Vegas Sun* (18 September 1998).

———. "Former Horseshoe Exec Binion Found Dead." *Las Vegas Sun* (18 September 1998).

German, Jeff, and Gary Thompson. "Horseshoe Owner to Appeal Order to Cash Chips." *Las Vegas Sun* (18 November 1998).

Glazer, Andrew N. S. "All Hail Harrington." Finaltablepoker.com (28 May 2004).

———. "The Dangers of Unexplored Territory—WSOP Day Three." Finaltablepoker.com (24 May 2004).

———. "Gentlemen, Start Your Engines." Conjelco.com (10 May 1999).

———. "Give No Quarter, Ask No Quarter, And Win 10 Million Quarters." (6 June 2003).

———. "Irish Eyes Are Smiling." Conjelco.com (13 May 1999).

———. "The Man Who Might Have Been King." *Card Player* (2 July 2004).

———. "A Nearly Perfect Champ, a Nearly Perfect Rumble; Watch These Nine, and Feel Quite Humble." Finaltablepoker.com (30 May 2004).

———. "A Rout Turns into a Close Shave." *Poker Digest* (27 June 2002).

———. "Step by Step, Inch by Inch." Conjelco.com (11 May 1999).

———. "Superstars." ESPN.com (16 June 2004).

———. "$10,000 No-Limit Hold'em Championship, Day One: And We're Off!" (25 September 2001).

———. "$10,000 No-Limit Hold'em Championship, Day One, Part II: Top Twenty to Terrorize the Tiny" (25 September 2001).

———. "$10,000 No-Limit Hold'em Championship, Day Two: Follow the Money" (25 September 2001).

———. "$10,000 No-Limit Hold'em Championship, Day Three: And the Aces Shall Inherit the Chips" (25 September 2001).

———. "$10,000 No-Limit Hold'em Championship, Day Four: The Hour of Living Dangerously" (25 September 2001).

———. "$10,000 No-Limit Hold'em Championship, Day Two: Survive and Advance." *Poker Digest* (23 May 2002).

———. "$10,000 No-Limit Hold'em Championship, Day Three: Why, Why, What If, and If Only" (28 May 2002).

———. "$10,000 No-Limit Hold'em Championship, Day Four: Think About It" (28 May 2002).

———. "$10,000 No-Limit Hold'em Championship, Day Five: A Rout Turns Into a Close Shave" (28 May 2002).

———. "There Can Be Only One." Conjelco.com (12 May 1999).

———. "Whether It's After Four or After Five, the Motto Now: Survive, Survive!" Finaltablepoker.com (27 May 2004).

———. "Winner on Table 112." Finaltablepoker.com (26 May 2004).

Glover, Randy. "Profile of David Roepke." PokerPages.com.

Goldman, Adam. "Agents Shut Down Gambling at Binion's Horseshoe in Las Vegas." *Las Vegas Sun* (9 January 2004).

———. "Finalists Vie for $5 Million Prize in Las Vegas Poker World Series." *Las Vegas Sun* (28 May 2004).

———. "Harrah's Entertainment Creates World Series of Poker Circuit." Associated Press (20 September 2004).

———. "Harrah's Entertainment Says It's Buying Binion's Horseshoe Casino." *Las Vegas Sun* (12 January 2004).

———. "Raymer Takes Home $5 Million Prize in Las Vegas' Poker World Series." *Las Vegas Sun* (29 May 2004).

Goldman, Dan. "Online Poker Revolutionizes the World Series." *Card Player* (20 June 2003).

Goodman, Michael J. "Courting the Heavy Hitters." *Los Angeles Times Magazine* (18 February 1998): 10.

Gordon, Phil, and Jonathan Grotenstein. *Poker: The Real Deal*. New York: Simon and Schuster Spotlight Entertainment, 2004.

Green, Marian. "Poker King Johnny Moss Dies." *Las Vegas Review-Journal* (20 December 1995): 1B.

Groover, Joel. "Josh Arieh." Pokerpages.com (April 2004).

Hale, H. D. *Gentleman Gambler: "Oklahoma Johnny" Hale on Poker & Las Vegas*. Las Vegas: Poker Plus Publications, 1999.

Hall, Michael. "The Skinny on Slim." *Texas Monthly* (May 2003).

Haney, Jeff. "Wild Wild West Unveils Innovative Baseball Contest." *Las Vegas Sun* (10 May 2000).

Harroch, Richard D., and Lou Krieger. *Poker for Dummies*. New York: Hungry Minds, 2000.

Hassell, Greg. "Road to Top Was Long for Poker Player." *Las Vegas Review-Journal* (29 May 1983).

Hayano, David M. *Poker Faces: The Life and Work or Professional Card Players*. Berkeley: University of California Press, 1982.

Hellmuth, Phil, Jr. "Attitude, Attitude, Attitude." *Card Player* (11 October 2002).

———. *Bad Beats and Lucky Draws*. New York: HarperCollins Publishers, 2004.

———. "Kept Up at Night Wondering, 'What If . . .'" *Card Player* (11 July 2001).

———. *Play Poker Like the Pros*. New York: HarperCollins Publishers, 2003.

———. "The 2004 World Series of Poker." *Card Player* (18 June 2004).

———. "2004 World Series of Poker Eliminations." *Card Player* (2 July 2004).

———. "Trying to Run Over Stu Ungar." *Card Player* (18 January 2002).

———. "Varkonyi's Qc10c." *Card Player* (13 September 2002).

———. "You Wanna Bet?" *Card Player* (18 July 2003).

Helming, Ann. "Nets Flush With Poker Options; Who Could Have Imagined Poker Would Be a Viewer- and Marketer-Favorite?" *Advertising Age* (31 May 2004): S14.

Hevener, Phil. "Entries to Series Finals Rise Sharply." *Las Vegas Review-Journal* (15 May 2004): 1D.

———. "Poker Players' Wives Say Good Life 'In the Cards.'" *Las Vegas Sun* (18 May 1980).

Holden, Anthony. *Big Deal: One Year as a Professional Poker Player*. London: Abacus, 1990.

Isaacs, Susie. "A World Champion in the Family." *Poker Digest* (11 January 2001).

Jaffrey, Allyn. "Phil Gordon—A Frog Turned Prince." *Card Player* (7 May 2004).
———. "Phil Hellmuth, Jr.: The Bad Boy of Poker." *Card Player* (9 April 2004).
Jenkins, Don. *Champion of Champions: A Portrait of the Greatest Poker Player of Our Time*, Odessa, Texas: JM, 1981.
Johnson, Linda. "Howard 'Tahoe' Andrew . . . One of the Golden Oldies." *Card Player* (5 December 2003).
———. "Matt Savage—A Rising Star." *Card Player* (29 March 2002).
———. "Robert Varkonyi: Poker's 2002 World Champion, Parts I & II." *Card Player* (30 August 2002 & 13 September 2002).
Jones, Chris. "Harrah's Purchase Clears Last Hurdle." *Las Vegas Review-Journal* (1 July 2004): 1D.
Kaplan, Michael. "Dealing With the Master." *L.A. Weekly* (16–22 May 2003).
———. "Gambling: Who Wants To Be a Poker Millionaire?" *Cigar Aficionado* (September/October 2003).
———. "The Original Showdown." *Las Vegas Life* (May 2003): 35–40.
Karp, Warren. "Moneymaker's Real Name Is . . ." *Card Player* (23 April 2004).
Katz, Jonathan M. "Not in the Cards." *Slate* (4 June 2004).
Kelly, Charles. "Pickup-Driving Poker Champ Says Perfectionism Helped Him to Title." *Las Vegas Review-Journal* (17 May 1993): 4B.
Knapp, George. "Knappster: Hard Rock Shuffle." *Las Vegas Mercury* (24 May 2004).
Koch, Ed. "Binion Followed Dad's Untamed Style." *Las Vegas Sun* (18 September 1998).
———. "Binion Pleased Beating Case Dropped." *Las Vegas Sun* (25 August 1992): 6B.
———. "Binion's Chip Immortalizes Poker Player." *Las Vegas Sun* (22 April 1996).
———. "Binion's Poker Tournament Getting Tougher for Only Champ Left in Field." *Las Vegas Sun* (13 May 1998).
———. "Binion's Tournament is Smaller, But It's On." *Las Vegas Sun* (9 February 1999).
———. "Binion's Used to Million-Dollar Pots." *Las Vegas Sun* (14 May 1993).
———. "Brunson Adds Page to Legend." *Las Vegas Sun* (6 May 1998).
———. "Brunson Reigns in Early Round of Poker Event." *Las Vegas Sun* (29 April, 1998).
———. "Celebrities Add to Poker Title Hunt." *Las Vegas Sun* (12 May 1998).
———. "Chan Makes Comeback in Poker Play." *Las Vegas Sun* (17 May 1989).
———. "Colorful Poker Player Wolford Dies." *Las Vegas Sun* (15 May 2003).
———. "Cotton-Pickin' Millionaire." *Las Vegas Sun* (14 May 1993): 1A.
———. "Famed Gambler Ungar Dies at 45." *Las Vegas Sun* (23 November 1998).
———. "Hall of Famer Moss Slows Down." *Las Vegas Sun* (16 May 1995): 4A.
———. "Hellmuth Goes for 3 in Row." *Las Vegas Sun* (10 May 1993).
———. "Hitting the Million Mark." *Las Vegas Sun* (3 May 1997).
———. "Hottest Players at Top." *Las Vegas Sun* (13 May 1993).
———. "Johnny Moss Wins $116,400 in Poker Event." *Las Vegas Sun* (3 May 1988).
———. "Key Hands." *Las Vegas Sun* (16 May 1997).
———. "Known for Poker Prowess, Ungar Had Deeper Side." *Las Vegas Sun* (27 November 1998).
———. "Moore Inducted to Hall of Fame." *Las Vegas Sun* (13 May 1997).
———. "Moss Eliminated From Poker Series." *Las Vegas Sun* (18 May 1988).
———. "New Experience for Binion's Poker." *Las Vegas Sun* (21 April 1997).

———. "Nguyen Collects $1 Million with Binion's Poker Crown." *Las Vegas Sun* (15 May 1998).

———. "Nguyen Sounds and Looks Like a 'Win' in Binion's Poker." *Las Vegas Sun* (14 May 1998).

———. " '92 Binion's Winner Out." *Las Vegas Sun* (11 May 1993).

———. "Past Poker Champions Run into Trouble." *Las Vegas Sun* (15 May 1991).

———. "Player's Passing Ends Era." *Las Vegas Sun* (20 December 1995): 1A.

———. "Poker Champion Smith Dies." *Las Vegas Sun* (1 March 1996).

———. "Poker Champ Takes On Computer for Charity." *Las Vegas Sun* (29 April 1990).

———. "Poker Chief: Let's Keep Growing." *Las Vegas Valley Times* (16 May 1984).

———. "Poker Promoter Albrecht Dies." *Las Vegas Sun* (20 October 2003).

———. "Poker Series Draws Record Field." *Las Vegas Sun* (3 May 1989).

———. "Recession Affects Poker." *Las Vegas Sun* (12 May 1992).

———. "Record Pot Taken in Binion's Poker." *Las Vegas Sun* (18 May 1990).

———. "Several Poker Players Mix Dual Careers." *Las Vegas Sun* (8 May 1988).

———. "Sparks Fly at Record Poker Final." *Las Vegas Sun* (17 May 1991): 1A.

———. "Strike Impact Doesn't Faze Poker Tourney." *Las Vegas Sun* (6 December 1990).

———. "Strikers Appeal to Poker Players." *Las Vegas Sun* (1 May 1990).

———. "Taxes Don't Keep Foreign Players from Poker Event." *Las Vegas Sun* (29 April 1996).

———. "$10 Million Prize Fund Is in the Cards." *Las Vegas Sun* (24 April 1995): 4A.

———. " 'Texas Dolly' Brunson Passes $1.1. Mil. Mark." *Las Vegas Valley Times* (20 May 1983).

———. "A Tough Pair to Draw On." *Las Vegas Sun* (14 May 1991).

———. "Ungar Eliminated in Binion Poker Series Action." *Las Vegas Sun* (16 May 1989).

———. "Ungar Wins World Series of Poker Finale for 3rd Time." *Las Vegas Sun* (16 May 1997).

———. "Veterans Shine at World Series." *Las Vegas Sun* (9 May 1997).

Koch, Ed, and Gary Thompson. "World Series of Poker in Doubt." *Las Vegas Sun* (6 July 1998).

Konik, Michael. *The Man with the $100,000 Breasts and Other Gambling Stories.* New York: Broadway Books, 1999.

———. *Telling Lies and Getting Paid.* Las Vegas: Huntington Press, 2001.

Koppelman, Brian. "Mayfair Club: An Elegy for a Carpet Joint." *New York Observer* (21 May 2001).

Lanning, Rick. "Texas Dolly." *Nevada* (July/August 1983): 17–20.

Larson, Barbara. "Horseshoe Lures Poker Champs." *Las Vegas Sun* (12 May 1975): 9.

Lauer, Kent. Title unknown. *Las Vegas Review-Journal* (17 May 1983).

Lederer, Katy. *Poker Face.* New York: Crown Publishers, 2003.

Leong, Grace. "Federal Agency Files Labor Complaint Against Binion's." *Las Vegas Sun* (3 February 2003).

Lubove, Seth. "All in the Family." *Forbes* (28 July 1997): 48.

Luo, Michael. "Poker Champion Tells Story of 'Dead Money.' " *Las Vegas Sun* (28 August 2003): 3C.

Macy, Robert. "Jury Finds Pair Guilty in Death of Well-Known Gambler." *Las Vegas Sun* (19 May 2000).

Marcus, Richard. *American Roulette*. New York: Thomas Dunne Books, 2003.

McCabe, George. "Side Games." *Las Vegas Review-Journal* (16 May 1991): 1D.

McEvoy, Tom. "The Beauty and the Beast." *Card Player* (23 May 2003).

———. "A Blast From the Past: Set Over Set at the 1978 World Series of Poker." *Card Player* (30 January 2004).

———. "A Bluff That Turned the Tide of Fortune." *Card Player* (6 December 2002).

———. "The '83 Class Reunion at the 2003 World Series of Poker." *Card Player* (20 June 2003).

———. "He Might As Well Bet $100,000 in the Dark." *Card Player* (22 June 2001).

———. "Set Over Set Turns the Tide in 1981." *Card Player* (11 April 2003).

———. "Tribulation, Triumph, and Tribute." *Card Player* (31 January 2003).

———. "What, Another Unknown Defeated the Pros?!" *Card Player* (4 July 2003).

———. "World Series of Poker Memories: Man Versus Machine." *Card Player* (6 June 2003).

McManus, James. *Positively Fifth Street: Murderers, Cheetahs, and Binion's World Series of Poker*. New York: Farrar, Strauss & Giroux, 2003.

Mikla, Pete. "Baldwin Wins Poker Tourney." *Las Vegas Review-Journal* (May 1978).

———. "Final Round of Poker Series Begins." *Las Vegas Review-Journal* (20 May 1980).

———. "High Stakes Keep Poker Players at Table." *Las Vegas Review-Journal* (5 May 1981).

———. " 'Non-Pro' Fowler Wins Poker Meet." *Las Vegas Review-Journal* (26 May 1979).

———. "Players Line Up for World Poker Tourney." *Las Vegas Review-Journal* (May 1979).

———. "Poker Champ Looks to Next Year's Tournament." *Las Vegas Review-Journal* (20 May 1978).

———. "Poker Meet to Kick Off." *Las Vegas Review-Journal* (25 April 1980).

———. "Poker Takes Over; Series Underway." *Las Vegas Review-Journal* (27 April 1978).

———. "Record 54 Enter World Poker Tournament." *Las Vegas Review-Journal* (22 May 1979).

———. "You've Got to Know When to Fold 'Em." *Las Vegas Review-Journal* (21 May 1980).

Miller, Len. "World Series: The Final Match." *Poker Player* (17 June 1985): 3.

Moneymaker, Chris, with Daniel Paisner. *Moneymaker: How an Amateur Poker Player Turned $40 into $2.5 Million at the World Series of Poker*. New York: HarperEntertainment, 2005.

Morrison, Jane Ann. "Horseshoe Crowns a New Poker King." *Las Vegas Review-Journal* (23 May 1986).

———. "Horseshoe Customers Hope New Owners Have Some of Benny Binion's Touch." *Las Vegas Review-Journal* (3 April 2004): 1B.

Munzer, Lee. "$10,000 No-Limit Hold'em Championship, Day One." Seiyuu.com (23 May 2002).

Nemeth, B. J. "No-Limit Hold'em World Championship Day One." *Card Player* (22 May 2004).

———. "No-Limit Hold'em World Championship Day Two." *Card Player* (22 May 2004).

———. "No-Limit Hold'em World Championship Day Three." *Card Player* (22 May 2004).

Noer, Michael. "The Last Article You Will Ever Have to Read on Executive Pay? No Way!" *Forbes* (20 May 1996): 177.

O'Connell, Peter. "The Binion Files." *Las Vegas Review-Journal* (24 June 2001): 25A.

O'Malley, Michael. "Party Poker Million (Final)." PokerPages.com (16 March 2002).

Odessky, Dick. "Now the Real Show at Binion's Tourney." *Las Vegas Valley Times* (26 April 1978).

Palermo, Dave. "Casino, Gamblers Ready for Poker Championship." *Las Vegas Review-Journal* (18 April 1993): 1B.

———. "Patient Puts Life on Line." *Las Vegas Review-Journal* (date unknown).

———. "Poker Players Ready to Draw at World Title." *Las Vegas Review-Journal* (10 May 1993): 1B.

———. "Standing Around Brings Poker Win." *Las Vegas Review-Journal* (15 May 1992): 1B.

Palermo, Dave, and Jeff Burbank. "Casinos Say Business Brisk." *Las Vegas Review-Journal* (27 December 1991): 1B.

———. "Gaming Analysts Predict Prolonged Slump." *Las Vegas Review-Journal* (22 December 1991): 1A.

Paris, Ellen. "The House That Boyd Built." *Forbes* (3 June 1985): 66.

Paulle, Mike. "We Cannot Stay Furlong" (1999).

———. "It's Dance Time—The World Series of Poker Championship." *Card Player* (29 May 1998): 22–23.

———. "World Series of Poker Championship: A Close Shave." *Card Player* (7 June 2002).

Peters, Pete. "Binion Back 'Home'; Keller in Poker Lead." *Las Vegas Sun* (17 May 1984).

———. "Binion Poker Field Narrows; McEvoy Out." *Las Vegas Sun* (16 May 1984).

———. "Defending Poker Champ Doesn't Like the Odds." *Las Vegas Sun* (16 May 1983).

———. "Five Locals in Horseshoe Poker Finale." *Las Vegas Sun* (19 May 1983).

———. "Keller Takes It All With a Pair of 10s." *Las Vegas Sun* (18 May 1984).

———. "Las Vegas McEvoy Wins Poker." *Las Vegas Sun* (22 May 1983).

———. "Oklahoman Wins Richest Poker Series Prize." *Las Vegas Sun* (23 May 1986).

———. "Poker Champion Says Thanks with $15,000." *Las Vegas Sun* (28 May 1982).

———. "Poker High Noon at Horseshoe Shootout." *Las Vegas Sun* (22 May 1982).

———. "Poker Leader Out for Biggest Win Ever." *Las Vegas Sun* (20 May 1983).

———. "Roach Takes Poker Lead; Flynt Hustles Comeback." *Las Vegas Sun* (18 May 1983).

———. "Squatty Catches Poker Lead." *Las Vegas Sun* (17 May 1983).

———. "Texan's Full House Banks $700,000." *Las Vegas Sun* (24 May 1985).

———. "$3 Million Ready for Horseshoe Poker Winners." *Las Vegas Sun* (24 April 1984).

———. "World Poker Series Bustin' Its Britches." *Las Vegas Sun* (10 May 1983).

———. "World Series of Poker Begins at Binion's." *Las Vegas Sun* (23 April 1984).

Peterson, Ivars. "Playing Your Cards Right." *Science News Online* (18 July 1998).

Peterson, Kristen. "Lost in the Shuffle: Chroniclers Scouring for Rare World Series of Poker Mementos." *Las Vegas Sun* (13 May 2004).

Pordum, Matt. "Tabish, Murphy Jury Deliberates for Second Day." *Las Vegas Sun* (22 November 2004).

———. "Tabish, Murphy Not Guilty of Killing Binion." *Las Vegas Sun* (23 November 2004).

Pordum, Matt, and Jace Radke. "Court 'Has a Lot of Options' in Sentencing Murphy, Tabish." *Las Vegas Sun* (24 November 2004).

Preston, Amarillo Slim, with Greg Dinkin. *Amarillo Slim: In a World Full of Fat People*. New York: HarperEntertainment, 2003.

Preston, Thomas. "Amarillo Slim." Personal interview (18 December 2004).

Pudaite, Paul, and Tom Sims. "1996 World Series of Poker—The Survivors." Conjelco.com (16 May 1996).

Radke, Jace, and Kim Smith. "Binion Family Feels Sentences Were Fair." *Las Vegas Sun* (25 May 2000).

Reid, Jean. "Irish Luck with 'Cool Hand' Collette?" *Las Vegas Valley Times* (19 May 1980).

———. "Poker Players Are Going to the Computers." *Las Vegas Valley Times* (9 May 1980).

———. "650 Poker Players Compete for $1,500,000 at Binion's." *Las Vegas Valley Times* (12 May 1980).

Reinert, Al. "Inside the World Series of Poker." *Texas Monthly* (August 1973).

Riley, Brendan. "Gaming Commission Hearing on Ted Binion Delayed." *Las Vegas Sun* (20 October 1997).

———. "Nevada High Court Grants Appeals in Ted Binion Murder Case." *Las Vegas Sun* (14 July 2003).

———. "Ted Binion Hearings Set for April in Las Vegas." *Las Vegas Sun* (28 February 1996).

———. "Three Charges Dropped Against Binion; but Two Others Remain." *Las Vegas Sun* (26 February 1998).

Ritter, Ken. "Harrah's Completes Deal, Plans to Reopen Binion's Horseshoe." Associated Press (22 January 2004).

Rubin, Neal. "He's Experienced Loser." *Las Vegas Sun* (16 May 1981).

———. "Side Games Spur Series." *Las Vegas Sun* (24 April 1981).

———. "The Teacher Does It." *Las Vegas Sun* (26 April 1981).

Ryan, Cy. "Binion Decries New Criminal Allegations." *Las Vegas Sun* (24 November 1997).

Ryan, Cy. "Binion Wins Round in License Fight." *Las Vegas Sun* (23 February 1996).

———. "Gaming Win Inches Up." *Las Vegas Sun* (10 December 2003).

———. "Strip Revenue Dips in March." *Las Vegas Sun* (13 May 1992).

Ryan, Harriet. "Defiant Lovers Get Life Sentences for Casino Murder." *Court TV Online* (15 September 2000).

Schichtman, Sondra H. "Berry and Rick Johnston." *Card Player* (18 April 1997).

Schumacher, Geoff. " 'Rise and Fall of Bob Stupak' a Towering Addition to Limited Las Vegas Bookshelf." *Las Vegas Sun* (15 May 1997).

Scott, Cathy. "Becky Behnen's Hubby Granted Work Card." *Las Vegas City Life* (24 July 2003).

Scott, Cathy, and Jeff German. "Metro Uncertain if Blitzstein Homicide a Mob Hit." *Las Vegas Sun* (8 January 1997).

Seligman, Dan. "The Winning Hand." *Forbes* (26 July 1999): 76.

Sexton, Mike. "Berry Johnston." *Card Player* (2 July 2004).

———. "Final Hand of the '97 World Series of Poker." *Card Player* (15 March 2002).

———. "Howard Lederer." *Card Player* (22 November 2002).

———. "Jack Binion." *Card Player* (27 February 2004).

———. "Luck or Destiny." *Card Player* (1 February 2002).

———. "Stu Ungar: Welcome to the Hall of Fame." *Card Player* (13 April 2001).

Shapiro, Max. "Fun and Games at the World Series of Poker." *Card Player* (20 June 2003).

———. "Hail to the King (On Day Three Anyway)." *Poker Digest* (23 May 2003).

———. "Reports of My Death Have Been Greatly Exaggerated." *Poker Digest* (20 May 2003).

Shemeligian, Bob. "Chess Match a Reminder of What Separates Man, Machine." *Las Vegas Sun* (13 May 1997).

———. "Winning Hand." *Las Vegas Mercury* (15 April 2004).

Shulman, Allyn Jaffrey. "Action Dan." *Card Player* (10 September 2004).

Shulman, Jeff. "Atop the World." *Las Vegas Review-Journal* (20 May 2000).

———. "Aviation Club, and an Interview With Chris Moneymaker." *Card Player* (20 June 2003).

———. "Bellagio to Host Poker Series." *Las Vegas Review-Journal* (22 February 2002): 1D.

———. "Binion's Distribution Plan Annoys Poker Players." *Las Vegas Review-Journal* (19 April 2001).

———. "Binion's Fires 12 Poker Dealers." *Las Vegas Review-Journal* (22 May 2002): 1D.

———. "Binion's Horseshoe: Poker Room Manager Out." *Las Vegas Review-Journal* (7 September 2001).

———. "Boss Plans Changes for Poker Room." *Las Vegas Review-Journal* (20 July 2001): 3D.

———. "Horseshoe Broke No Rules in Dividing Poker Prizes, Regulators Say." *Las Vegas Review-Journal* (16 November 2001): 7D.

———. "The Horseshoe Closing: Blame Becky." *Las Vegas Review-Journal* (18 January 2004).

———. "Horseshoe May Be Shopping Series." *Las Vegas Review-Journal* (31 December 2003).

———. "Horseshoe Turns 50." *Las Vegas Review-Journal* (15 August 2001): 1D.

———. "More Signs of Bad Times at Horseshoe." *Las Vegas Review-Journal* (23 December 2003).

———. "MTR: Binion's Deal on Track." *Las Vegas Sun* (10 March 2004).

———. "Nevadan at Work: Bob Thompson—World Series of Poker Tournament Director." *Las Vegas Review-Journal* (22 April 2001): 1F.

———. "Online Poker Player Scores $1 Million Payoff." *Las Vegas Review-Journal* (22 March 2002): 2D.

———. "Player Barred from Series." *Las Vegas Review-Journal* (21 April 2001).

———. "Regulators Scrutinize Payouts to Card Tournament Workers." *Las Vegas Review-Journal* (5 June 2001).

———. "Sale of Riverboat Company Rumored." *Las Vegas Review-Journal* (30 July 2003).

———. "Shuffle Up and Deal." *Las Vegas Review-Journal* (20 April 2002): 1D.

———. "Winning Hand." *Las Vegas Review-Journal* (15 August 2000).

———. "Woman the Chip Leader at World Series of Poker." *Las Vegas Review-Journal* (18 May 2000).

———. "World Series of Poker Opens Today." *Las Vegas Review-Journal* (20 April 2001): 3D.

Sims, Tom. "1997 World Series of Poker Daily Report." Conjelco.com (16 May 1997).

Sklansky, David. "The World's Greatest Poker Players." *Gambling Times* (May 1978).

Smith, Dana. "Byron 'Cowboy' Wolford, 1930–2003: A Tribute to a Rodeo Champion and Poker Legend." *Card Player* (6 June 2003).

———. "Erik Seidel." *Card Player* (27 April 2001).

———. "Noel Furlong: The 1999 World Champion of Poker Pays Tribute to a Dear Friend." GamblingTribune.org (11 June 2003).

Smith, Dana, Tom McEvoy, and Ralph Wheeler. *The Championship Table at the World Series of Poker: 1970–2002*. Las Vegas: Cardsmith Publishing, 2003.

Smith, John L. "Binion's Employees Say Casino's Failure Not Difficult to Explain." *Las Vegas Review-Journal* (13 January 2004).

———. "Gaming Suffers New Blow Before Its Critics: Stupak's Lawsuit." *Las Vegas Review-Journal* (12 November 1998).

———. "Good Fortune Appears to Have Slipped Away from Binion's Horseshoe." *Las Vegas Review-Journal* (13 February 2002): 1B.

Smith, Raymond. *Better One Day as a Lion*. Dublin: Sporting Books Publishers, 1996.

———. *The Poker Kings of Las Vegas*. Dublin: Aherlow Publishers, 1982.

Smith, Rod. "Binion's Horseshoe Reopens." *Las Vegas Review-Journal* (2 April 2004).

———. "Horseshoe Woes Continue." *Las Vegas Review-Journal* (28 January 2004): 1D.

Spanier, David. *Total Poker*. New York: Simon and Schuster, 1977.

Strow, David. "Horseshoe Retires $1 Million Display." *Las Vegas Sun* (20 January 2000).

———. "Luck Prevails Over Skill at Poker Tourney." *Las Vegas Sun* (19 May 2000).

———. "Mortensen Claims Poker Championship" (18 May 2001).

———. "Poker Championship Leaves Spaniard Flush with Cash." *Las Vegas Sun* (21 May 2001).

Stutz, Howard. "Card Playing is a Full-Time Job for 'Grand Old Man' of Poker." *Las Vegas Review-Journal* (9 May 1988).

———. " 'Golden Boy' Plays His Hand." *Las Vegas Review-Journal* (19 May 1989): 1A.

———. "Harrah's Hires Consultant to Negotiate Series Deal." *Las Vegas Review-Journal* (11 January 2005): 1D.

———. "Iranian Businessman Takes Poker Title." *Las Vegas Review-Journal* (18 May 1990).

———. "NBC to Air Poker Tourney." *Las Vegas Review-Journal* (14 February 2005).

———. "Norwegian Victorious in Poker Series Event." *Las Vegas Review-Journal* (10 May 1988): 2B.

———. "178 Vie for World Poker Championship." *Las Vegas Review-Journal* (16 May 1989): 3B.

———. "Poker Classic On Despite Strike." *Las Vegas Review-Journal* (22 April 1990).

———. "Reigning Poker Champ Out of Game." *Las Vegas Review-Journal* (16 May 1990).

———. "Sparks Gambler Wins Poker Title." *Las Vegas Review-Journal* (17 May 1991): 1B.

————. " 'World' Poker Champ: I'll Win Again." *Las Vegas Review-Journal* (22 April 1990): 11B.

Sweeney, Tony. "Bookie Who Believed Even Punters Merit Heaven." *The Irish Times* (9 November 1999): 8.

Sweetingham, Lisa. "In Dramatic Closing, Tabish Lawyer Invokes Caesar, God, a Holy Cow." *Court TV Online* (19 November 2004).

Thackery, Ted, Jr. *Gambling Secrets of Nick the Greek*. Chicago: Rand McNally, 1968.

Thompson, Gary. "Irishman Captures Crown at World Series of Poker." *Las Vegas Sun* (14 May 1999).

————. "Poker World Series to Stay at Binion's." *Las Vegas Sun* (7 July 1998).

————. "Stupak Challenges Horseshoe." *Las Vegas Sun* (17 November 1998).

Varkonyi, Robert. "I'd Rather be Lucky Than Good." *Card Player* (12 March 2004).

Velotta, Richard N. "Behnen: Dealers Tried 'Absolute Extortion.' " *Las Vegas Sun* (23 May 2002).

————. "Dealers Fired in Dispute at World Series of Poker." *Las Vegas Sun* (22 May 2002).

————. "Harrah's Plots Strip Strategy." *Las Vegas Sun* (30 April 2004).

Waddell, Lynn. "IRS Rule Decried." *Las Vegas Sun* (21 October 1992): 1A.

Wagner, Angie. "Irishman Wins $1 Million and Poker's Top Title." *Las Vegas Sun* (14 May 1999).

Wayner, Peter. "Online Poker Changes Nature of Game." *Las Vegas Sun* (10 July 2003).

Werner, Larry. "Binion's '83 Poker Tourney Hits Jackpot." *Las Vegas Review-Journal* (22 May 1983).

Wilen, John. "Sister's Horseshoe Buy Approved." *Las Vegas Sun* (12 June 1998).

Wolfe, Frank. "Inherited Talents." *Forbes* (17 October 1994): 76.

Wolford, Byron. "Aimworth, Sawmill, and Everett." *Card Player* (20 November 2002).

————. *Cowboys, Gamblers & Hustlers*. Las Vegas: Cardsmith Publishing, 2002.

————. "Fadin' the White Line." *Card Player* (20 December 2002).

————. "Gamblin' With the Boys in Dallas." *Card Player* (11 April 2003).

————. "Jesse and the Big Bluff." *Card Player* (10 May 2002).

————. "Smith Sets the Record for Gettin' Busted." *Card Player* (17 January 2003).

————. "Treetop and the Ponies." *Card Player* (25 October 2002).

World Series of Poker. Videos: 1973, 1979, 1983, 1987, 1988, 1989, 1990, 1991, 1992, 1993, 1994, 1997, 1998, 2003, 2004.

Young, Rick. "Q-10—The Greyhound." *Card Player* (27 September 2002).

Zamost, Scott A. "Luck of Irish May Rest With O'Dea." *Las Vegas Sun* (11 May 1982).

Zipay, Steve. "Dip in Super Rating." *Newsday* (8 February 2005).

INDEX